D0092938

Population Policy
Analysis

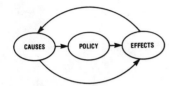

Policy Studies Organization Series

Population Policy Analysis

Issues in American Politics

Edited by

Michael E. Kraft
University of Wisconsin

Mark Schneider
State University of New York

Lexington Books
D.C. Heath and Company
Lexington, Massachusetts
Toronto

Library of Congress Cataloging in Publication Data

Main entry under title:
  Population policy analysis.

  (Policy Studies Organization series ; 17)
  "Collection of studies originated with a symposium on population policy which appeared in the winter, 1977 issue of the Policy studies journal."
  Includes index.
  1. United States—Population policy—Addresses, essays, lectures. 2. Population policy—Addresses, essays, lectures. I. Kraft, Michael E. II. Schneider, Mark. III. Series: Policy Studies Organization. Policy Studies Organization series ; 17.
HB3505.P657   301.31   77-221
ISBN 0-669-01456-7

Contents

List of Figures

List of Tables

Acknowledgments

This collection of studies originated with a symposium on population policy which appeared in the Winter 1977 issue of the *Policy Studies Journal.* Most of the original articles have been considerably revised and expanded, and three chapters appear here for the first time. The symposium was made possible through the generous assistance of the Rockefeller Foundation. Again we wish to thank the foundation and Dr. Mary Kritz, assistant director for the social sciences. As coordinator of the *Policy Studies Journal* and secretary-treasurer of the Policy Studies Organization, Stuart S. Nagel was instrumental in arranging for publication of the symposium.

During the 1976-1977 academic year, the Center for Demography and Ecology at the University of Wisconsin-Madison provided one of the editors (M.K.) with a postdoctoral fellowship under the National Institutes of Health National Research Service Award Program. A year free from normal university obligations combined with full access to the staff and facilities of the Center proved of invaluable assistance. Both the University of Wisconsin-Green Bay and the State University of New York, Stony Brook provided the usual logistical support so necessary for assembling and editing such a collection. All conclusions and interpretations, of course, are those of the individual authors and do not necessarily reflect the views of the persons and organizations whose assistance is acknowledged.

Finally, our special thanks go to the individual contributors to the volume. Without their willingness to participate in the original symposium and to undertake successive revisions of their manuscripts (often much more extensive than they had imagined would be asked), this book would not have been possible.

The Editors

xi

1

Introduction: Analyzing Population Policy

Michael E. Kraft and
Mark Schneider

Population patterns—size, composition, distribution, and rates of change—rank among the most important factors shaping the quality of human life in any society. As governments increasingly have attempted to influence those patterns to achieve desired social goals, considerable scholarly interest has developed in the relationship between population patterns, government, and public policy. There are two broad lines of inquiry in the study of population and politics. One set of questions concerns the effect of population change on the type and level of demands citizens make upon government, and on the distribution of political power, and how well government performs in response to changing population characteristics.[1] The other set of questions asks what impact government and politics have on population change. Of special interest here are alternative population policies and their consequences, and the processes by which population problems are considered by government, and by which public policies are adopted and implemented. The essays written for this book examine both sets of questions, with a predominant focus on the second: population policy analysis.

In the fall of 1975, as plans were made for the symposium on population policy on which this book is based,[2] one could point to a small but growing literature on population and politics. Most of that work was of recent origin, with some twelve volumes published between 1972 and 1975.[3] Not unexpectedly for a developing literature on controversial policy issues, this work has been criticized for a variety of failings or omissions: insufficient coherence in edited collections; lack of agreement on concepts, theories, and methods; uneven quality; questionable utility, both for scholars and practitioners; and a concentration on population growth issues of the developing nations to the neglect of questions of composition and distribution and of policy issues in developed nations. Even by the usual standards of political science, studies of population and politics reveal markedly different perspectives on the nature of population trends, their causes and consequences, appropriate policy actions, and the legitimate roles for the analyst.[4]

The present collection might be faulted for some of the same reasons. And it may well represent a more modest contribution to knowledge and to the development of public policy than the authors and editors would like to believe. However, the book does differ from previous volumes in a number of significant respects: (1) questions of population size, growth rates, composition, and distribution are all examined, albeit with unequal coverage; (2) there is a nearly exclusive focus on issues in American politics, although some comparisons are

1

made to issues and policies of other developed nations; (3) there is a heavy emphasis on public policy and policy analysis, at both national and state and local levels.

The first two points need little comment; the third will be explained at greater length to clarify the meaning of public policy, population policy, and policy analysis. Growth and nongrowth continue to be major issues, and they receive the lion's share of the space here. But since in the past issues related to composition and distribution have received less attention than deserved, we have tried to moderate that imbalance. The focus on American politics derives from a desire to add more coherence to this collection than has been the case in similar volumes. While this has meant excluding a great deal of interesting and important work on developing nations, we hope the result is indeed a more cohesive set of related studies sharing at least some common assumptions and goals.

The focus on public policy and policy analysis follows the general purpose of the *Policy Studies Journal* and the Policy Studies Organization Series: to promote the application of political and social science to important policy problems. We are attempting as well to respond to the critique that research on population and politics has not been sufficiently policy-relevant. Policy-relevance is not easily defined. At one extreme, it implies very specific, short-range, and highly practical analysis with governmental policy makers as the intended audience or "client" (such as, government supported evaluation of an ongoing program). At the other extreme, research may be called policy-relevant if it adds to our knowledge of social relations and social change in a manner that might influence (directly or indirectly) the design or implementation of policy.[5] The contributions here reflect these diverse interpretations of policy-relevance; each author has chosen his or her own topic, approach, and methods, while the editors refrained from imposing restrictive guidelines in this respect.

A brief review of what constitutes public policy might be useful. Policy is sometimes taken to mean goals or ends to be achieved, plans or proposals (means) to achieve them, formal or authorized programs and their effects, or specific decisions or actions taken in setting goals, formulating plans, and implementing programs.[6] Given these multiple meanings, Charles O. Jones suggests that a wise analyst would avoid "immutable formulations" of what public policy is. Instead, one should remain sensitive to the complexity of policy, and seek out the contents of specific policies through whatever devices are appropriate to the case at hand. It is especially important to note that the nature of public policy in a given area is rarely self-evident. It must be specified by the analyst. And answers are not to be found exclusively in policy makers' statements of intentions or goals, in the formal language of statutes and administrative regulations, or in the observable policy decisions of government officials. There may be more (or less) than meets the eye.

Confusion and disagreement over the meaning of public policy in general extends to substantive policy areas as well, of course. This seems particularly the case with population policy. Thus, in an empirical search for whatever common ground exists, Oakley identified thirty-four definitions of population policy, the "sum total of definitions that could be found in available literature."[7] She examined the thirty-four definitions on sixteen separate elements, noting the usual distinctions between explicit and implicit policies, direct and indirect policies, and population influencing and population responsive policies. By this analysis, there seems to be substantial agreement that population policy refers to government participation in some fashion, that some demographic effect is intended or is produced, and that both indirect and direct policy actions should be included. Based upon that apparent agreement, Oakley suggests a straight-forward, uncomplicated definition: "those actions of government that affect or attempt to affect births, deaths, and migration of human beings."[8] This definition is broad enough to capture the variety of policies studied by those interested in population and politics, while allowing at least some distinction between general social policies and those which merit the label "population policy."

The field of public policy analysis itself is also characterized by disparate definitions, approaches, and methods. For some, policy analysis involves the study of policy-making processes, and therefore is concerned chiefly with describing and explaining the determinants of public policy.[9] For others, policy analysis is a new discipline devoted to the systematic study of policy alternatives and their consequences.[10] By population policy analysis, we refer simply to the application of the various approaches and methods of public policy analysis to the substantive issues of population policy. The division of the book into three sections helps to organize the individual contributions in these terms. Part I is devoted to the political (including policy) consequences of population change, the second and third sections to policy alternatives and their consequences and to the processes by which public problems reach government agendas, and by which policy proposals are formulated, legitimated, implemented, and evaluated. In Part II we have collected those essays taking a predominantly national perspective and in Part III those with a state and local perspective.

Political Consequences of Population Change

Three chapters form the first section on the political consequences of population change. Together they illustrate that although it is certainly true that demographic makeup and changes have an impact on political processes and policy decisions, the exact relationship between population characteristics and policy is still unclear.

There is substantial agreement among the three authors that in the United States, the demographic history of the past forty years has had, and will continue to have, significant policy consequences. The juxtaposition of the baby boom of the post-World War II era with low fertility periods in the 1930s and in the 1970s has created an uneven demand for many social services in the past and will continue to do so in the future. The extraordinary demand for schools and educational services created by the baby boom cohort has passed, and the education establishment is now faced with a declining school-age population. Disruptions of a similar nature in other services is quite evident.

Most notably, the low fertility of the 1970s, if continued into the future, inevitably means an aging of the American population. Indeed, as Cutler shows (table 3-1), there has been a continual growth in the proportion of the American population aged 65 or older from 5 percent in 1930 to 10 percent in 1970, with a projected increase to 15 percent by 2050. Old age dependency ratios, reflecting the proportion of the population age 65 and above compared to the population 18-64, will increase throughout this century, and will increase dramatically after the year 2000, as the children of the baby boom reach age 65. This aging of the population is already having a significant impact on social security legislation; other aspects of American society will be affected as well, though not with totally predictable consequences.

The aging of the American population reflects both the aging of the baby boom cohort and the declining fertility found in the United States. As Finkle and McIntosh inform us, this declining fertility is not limited to the United States; it is a phenomenon found in most of the developed countries of the world. According to recent studies, between 1950 and 1975, thirty-four of the thirty-five countries classified as "more developed" experienced declines in birth rates, Ireland being the only exception. In many of these nations, the declining birthrate and the subsequent change in the population structure has already touched off significant reactions; pronatalist policies designed to increase fertility have been adopted or are being seriously considered.

In general, most national policy-makers seem to assume that declining fertility and subsequent changes in the population will weaken the national power base of the country or have significant effects on the nation's economy, leading to stagnation and decline. However, the desire or the ability to respond to declining fertility in developed countries is not uniform. First, the fact of declining fertility has to be perceived as a potentially deleterious factor by political elites. Petersen's discussion of the Zero Population Growth movement and the Rockefeller Commission (along with the observations made by Finkle and McIntosh) suggests that in the United States most elites are not yet concerned about declining fertility and, in fact, are in favor of zero population growth. Furthermore, even if policy makers wanted to reverse declining fertility rates, the ability to intervene may be circumscribed in western democratic countries. This restriction results in part from the pluralistic demands on government; regardless of the preferences of national policy makers, many citizens are in favor of reduced childbearing for themselves or for others. In response, democratic governments which prefer to increase fertility may at the same time be forced into supplying family planning, contraceptive, and abortion services that help keep the birthrate low.

In short, there is agreement that changes in population structure will have major policy implications for American society. In particular, a changing age structure will produce changes in demands for services and perhaps a more salient generational conflict between the old and the young than in the past. However, the exact form of these conflicts, the severity of them, and the actual long-run effects of the population and age structure on economic and social conditions and policies is still a matter of considerable debate.

Population Policy: National Perspectives

Several of the general issues addressed in these opening essays are returned to in more specific detail in the second section dealing with population policy from a national perspective. The first four chapters in this section, A.E. Kier Nash on the Population Commission, James Sundquist on population distribution policy in the United States and in Europe, David North on immigration policy and John Ostheimer on abortion policy, all illustrate various successes and failures in the political and policy process in the United States in dealing with aspects of population policy.

Perhaps the most significant attempt in the recent history of the United States to treat population policy issues in a comprehensive manner was the National Commission on Population Growth and the American Future.[11] Yet the operation of the Commission has been criticized by Bachrach and Bergman as an "opportunity forfeited."[12] Faced with the diffuse nature of population policy questions, the Commission adopted an emphasis on reducing unwanted fertility—the most consensual possible policy option for controlling population growth. This option has been criticized on a variety of grounds. Yet Nash, from his perspective as staff director for political research for the Commission, introduces another criticism. Rather than any conscious choice in selecting the reduced fertility option, Nash argues that the policy proposals recommended by the commission can be traced to chance in the appointments process and in the deliberations process. In general, his analysis then leads one to question first the validity of the use of presidential commissions as a device for generating information and policy guidance (assuming that the Population Commission's decision making is comparable to that of other commissions). But more specifically, Nash's analysis leads one to wonder how a rational policy perspective can be introduced into the population policy-making process. If the leading scholars of population problems cannot agree upon solutions, and if the solutions chosen by the Commission were so heavily influenced by chance processes, what does that tell us about the politics of population policy-making?

To what extent should one expect population policy analysis of the type recommended, and to some extent illustrated, in this book to play an influential role in future decision making? The creation of a Select Committee on Population in the U.S. House of Representatives in the fall of 1977 may provide another testing ground for hypotheses on the utilization of population research in policy formulation.

Sundquist indicates another source of potential failure in population policy. His paper is specifically concerned with questions of population distribution—in particular, the role of government policy in balancing the concentration of growth in certain regions of countries against the stagnation and decline of other regions. In contrast to the general lack of policy goals articulated by the Population Commission, Sundquist argues that in the late 1960s and early 1970s, the Federal government had made a clear and articulated policy decision to develop a national growth policy. At various times in the recent past, similar decisions to develop growth policies were also made in five European countries studied by Sundquist. However, in each of these countries, articulated policies were actually adopted and implemented. In the United States, no policy was adopted. The problems of securing widespread agreement on proposed policies, particularly in the pluralistic American political system, is an increasingly important topic of concern in policy analysis. Sundquist's essay illustrates those problems with regard to one important aspect of population policy.

North's analysis of immigration policy highlights still another problem with population policy. Immigration is an increasingly important component of population growth in the United States, accounting for approximately 25 percent of the annual growth rate at present (counting only legal immigration). Given declining fertility, immigration will become even more important in the future. Yet at best there is only fragmentary data on the extent of immigration into the United States. Since good data is a prerequisite for good policy analysis, our capacity to formulate immigration policy is weakened.

North also points out several other significant characteristics of immigration policy. Historically, American policy has been bifurcated into a restrictive practice incorporated in law and quotas as opposed to a much less restrictive practice allowing into the U.S. large numbers of illegal immigrants, from Latin America and Mexico, in particular. This de facto system of nonrestrictive immigration has been used by employers to supply a cheap and compliant labor force, and serious attempts to curtail it have been unsuccessful. Yet some rationalization of this system of immigration is necessary. President Carter has begun to consider several possibilities, and has sent his proposals to Congress. Given this new attention, it is possible that better data on immigration will be generated, that a rational choice procedure for selecting who will be allowed to immigrate into the United States will be established, and that the split between de facto and de jure immigration practices will be ended.

While immigration is an issue that at times excites emotional reaction and debate, the issue of abortion discussed by Ostheimer seems to be debated in the most emotional terms possible. Ostheimer is concerned with the politics of abortion policy in terms of coalitions and conflicts. In general, given the high level of emotion attached to the issue, it is not surprising that elected political elites have tried to shy away from taking stands unless forced to do so; they feel that they can only lose on this issue. Given this hesitation by elected officials to join the battle, most of the major political debates have focused on the courts, in particular on the Supreme Court's 1973 decision liberalizing abortion (*Roe* v. *Wade*). Although recent action in the Congress has seriously redefined the availability of abortion for low-income women, and may foretell a greater inability of elected officials to avoid abortion as an issue, it is likely that many of the future battles concerning abortion will still be fought in the courts.

Changing the tone of the analysis somewhat, both Stetson and Godwin/Shepard are concerned with developing more theoretical approaches to the study of population policy. Stetson notes that attempts to control fertility in the United States are only one part of population policy. She is concerned with the general "pro-natal" or "anti-natal" impact of a variety of government policies regulating family life, taxes, and child support, that have an effect on the incentives or disincentives to families to have additional children. While the United States has not adopted an explicitly articulated population policy as found, for example, in Britain, France, or Canada, a variety of government policies nonetheless have an impact on the number of children born. Stetson provides a framework for evaluating the effects of such implicit population policies.

Godwin and Shepard are also concerned with developing a theoretical framework for the analysis of population policy. In particular, they are interested in the potential of public choice theory. Using game theoretic concepts, they examine the possibilities of conflict and cooperation between actors concerned with population policy and behavior, for issues related to fertility, mortality, and mobility. They argue the merits of this approach for identifying potential policies and the distribution of their costs and benefits, giving numerous examples to illustrate the utility of public choice theory in this area.

Population Policy: State and Local Perspectives

The final four chapters deal with population policy from a subnational perspective. The most essential characteristic of local population policy is, as Dye and Garcia note in their chapter, that such a policy cannot really be a "growth" policy but must, in fact, be a "distribution" policy. With minor exceptions, local governments do not seem to be capable of having much effect on the rate of population growth in the nation. It is true that certain local governments, such as New York, can make a determination to supply abortions even as the Federal government backs out of such policy commitments. But in general, given the limited jurisdictions of even the largest cities, local governments cannot really control population growth. However, local policies can more strongly affect the distribution of population, and more importantly, can affect the location of class and racial groups in the population.

In viewing this question of population distribution at the local level, it is important to note the "fragmented" nature of metropolitan regions. Political boundary lines divide what may be economically and socially unitary metropolitan areas into separate political jurisdictions. The tradition of local autonomy and local provision of services in the same region has important effects in determining local population distribution policy. Consider, for example, the division of metropolitan regions into central cities and suburbs. We know that many central cities are in desperate fiscal straits. In large part this is the result of population redistribution—upper- and middle-class city residents have left the central city for residence in the suburbs. Given the limited taxing jurisdiction of central cities, these suburban residents can now enjoy central city services while avoiding the taxes necessary to pay for them.

In contrast, central cities become disproportionately populated with lower income and minority populations and must face the financing of local services with a declining tax base. A similar pattern occurs with the more recent movement of industry and commercial activity out of the central cities. Within the past twenty years, economic activity has begun to abandon the central city for suburban locations, further depleting the central city tax base.

Within the suburban part of the metropolis a similar process unfolds. Here the competition for desirable residents and economic development can be intense, as local governments seek to protect their own tax base against an influx of undesirable economic development and of low-income residents (bottling them up either in central cities or in poorer suburbs). This theme informs the chapters by Logan and Schneider and by Dye and Garcia.

Government policies can have an exacerbating effect on differences between cities and suburbs and between suburbs themselves. Perhaps one of the most hotly argued subjects concerning metropolitan development at present is the debate over "white flight" from busing. It has been argued by James Coleman and others that forced school busing has a deleterious effect on the racial and class composition of central cities by encouraging white flight to the suburbs. This, it is argued, is particularly true in northern and western regions where the central city school district is surrounded by independent suburban school districts immune to central city school busing orders. Thus government policy, by forcing central city school busing while allowing suburban school districts to operate independently of the central city schools, fosters the further deterioration of racial and class balance in metropolitan areas. The chapter by Taeuber and Wilson throws some cautionary light on the acceptance of this argument.

Basically, most arguments purportedly documenting white flight rely upon the change in white enrollment in public school systems faced with or undergoing school busing as the indicator of white flight. Taeuber and Wilson show the multitude of problems associated with the use of this measure. Using concepts and approaches developed by demographers, in particular the use of cohorts as the unit of analysis, they show how the dependent variable used in studies of white flight can be more accurately measured and how the components of change more precisely specified, so that the effects of school busing can be more effectively measured. In addition, they also suggest an agenda for future research. The end result of their chapter is that they point to a possible solution to the "battle of the sociologists" that has plagued government attempts to understand the effects of school busing on metropolitan population distribution.

Other policies affect the distribution of population. Logan and Schneider's chapter and, more specifically Marilyn Whisler's chapter, are concerned with the effects of local zoning policy on population distribution. The former chapter shows how zoning decisions can produce a situation in which certain suburbs can attract both high income residents *and* taxable commercial development to win in the growth process, while forcing the costs of low income residential and less attractive commercial development onto other "losing" suburban communities. Whisler's chapter details some attempts by federal, state, and local governments to change local policy options to avoid such inequality in the metropolitan development.

The thirteen chapters which follow are not the last word on population policy. We hope, however, that taken together they indicate the potential of public policy analysis for explaining the causes and consequences of demographic trends, for clarifying the issues raised by those trends, for assessing policy alternatives, and for elucidating the policy-making process.

Notes

1. Myron Weiner, "Political Demography: An Inquiry into the Political Consequences of Population Change," in the National Academy of Sciences, *Rapid Population Growth: Consequences and Policy Implications* (Baltimore: Johns Hopkins Press, 1971), pp. 567-617.

2. Michael E. Kraft and Mark Schneider, eds., "Symposium on Population Policy," *Policy Studies Journal* 6, 2 (Winter 1977):142-238.

3. A.E. Keir Nash, ed., *Governance and Population: The Governmental Implications of Population Change* (Washington, D.C.: U.S. Government Printing Office, 1972); Richard L. Clinton, William S. Flash, and R. Kenneth Godwin, eds., *Political Science in Population Studies* (Lexington, Mass.: Lexington Books, D.C. Heath and Company, 1972); Richard L. Clinton and R. Kenneth Godwin, eds., *Research in the Politics of Population* (Lexington, Mass.: Lexing-

ton Books, D.C. Heath and Company, 1972); Richard L. Clinton, ed., *Population and Politics: New Directions in Political Science Research* (Lexington, Mass.: Lexington Books, D.C. Heath and Company, 1973); Peter Bachrach and Elihu Bergman, *Power and Choice: The Formulation of American Population Policy* (Lexington, Mass.: Lexington Books, D.C. Heath and Company, 1973); Elihu Bergman, David Carter, Rebecca J. Cook, Richard D. Tabors, David R. Weir, Jr., and Mary Ellen Urann, eds., *Population Policymaking in the American States: Issues and Processes* (Lexington, Mass.: Lexington Books, D.C. Heath and Company, 1974); Nazli Choucri, *Population Dynamics and International Violence* (Lexington, Mass.: Lexington Books, D.C. Heath and Company, 1974); Terry L. McCoy, ed., *The Dynamics of Population Policy in Latin America* (Cambridge, Mass.: Ballinger, 1974); Virginia Gray and Elihu Bergman, eds., *Political Issues in U.S. Population Policy* (Lexington, Mass.: Lexington Books, D.C. Heath and Company, 1974). James L. Sundquist, *Dispersing Population: What America Can Learn from Europe* (Washington, D.C.: The Brookings Institution, 1975); Warren F. Ilchman, Harold D. Lasswell, John D. Montgomery, and Myron Weiner, eds., *Policy Sciences and Population* (Lexington, Mass.: Lexington Books, D.C. Heath and Company, 1975); R. Kenneth Godwin, ed., *Comparative Policy Analysis: The Study of Population Policy Determinants in Developing Countries* (Lexington, Mass.: Lexington Books, D.C. Heath and Company, 1975).

4. Philip Coulter, "In Search of the Master Science: Population Policy in the Seventies," *Public Administration Review* 34 (July-August 1975): 419-423; Terry L. McCoy, "Political Scientists as Problem-Solvers: The Case of Population," *Polity* 5 (Winter 1972):250-259; Richard L. Clinton, "Population, Politics, and Political Science," in *Population and Politics*, pp. 51-71.

5. Laurence Lynn, "Policy Relevant Social Research: What Does it Look Like," in *Policy Analysis on Major Issues*, U.S. Congress, Senate, Commission on the Operation of the Senate, 94th Congress, 2nd session, 1977, pp. 59-71, esp., p. 68; Carol Weiss, ed., *Using Social Research in Public Policy Making* (Lexington, Mass.: Lexington Books, D.C. Heath and Company, 1977); James S. Coleman, *Policy Research in the Social Sciences* (Morristown, N.J.: General Learning Press, 1972); and Warren F. Ilchman, "Population Knowledge and Fertility Policies," in *Policy Sciences and Population*, pp. 15-63.

6. Charles O. Jones, *An Introduction to the Study of Public Policy*, 2nd ed. (North Scituate, Mass.: Duxbury Press, 1977), p. 4.

7. Deborah Oakley, "The Development of Population Policy in Japan, 1945-1952, and American Participation" (Ph.D. diss., University of Michigan, 1977).

8. For a more extended discussion of definitions of population policy, see Elihu Bergman, "American Population Policy: An Agenda for Expanding Opportunity," in *Political Issues in U.S. Population Policy*, ed. Gray and Bergman, pp. 4-7; and Bernard Berelson, ed., *Population Policy in Developed Countries* (New York: McGraw Hill, 1974), esp., pp. 6-7.

9. Jones, *An Introduction to the Study of Public Policy*, and Thomas R. Dye, *Understanding Public Policy*, 3rd ed. (Englewood Cliffs, N.J.: Prentice-Hall, 1978).

10. Jacob B. Ukeles, "Policy Analysis: Myth or Reality?", *Public Administration Review* 37 (May/June 1977):223-228; Yehezkel Dror, *Public Policy-making Re-examined* (San Francisco: Chandler, 1968); and E.S. Quade, *Analysis for Public Decisions* (New York: Elsevier, 1975).

11. The Commission on Population Growth and The American Future, *Population and the American Future* (Washington, D.C.: U.S. Government Printing Office, 1972).

12. Bachrach and Bergman, *Power and Choice*, p. 26.

Part I
Political Consequences
of Population Change

2

Population Policy and Age Structure

William Petersen

Even in the bizarre annals of popular mass movements, one must denote the recent attempts to effect a zero population growth in the United States a remarkable phenomenon. Initiated during a period of only moderately high fertility, the campaign for Zero Population Growth (ZPG) reached a climax as a paradoxical counterpoint to the lowest birthrates in the nation's history. The effects of a static or declining population on the economy and the society, which a generation earlier had excited awesome fears, were now typically assumed to be negligible, if not actually beneficent.

Who Was Responsible for ZPG?

The most obtrusive of the pressure groups that conducted this campaign was Zero Population Growth, Inc., which reflected the well-publicized views of its first president, Paul Ehrlich, author of *The Population Bomb*. In 1970 and 1971, according to successive surveys of the organization's membership, it was virtually entirely white and predominantly male, with an education far above the national norm.[1] The most striking characteristic of the members was their youth. In both surveys the respondents' median age was under thirty, and the proportion of full-time students among them rose in the one year from 37 to 46 percent. To the degree that this organization can be taken as typical of the movement, then, the pressure for ZPG was generated largely by male college students and young men who had recently graduated from college. These were the boom babies.

In 1947, America's birthrate had reached a high of 26.6 per 1,000 population, contrasted with a low of 18.4 during the 1930s, and it remained high throughout the 1950s. The members of the small cohorts born during the interwar depression had grown up to expect rather little from life. When as young adults they entered the labor market, their small numbers (among other factors) enabled them to move up very rapidly, so that at early ages they were often earning enough to overwhelm their modest anticipations. Under no pressure to spend their salaries otherwise, many of them had more children than their parents had had.[2] In the 1960s, each of these conditions was repeated in reverse. The boom babies, growing up in homes where rising prosperity was seen as the rule, extrapolated this upward trend in their own anticipations. Partly for this reason, a much larger proportion went to college than in the prior generation. Because of the extraordinarily large numbers seeking jobs over a few years, they formed a glut not only in low-level occupations but often in those demanding graduate degrees. Expecting more from life than their fathers and frequently able to get less, they took steps to reduce their family responsibilities. The periods of both high and low fertility, therefore, resulted from a combination of economic conditions with the relative size and social aspirations of the cohorts entering the labor force.

A generation that from primary grades on had been squeezed into institutions too constricted to hold its members as comfortably as they wished was even more frustrated when they flooded into colleges and then went out to compete for scarce job openings. The negative view that many of them developed of "the establishment" was expressed especially in demands for ecological reforms, for as they saw it, the United States was already overcrowded. The first relation between population policy and age structure, that is to say, is the opposite of what one expects; because of the abnormal distribution by age in the 1950s, many young people were stimulated by their common life experience to advocate the immediate cessation of America's population growth. The youthfulness of the movement, and thus the relative inexperience and ignorance of the typical member, may account for its naiveté. Most of those who believed that no one over thirty was to be trusted, and who devoted much time and effort campaigning in an organization like ZPG, were certainly unaware of the fact that in a stationary population the "trustworthy" would be proportionately far less numerous.

Population Growth and Age Structure

The term "zero population growth" has been used with several meanings, not all of them accurate. For several years after the ZPG organization came into existence, its brochures passed on the simplistic assumption that if each two parents had only two children, the population would not increase from one generation to the next any more than each family in it. This elementary error passed over the fact that as the boom babies reached childbearing age, the number of families formed could be so large that even if each produced only a few progeny the total number of children could be proportionately much larger. That is why virtually every demographer believed that the baby boom would have an "echo"; the actual decline in American fertility was the unexpected consequence of a fall in family size so drastic that it more than made up for the far larger number of young people in the prime reproductive ages.

A second meaning given to ZPG is also simplistic—that the total population remains more or less constant from one year to the next. But it is an axiom of demographic analysis that the rate of a population's growth and its distribution by age are closely interlinked. With no change in size over a short period, the resultant shift in the age structure would in all likelihood result in sizable changes in the rate of growth over the following period. Thus, the slogan calling on us to achieve ZPG by the end of this century is utopian, for it assumes that each year there can be revisions up or down in age-specific birth and death rates sufficient to maintain the sum constant.

If we ignore migration, and if age-specific birth and death rates remain the same for as much as a century, the fluctuations in the growth rate end. In the so-called stable population that is thus brought into being, both the age structure and the rate of growth (which can be zero or negative, as well as positive) remain fixed. A stable population with no growth is called stationary, or one of which both the age structure and the size are permanently fixed. This is the meaning that professional demographers would assign to "zero population growth."

It is useful to distinguish three fixed patterns of interaction between population structure and fertility plus mortality.[3] These three stable populations are (1) expansive, with a broad base to the population pyramid, indicating a high proportion of children and a small proportion in the advanced ages most susceptible in this era to death; (2) stationary, with a narrower base to the pyramid, indicating a rate of reproduction just large enough to match those who die off; and (3) constrictive, with a base narrower than the middle of the pyramid, indicating a proportion of children insufficient to maintain the population's size. In the accompanying figure, three stylized pyramids are matched with three actual population structures that approximate their shape. The expansive type could have been exemplified as well by the structure of almost any population of a less developed country over the past several decades. Switzerland in 1947 (with an indicated revival of fertility too great, given the very low infant mortality, to make it precisely a stationary type) might have been almost any country of Western Europe after the postwar rise in fertility got under way. And the constrictive type could have been illustrated by France, Germany, or England, for example, at the same date of 1935.

If we assume that the current growth of the American population approaches nil and remains more or less at that level, its age structure will fluctuate for several decades and then move toward that of a stationary population. If we assume that the life expectation at birth will be seventy years (or more or less what it is now), then the bar graph representing this future age distribution will have a decidedly different shape. From birth to ages fifty or fifty-five, the successive steps will form a virtual rectangle; the usual pyramid will begin only with persons close to retirement. There will be as many persons over sixty as under fifteen; the median age will be about thirty-seven.

The proportionate growth of the elderly is the one element of this change in age structure to which much analysis has been devoted. If the proportion of children declines and that of the retired population increases, the collective burden on those in the middle need not rise appreciably. It is rather the way this burden will be carried that will change. The cost of rearing children is borne in large part by their parents, but for those beyond working age the state has

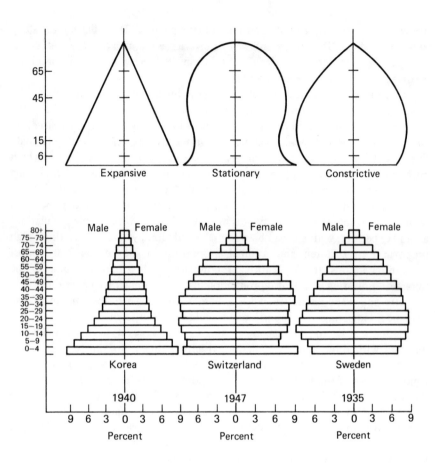

Source: William Petersen, *Population* (New York: Macmillan, 1975), p. 92. Reprinted with permission.

Figure 2-1. Stylized Population Pyramids and Three Comparable Population Structures

increasingly provided its very often inadequate, inefficient, and expensive care. Unless present institutions undergo a highly improbable reversal, that a different sector of the population receives society's main support would seem to mean a trend away from the personal toward the impersonal, from the familial to the bureaucratic. With a high proportion of the electorate over sixty, moreover, American politics will probably move toward a narrow concentration on pensioners' day-to-day requirements. As analysts of voting behavior have documented time and again, in constituencies with many elderly voters it is notoriously difficult to get school bonds passed, for example, or more generally to build any base for a better future. To be sure, we cannot be certain that such proclivities will continue, but the grim possibility is worth more serious consideration than it has usually been given.

Population Growth and Social Structure

With its typical insouciance, the Rockefeller Commission held that "it does not appear, for several reasons, that a lower population growth rate will cause serious problems for *any* industry or its employees."[4] But inevitably those serving young people will see their job market contract, and the fact that sectors serving the aged may become larger will not eliminate the strain. In Great Britain, which apart from the migration balance had a static population in 1975, the government responded by closing a number of the schools that train teachers. This first short step toward the massive adaptation that will be needed in elementary, secondary, and eventually higher education elicited an all but universal hostility from the young people whose planned careers were now labeled "closed," from the administrators and faculty of defunct institutions, and from the professional planners who are supposed to guide the nation through this kind of crisis.[5]

The recent trends in American higher education also illustrate how a stationary population will probably affect social mobility. During the 1960s, when faculties grew far faster than the usual supply of replacements, young scholars (including some whose scholarly qualifications were dubious) moved up with a speed that they found gratifying. Presently, with academia merely holding its own or facing the prospect of early retrenchment, new Ph.D.s do not find positions easily, and most of the young professors with a foot on a lower rung see all those above them already fully occupied. Promotion in American universities is seemingly moving toward the pattern of nineteenth-century Europe, when underlings typically had to wait for the retirement or death of a professor before they could hope to inherit his chair.

Generally, the open society of which Western democrats are deservedly proud has depended to some degree on the rapid expansion of economic and social institutions, which grew partly in response to the needs of an increasing population.[6] The racial minorities now clamoring for posts nearer the top of the social scale will be welcomed with far less enthusiasm if each black displaces a white, rather than moving up to his side. Women, it is true, will benefit in the occupational market from the smaller number of children they bear and raise,[7] but this advantage may be cancelled by the same sharpening of competition with the males already holding the power implicit in their higher status.

What is the general effect of a slower growth of population on the economy, and thus on the chances for advancement of the average person? In the 1930s, when ZPG was seen as a likely but fearsome fate for most Western countries, one of the main reasons for this attitude was the belief that a free economy needs an

20

injection of people each generation to flourish. In his enormously influential *General Theory*, Keynes revived a thesis from Malthus that had disappeared from conventional economic theory for the whole of the intervening century—namely, that the automatic circuit between production and consumption is completed only in the special case when planned savings and planned investments are equal. In all other cases (hence, the "general" theory), a portion of potential purchasing power is siphoned off into "hoards," or savings that remain idle for lack of attractive investment opportunities. Particularly in wealthy countries (that is, those deemed at the time to be suffering from an "incipient decline" in population) investment tended to be inadequate, for two reasons: because a smaller proportion of the far greater national income was consumed and thus a larger proportion was left to be invested, and because the already existent capital stock meant that new investment opportunities were more difficult to find. In short, the marginal efficiency of capital is lower, ceteris paribus, the greater the existing amount of capital. Why then did not the marginal efficiency of capital decline during the nineteenth century? Because, as Keynes put it, "the growth of population and of invention, the opening up of new lands, the state of confidence, and the frequency of war over the average of (say) each decade seem to have been sufficient."[8]

If we use this list to diagnose our present situation, we can get some suggestive answers. There are hardly any more new lands to open up, and war has become far too terrible to advocate, even halfheartedly, for its beneficial effect on the economy. And to depend in each generation on the invention of an automobile or a television would seem to be inordinately risky. True, the redistribution of income through social welfare programs has typically shifted money to those who will spend it from those who seek to invest it; but most Western countries have already traveled farther along that road than either economic good sense or political justice would warrant. In short, a continuing growth of population, rather than a continued transfer of entrepreneurial functions from private firms to the state, would seem to be a partial and temporary therapy for the ills that Keynes spoke of.

Population Optima

One paradoxical characteristic of the recent campaign to lower American fertility has been the relative indifference to how population size and growth relate to the economy, the environment, and the society. In contrast, demographers of the 1930s and 1940s spent a great deal of effort in trying to define the optimum population. In its original formulation, this concept derived essentially from Malthus' two progressions. If, as he wrote, the American colonies benefited from their rapid increase in numbers and if most countries of Europe had too many people, then somewhere between two such poles there must be for each particular area a population that would result in the maximum feasible economic return per capita. In fact, however, there are two economic optima, one related to the resources available and the other, as we have noted, to the maintenance of a demand for investment; and the two have never been satisfactorily reconciled. Moreover, as analysts began to ask, why should the optimum be stipulated exclusively by one set of conditions rather than all that are pertinent? Penrose, for example, set the optimum as "the number socially desirable," a definition that still implied that all of the factors necessarily coalesce into a single figure.[9] It may well be, on the contrary, that the number of persons required for the best military defense, say, is considerably higher than the one that would yield the highest economic return in the given natural, cultural, and social environment or, to introduce another dimension, in some extrapolation of current trends to a supposedly more efficient economy or better society of the future. There is a further dilemma more closely related to the topic of this paper—"To grow or to age, a conflict between population structure and population size."[10] As ever more variables were included, the debate became more and more complicated, and some concluded that the theory of optimum population is "one of the most sterile ideas" ever developed in economics.[11] Yet the idea underlying the concept, that national income (or welfare, generally) can sometimes be increased by adjusting the population to the economy and other factors, is the rationale implicit in *any* population policy including, for example, the pronatalist program that Myrdal helped develop in Sweden during the interwar period.

The proper conclusion from the earlier debate, at least for would-be policymakers, is rather that the problem is considerably more complex than most of the antagonists of that time assumed. A nation has many legitimate goals, and the population best suited to each of them is likely to be specific to it. Any overall best, then, can be defined by only the loosest compromise among all the optima related to these various purposes. Except for areas that obviously are overpopulated or have an excessively high rate of growth (India, Egypt, Central America, and so on), it is probable that the specification will in fact depend on which of the national goals is deemed to be most important.

As it became obvious to serious demographers that in a country like the United States any optimum population would have to be an approximate balance between the advantages and disadvantages associated with any single figure, the demands for an immediate cessation of growth became ever more frenetic. By most obvious criteria, the United States is hardly overpopulated. A tiny fraction of the labor force produces enough food to keep many Americans overweight and to supply some of the gaps in production of less developed or Communist countries. As Ansley Coale noted in a presidential address to the Population Association of America, population density is four and a half times greater in France, ten times greater in the United Kingdom, and thirty times greater in the Netherlands. "Even if our population were to rise to a billion, its average density would not be very high by European standards."[12]

When such guidelines were dismissed, what were substituted by proponents of ZPG to justify their program? The most often repeated, perhaps, has been the obvious contention that there must be a limit to population growth at some point. "Recognizing that our population cannot grow indefinitely, and appreciating the advantages of moving now toward the stabilization of population, the Commission recommends that the nation welcome and plan for a stabilized population."[13] The logic is hardly impeccable, however, that moves from an eventual necessity to an immediate policy. In fact, there is no urgency to reduce the fertility of the United States, not only because it is already very low but also because population, in rational rather than ideological terms, is hardly a current issue. It has been made one by arguments that are false, irrelevant, or at best contentious.

That certain other countries are manifestly overpopulated (and that some of their more nationalist spokesmen have denounced American-sponsored birth control programs as "genocide") provides no reason to apply parallel programs to a totally different setting. Pollution is indeed a serious problem, a political-fiscal-engineering problem that has nothing to do with population—cities as different as London and Pittsburgh have been transformed from their prior notorious state without the expulsion of a single person. As Coale pointed out, of the American gross national product of about $4,500 per capita, the raw-materials component is less than $100, or relatively no higher than it was at the beginning of the century.[14] In a passing comment, one cannot draw a balance between partisan statements on both sides of the debate over energy, but it is worth making two points. Anti-industrial enthusiasts have attacked the Alaska pipeline, blocked oil refineries on the East Coast and nuclear power plants anywhere, opposed strip mining, denounced the construction of port facilities for importing liquefied natural gas; in short, they have campaigned against one major source of energy after another, with an eventual effect on its production. Also, that the United States uses more energy per capita than India, for instance (a fact that is supposed to generate guilt in every American), is the base of a productive system efficient enough, say, to help feed Indians.

The situation today is similar to that during the interwar period, when the trend toward a static population led to an international demand that fertility be actively stimulated. The pronatalist measures adopted were seldom effective, which is the main reason why it would be inappropriate to advocate one today. But if, as I have argued, (1) the realization of a static population will bring not only benefits but also serious problems, particularly but not exclusively those associated with a shift in the age structure, and (2) the necessary adjustment to these problems will be far easier if the change can be made gradually, then one should seek a way of slowing down a stabilization of the population and thus of mitigating its negative effects. And there is such a policy that does not depend on pronatalist measures—namely, to admit more immigrants.

Immigration Policy

The definition of good immigration policy has been intermittently disputed in this country for more than a century, and over most of this period the groups arrayed on either side have remained fairly consistent. For different reasons, businessmen and liberal academics have been for a freer entry, trade unions and racists for a more restricted one. The principle that a potential immigrant should be judged mainly by his individual worth, eventually effected in the abandonment of national quotas, was the declared goal of an earlier population commission, which as *its* guide to policy wrote *Whom We Shall Welcome.*[15] True, this earlier report concentrated on the moral and legal underpinnings of policy, partly because for the past two generations movement to this country has hardly mattered demographically. The average annual immigration rate per 1,000 of the total population was cut from 7.5 in 1861-1910 to 1.8 in 1911-1970. The proportion of the population that is of foreign birth has remained at around 5 percent, and of the low total growth between 1960 and 1970, only 16 percent was due to net immigration.

These figures are taken from the *Report* of the Rockefeller Commission,[16] and they are a strange introduction to some remarkable commentary and recommendations. Once the country dismissed the premise in the 1924 law that West Europeans are superior types, as the *Report* pointed out, this "affected the racial composition of immigrants, increasing the number of nonwhites." Many of those who come enter the country illegally, and the Commission recommended that Congress "impose civil and criminal sanctions on employers of illegal border-crossers or aliens in an immigration status in which employment is not authorized." The Commission revived the hoary theory, debated at length in the 1920s, that immigrants who succeed take away jobs and careers from natives; by their reasoning, it is not only illegal immigrants who harm the economy but at least some who enter with proper documentation. Thus, more generally, the Commission recommended that "immigration levels not be increased and that immigration policy be reviewed periodically to reflect demographic conditions and considerations."

No section of the *Report*, perhaps, shows more clearly the single-minded obsession of ZPG proponents with attaining that one goal, even to the point of proferring dubious arguments to block the entry of a body of newcomers that by a demographic measure is too small to matter very much. In other ways immigrants bring much to this country that it needs. They fill in gaps in the occupational structure, from physicians and nurses down to stoop labor on farms of the Southwest. They bring new diversity to a culture that always seems to be tending toward a monolingual sameness. They constitute a means by which, with little cost to itself, the United States can alleviate the hardship of some of the world's millions of refugees—our former allies in Vietnam, for example, some of whom sailed for months about the South China Sea looking for a port where they would be allowed to land. More pertinently in this context, they reinforce the slim ranks of the age category on which the burden falls for the support of children and the aged. Otherwise stated, they slow down the trend toward population stabilization and thus help the country adapt to a new age structure.

Consider specifically the issue of illegal Mexican immigrants. On the face of it, their temporary residence in the United States benefits everyone concerned. The workers themselves earn far more than they could in Mexico and are often able to accumulate enough to improve their prospects at home. Employers benefit by their availability, as does the American consumer by the greater supply of fruit and vegetables at prices not more exorbitant than they have become. Mexico benefits from the work that some of her unemployed get and from the money they bring back with them; Jorge A. Bustamante, the principal Mexican expert on the question, is appalled at the several bills that Congress is considering.[17] The proposals include a massive attempt to close the border and the provision recommended by the Rockefeller Commission that employers who hire illegal migrants would be criminally responsible.[18] Pressure for this draconian program has come mainly from trade unions, for it is alleged that Mexicans are taking work from American citizens. But just as the minimum wage has resulted mainly in keeping unskilled teenagers out of the labor market, so setting union rates and conditions for the work that Mexicans do would push the price of many agricultural commodities so high that it would not be feasible to produce them, even if enough Americans could be found to accept that kind of hard manual labor.[19] Mexicans are like Europe's *Gastarbeiter*, aliens who do work that natives refuse to do. European countries have institutionalized their temporary place in the labor force with various types of permits, and it would seem to be in the best interest of both the United States and Mexico to imitate this system.

Conclusion

The realization of a static population will bring with it many problems, some quite serious and most related to the changed age structure. That young people will be relatively less numerous and the aged far more so will bring about changes in the culture that are difficult to foresee, but many of them are hardly to be welcomed. The shift in the economy will come faster; in education it has already become discernible.

"The population problem," contrary to ZPG enthusiasts, is not at all urgent in the United States, and good policy would consist in weighing the benefits of a stationary population against its disadvantages. On balance, adjustments to the new age structure will be far less painful if they can be made gradually. With the country's current low fertility, such a policy means that another source of a continuing moderate increase in population might be considered—that is, immigration. Immigrants have the considerable advantage, moreover, that since most of them are in the middle age range, they would build up the portion of the population on which the growing numbers of old people will depend.

Notes

1. Larry D. Barnett, "Zero Population Growth, Inc.," *BioScience* 21 (1971):759-765; Larry D. Barnett, "Zero Population Growth, Inc.: A Second Survey," *Journal of Biosocial Sciences* 6 (1974):1-22.

2. Richard A. Easterlin, "The American Baby Boom in Historical Perspective," *American Economic Review* 51 (1961):869-911.

3. Cf. William Petersen, *Population* (New York: Macmillan, 1975), chapter 3.

4. Commission on Population Growth and the American Future, *Population Growth and the American Future* (Washington, D.C.: U.S. Government Printing Office, 1972), p. 40. Emphasis added.

5. Cf. Martin Trow, "The Implications of Low Growth Rates for Higher Education," *Higher Education* 5 (1976):377-396.

6. Nathan Keyfitz, "Individual Mobility in a Stationary Population," *Population Studies* 27 (1973):335-352.

7. Suzanne Keller, "The Future Status of Women in America," in Commission on Population Growth and the American Future, *Demographic and Social Aspects of Population Growth* (Washington, D.C.: U.S. Government Printing Office, 1972), pp. 267-287.

8. John Maynard Keynes, *The General Theory of Employment, Interest, and Money* (New York: Harcourt, Brace, 1935), p. 307.

9. E.F. Penrose, *Population Theories and Their Applications with Special Reference to Japan* (Stanford, Calif.: Food Research Institute, 1934), p. 90.

10. Alfred Sauvy, *L'Europe et sa population* (Paris: Editions Internationales, 1953), p. 119.

11. Gunnar Myrdal, *Population: A Problem for Democracy* (Cambridge, Mass.: Harvard University Press, 1940), p. 26.

12. Ansley J. Coale, "Should the United States Start a Campaign for Fewer Births?," *Population Index* 34 (1968):466-474.

13. Commission on Population Growth and the American Future, *Population Growth and the American Future*, p. 110.

14. Ansley J. Coale, "Man and His Environment," *Science* 170 (1970):132-136.

15. President's Commission on Immigration and Naturalization, *Whom We Shall Welcome* (Wahington, D.C.: U.S. Government Printing Office, 1953).

16. Commission on Population Growth and the American Future, *Population Growth and the American Future*, chapter 13.

17. *New York Times*, 27 May 1977.

18. Vernon M. Briggs, Jr., "Mexican Immigrants and the Labor Market," *Texas Business Review* 49 (1975):85-90.

19. Ellwyn R. Stoddard, "Illegal Mexican Labor in the Borderlands: Institutionalized Support of an Illegal Practice," *Pacific Sociological Review* 19 (1976):175-210; Austin T. Fragomen, Jr., *The Illegal Alien: Criminal or Economic Refugee* (New York: Center for Migration Studies, 1973).

3 The Consequences of Population Dynamics for Political Gerontology

Neal E. Cutler

As the articles in this volume suggest, the characteristics of a nation's demographic metabolism have a profound and direct impact upon the nature and future of the country's politics and public policy. This article suggests that the dramatic increases in the proportion of older persons in the United States—"the graying of America"—is one such area of profound and direct political and policy impact.[1] As our analysis will demonstrate, not only are there increasing numbers of older persons, but the politically relevant characteristics of tomorrow's elderly differentiate them from today's and yesterday's elderly. It has been argued that the aged and the issue of aging are not increasingly salient aspects of politics in the United States. This article will summarize a number of recent findings which contradict this view. Finally, although space does not permit a detailed or complete enumeration of the policy implications of the political gerontology perspective, a brief consideration of the social security issue highlights the potential importance of this perspective.

Demographic Dynamics

Table 3-1 illustrates the growth of the older (i.e. 65+) population since 1930, and projections to the year 2050. As can be seen, the older population is characterized by uninterrupted growth over this period; at the time of the 1970 census, this group included 20 million persons. If political influence were measured only in electoral terms, then this group has a strong potential impact, since by 1970 old people constituted 15 percent of the potential electorate.

The policy importance of the growing older population, as contrasted to the potential political or electoral impact, is actually greater since table 3-1 reflects only decennial *net* growth. In fact, in the period between the 1960 and 1970 censuses, an estimated 14.2 million persons passed their sixty-fifth birthday. Added to the 16.5 million persons already age sixty-five in 1960, this means that almost 31 million people age sixty-five and older were part of the American political and social systems sometime during this decade. While all 31 million

The research program of which this paper is a part has been funded by Administration on Aging grant no. 90-A-1009. The author holds a joint appointment in the Department of Political Science and as Laboratory Chief, Social Policy Laboratory, Andrus Gerontology Center, University of Southern California. This paper is a revised version of an article appearing in the Winter, 1977, issue of the *Policy Studies Journal*.

Table 3-1
Basic U.S. Census Data for Three Age Groups, 1930-2050

Percentage of Total Population	1930	1940	1950	1960	1970	2000	2020	2050
Young (under 18)	38.8	34.4	31.1	35.8	34.3	27.4	25.6	24.7
Work Force (18-64)	55.8	58.7	60.8	55.0	55.9	61.7	61.3	59.9
Old (65+)	5.4	6.9	8.1	9.2	9.9	10.9	13.1	15.4
Old (65+) as % of 18+	8.8	10.3	11.8	14.4	15.0	15.0	17.6	20.5
Old Age Dependency Ratio	.097	.118	.133	.167	.177	.177	.213	.257
Total Dependency Ratio	.792	.704	.645	.818	.791	.621	.631	.669

Source: (1930-1940) U.S. Bureau of the Census, *U.S. Census of Population: 1940. Characteristics of the Population*, table 8, p. 26. (1950-1970), U.S. Bureau of the Census, *Statistical Abstract of the United States: 1972*, table 37, p. 32. (2000) (Based on Series E. Projections) Herman B. Brotman, "Projections of the Population to the Year 2000," Statistical Memo #25, Department of Health, Education and Welfare, Administration on Aging, June 1973, p. 3. (2020, 2050) (based on Series E and Series W respectively) prepared by Dr. David M. Heer, Population Research Laboratory, University of Southern California, February 1974.

were not alive at any one time, the overall "throughput" of the institutions and mechanisms of public policy was greater than that described simply by net growth figures.[2]

In terms of policy choices and potential future political conflict, population numbers and percentages are only the beginning point. As recent controversies over the financial integrity of the Social Security system have highlighted, it is the relationship of the retired population to the working population which provides a basis for possible policy and political conflict. In table 3-1 this relationship is summarized by the Old-Age Dependency Ratio, which simply represents the percentage 65+ divided by the percentage 18-64. These OADRs, like the older age group percentages, demonstrate an uninterrupted increase from 1930 through 2050.

The demographic reasons for these trends are fairly well known.[3] By the first decades of the next century, the baby boom cohorts of 1940-1950 will arrive at "old age" (i.e. 65+). At the same time, the 1970s are characterized by a "baby bust," as the fertility rate in the United States has continued to decline. A recent Census Bureau study indicated that the current total fertility rate is 1.8 births per woman of childbearing age, exactly half the 1957 rate.[4] The current baby bust cohorts will provide the labor force when the aging baby boom begins its period of dependency. Hence, a diminishing labor force will be increasingly called upon to support a growing dependent population.

Some critics have argued that the Old-Age Dependency Ratios provide a biased view of the overall situation of demographic-economic dependency. After all, it may be argued, if the number of children is indeed declining, then the *total* dependency within the population system will either decline or at least not change as oldsters replace youngsters. Indeed, the Total Dependency Ratios presented in table 3-1 do decline somewhat between 1960 and 2020. This stability or slight decline of the Total Dependency Ratios, however, does not detract from the potential political and policy impact of the Old-Age Dependency Ratios. While this latter trend clearly indicates the increased relative growth of the older population, the "Total" trend does not guarantee that financial and service reallocations will in fact be made from youth programs and facilities to old-age programs and facilities. For example, the closing of the third elementary school in five years in the small tranquil town of Hermosa Beach, California, in response to a declining population of youngsters, does not guarantee the reallocation of the "savings" to senior citizens. A whole range of other local programs, old and new, as well as inflation, compete for the limited resources; senior citizens are among the competitors. The point, of course, is that the changing age structure of the population summarized in the Old-Age Dependency Ratios is more relevant to the possible conflict over policy allocations than is the scenario described by the Total Dependency Ratios.

Cohort Futures

Most political scientists conceptualize chronological age in terms of the life cycle processes of maturation and "aging." Yet the perspective of political gerontology, influenced by demographic analysis, suggests a consideration of the generational or cohort interpretation of age differences and age phenomena.[5] The concept of *cohort* has already been suggested by reference to the "baby boom": *individuals born in a definable time period*, who experience a contemporaneous exposure to history, and—relevant to the present discussion—arrive at old age in the same general time frame.

Yet while in one context the cohort concept simply identifies a statistical aggregate which can be traced through the population system, it is also the case that the flow of cohorts through the population is a source of social and political change.[6] Three basic functions can influence the role of a given cohort in the processes of societal change: the size of the cohort, the comparative nature of adjacent cohorts, and the characteristics of the cohort. From the vantage point of political gerontology, the baby boom cohort of the 1940-1950 period is affected by the intersection of all three of these factors.

The large size of this cohort has already been mentioned. Also relevant is the fact that the baby boom followed the low fertility period of the 1930s. Hence in its younger years the baby boom cohort encountered facilities designed to meet the needs of prior, smaller cohorts, thereby precipitating shortages in, for example, maternity wards and educational facilities around the country for several years. Just as the baby boom was preceded by the low fertility 1930s, it is being followed by the low fertility 1960s and 1970s. Thus, the juxtaposition of cohorts of different sizes does represent the potential for social dislocations whose resolution must be found in the dynamics of public policy.[7]

The third factor, that of the compositional characteristics of successive cohorts, is also relevant here. One example of compositional differences between cohorts is the attribute of educational attainment. As a large number of studies of political behavior has shown, the higher the education, the greater the participation, awareness, information, sophistication, efficacy, opinionation, skill, membership, and other orientations of political relevance.[8] Defining "high" educational attainment as completion of high school (or more), only 19 percent of the 65+ age group in 1952 had a high school education; by 1972, 30 percent of the 65+ group was in the high education category. The dramatic differences, however, are seen when we examine those young people who will be the 65+ group in the first decades in the next century. The cohort which was in its early twenties in 1972, the survivors of which will be 65+ by the year 2015, will have approximately 85 percent in the "high" education category.

Thus, tomorrow's older population will be much more educated than the elderly of yesterday or even today. Similarly, tomorrow's elderly will have been self-conscious in terms of age, and public policy issues concerning age, for a much longer part of its own life cycle than has previously been the case. Ironically, as one consequence of increased voluntary retirement at ages younger than sixty-five,[9] tomorrow's elderly are also likely to be younger. This phenomenon has lead Neugarten to suggest that the "young-old" (as contrasted to the "old-old") of the year 2000 will be very different from the "old people" of today. The young-old, she suggests, will be healthier, wealthier, better educated, and politically more interested, experienced, and skilled than old persons of the past.[10] In short, the flow of cohorts through the population system does not simply represent the iteration of similarly composed statistical aggregates defined in terms of the year of birth; rather, it represents the succession of potentially unique generational entities whose characteristics and location in the flow of population can substantially influence society and politics.[11]

Policy Conflicts

A final consideration concerns how the population pressures engendered by a dramatically changing age structure may affect policy and politics. The most explosive policy issue deriving from the changing age structure of the American population surrounds the national Social Security system. Officially this system is known as OASDHI—the Old Age, Survivors, Disability, and Health Insurance system. As the string of adjectives suggests, OASDHI, or Social Security, finances more than just old-age pensions. Nonetheless, the old-age pension is the original as well as the most critical of the needs served. In 1975, over 92 percent of the 65+ population was estimated to be receiving pension benefits. While some older persons are fortunate enough to have private pensions or other supplementary resources, in 1974 Social Security benefits accounted for over 50 percent of the money income for over 60 percent of older persons living alone.[12]

Controversies surrounding Social Security are receiving increasing public attention, and the number of problems identified seems outnumbered only by the number of solutions proposed. Although such problems as unequal treatment of men and women, inequities which allow some individuals to benefit from more than one pension, and the like, are often discussed, perhaps the most controversial issue concerns the financial integrity of the system. Clearly, Social Security is not "fully funded"—that is, Social Security does not currently hold sufficient assets to pay off the claims which are building on the part of those workers who are currently contributing. In a word, current income is not being acquired at a rate sufficient to finance the pensions of current workers; rather, as is well known, income derived from current contributions is being used to finance the pensions of currently retired workers.

Whether this is a major problem is a viewpoint associated with major philosophical issue differences. Currently, Social Security embraces both sides of the following pair of objectives: the "insurance concept," in which the pension represents an adjusted replacement of the individual's income, and thus is or should be scaled to what that income was during the individual's working years; and the "welfare concept," in which the primary function of the federal pension is to assure an adequate minimum income for all families regardless of lifetime earnings or contributions.

Clearly, a detailed consideration of these issues is beyond the scope of this discussion.[13] It can be noted, however, that the two objectives imply different priorities as far as the financial status of the system is concerned. One of the most important facets of the insurance concept is that workers receive a financial product of their own (including their employer's) contributions, and are not simply recipients of welfare programs. Whether or not the insurance concept is fiscally credible in the contemporary operation and financial structure of the system, the insurance image of the system has been an important element in the historical genesis of public support for the system. Such support is particularly noteworthy given the fact that the Social Security tax is a substantially regressive tax, which has risen at a faster rate over the past twenty-five years than has the federal income tax.

Perhaps the only conclusion to be drawn from this discussion is that no simple conclusion is apparent. Alternatively, the predicted "bankruptcy" of the Social Security system is more a theoretical alternative than empirical prediction, since such bankruptcy would be a function of such factors as the demographic profile of the society, the changing priorities among objectives mandated for the Social Security system, structural changes in the non-old-age segments of OASDHI, and alternative financing arrangements. In sum, as most economists would agree, while the operational solutions might be fiscal or economic in nature, the fundamental decisions are derived from political philosophy and political dynamics.[14]

Political Dynamics

Policy responses to demographic pressure will be a product of political dynamics. Two extreme positions describing the future politics of old age may be identified. On one extreme, it may be suggested that the graying of America will include the graying of politics to such an extent that the only salient social cleavage will be old vs. young, and the only issues will derive from the political-economic dynamics suggested by Old-Age Dependency Ratios.[15] On the other extreme, it may be suggested that old people will never directly influence politics, either through electoral bloc strength or pressure group activity, for the simple reason that the onset of old age does not erase such lifelong and politically-relevant identifications as ethnicity, social class, regionalism, and partisanship.[16] Virtually by definition the actual situation is likely to be somewhere between these two extremes; it is unlikely that the single issue of age will totally dominate politics, and it is unlikely that tomorrow's elderly will have absolutely no impact upon the shape and direction of American politics.

The following areas of political inquiry describe the likely foundation of old-age influence upon American politics, with the recognition that such influence will be conditioned by competing interests, issues, and constituencies:

1. *Political Participation:* Despite the common myth that old people "disengage" from politics as a "natural consequence" of the aging process, there is substantial evidence that people remain politically active through their sixties relative to voting behavior, awareness of and interest in political issues, and participation in political activities.[17] To a large extent the declining rates of participation often associated with increasing age are in fact the consequences of the lesser participation of females and lower socioeconomic status groups. Since the older population is, for a variety of reasons,[18] more female and of lower status than younger age groups, any observed decline in political participation associated with older age groups is likely to be highly affected by the sex and status composition of the different age groups. Indeed, when the appropriate multivariate statistical controls are introduced, rates of political participation do not exhibit an age-related decline.[19]

2. *Political Attitudes:* Another myth suggests that older persons are inherently conservative in matters of political philosophy, and are thus unlikely to turn to the federal government for the provision of services. Consideration of contemporary younger cohorts, however, suggests that tomorrow's elderly might be quite profederal in orientation. Yet even among contemporary and recent

groups of older persons, such self-interest issues as the financing of medical care have evoked substantially "liberal" responses, as measured in both cross-sectional and cohort trend studies.[20] That is, it has been found that aging at the older end of the life cycle is associated with increased attitudinal support for the federal role in medical care financing.

3. *Partisan Flexibility:* To some extent the older person has an image of being psychologically rigid and less likely to respond flexibly to changing circumstances. Whether or not such an image is true in generic psychological terms, it is not the case that older persons are more rigid in their partisanship than younger persons when it comes to voting behavior. A comparison of partisan flexibility in presidential voting in 1964, 1968, and 1972, revealed that in none of these three electoral contests were the older voters less flexible in voting for the candidate of the "other side" (opposite of their own party identification) than younger voters.[21]

4. *Organizational Activity:* In contrast to old-age organizations of the past, contemporary old-age organizations which have either manifest or latent political functions are less likely to be organized around a single issue or a single charismatic leader. In the past, such single-issue organizations tended to dissolve with the passing of the leader or the issue. By contrast, the modern organizations are bureaucratically organized, are financed by a combination of member dues and outside sources, are concerned with a range of sociopolitical issues, and perform their roles as representatives of political advocates of the elderly as but one of several services provided to their memberships.[22] Furthermore, recent research has demonstrated that, when age and membership rates are carefully considered (as contrasted with the "control variable" function which age typically serves in analyses of this type), large proportions of the older population are involved in voluntary associations; and involvement in even nonpolitical associations can serve to heighten the member's political awareness and activity.[23]

5. *Age Consciousness:* Perhaps one of the biggest differences between the older population of today and tomorrow is the proportion of their respective lives in which they—and the society around them—have been concerned with aging as a social and political issue. One consequence of this is the development of *age consciousness* as a potential source of political interest and political demands.[24] Recent research suggests that many older persons do indeed subjectively identify with "the older population" in general. Furthermore, the subjectively old (among the chronologically old) differ attitudinally from those who do not subjectively identify themselves as old in ways that suggest the likelihood of their looking to politics as a resource for the amelioration of the problems of the elderly.[25]

Although the future of public policy and the aged is not completely predictable, the parameters of this future are already known. The population of the United States is getting older as the large numbers of baby boom babies survive into old age during a time when the number of new babies born is declining. Generational or cohort attributes of this demographic pattern suggest that the years 2000-2010 will yield an older population whose experience, educational composition, age consciousness, and political involvements will combine with their greater population numbers to produce a political force which has great potential influence. Many of the most important policy issues which influence older persons do in fact represent societal allocations in the form of intergenerational financial transfers; yet in the first instance even financial allocations are the function of political philosophies and political decisions. Predictions that population patterns are likely to produce political controversies, and that in this context age is likely to grow as a political issue, should not be surprising.

Notes

1. See also Neal E. Cutler, "Demographic, Social Psychological, and Political Factors in the Politics of Age: A Foundation for Research in Political Gerontology," *American Political Science Review* 71 (1977):1011-1025.

2. Herman B. Brotman, "The Older Population Revisited: First Results of the 1970 Census," *Facts and Figures on Older Americans*, 1971, no. 2, Administration on Aging, Washington, D.C., SRS-AOA Publication #182.

3. See for example Neal E. Cutler and Robert A. Harootyan, "Demography of the Aged," in Diana Woodruff and James Birren, eds., *Aging: Scientific Perspectives and Social Issues* (New York: Van Nostrand, 1975), pp. 31-69.

4. United Press International, "U.S. Fertility Rate Drops to Record Low," February 11, 1977.

5. Vern L. Bengtson and Neal E. Cutler, "Generations and Inter-Generational Relations: Perspectives on Age Groups and Social Change," in Robert Binstock and Ethel Shanas, eds., *Handbook of Aging and the Social Sciences* (New York: Van Nostrand, 1976), pp. 130-159.

6. Norman B. Ryder, "The Cohort as a Concept in the Study of Social Change," *American Sociological Review* 30 (1965):843-861.

7. Matilda White Riley, "Age Strata in Social Systems," in Robert Binstock and Ethel Shanas, eds., *Handbook of Aging and the Social Sciences* (New York: Van Nostrand, 1976), pp. 189-217.

8. Lester W. Milbrath and M.L. Goel, *Political Participation: How and Why Do People Get Involved in Politics?* (Chicago: Rand McNally, 1977).

9. Erdman B. Palmore, "Retirement Patterns Among Aged Men: Findings of the 1963 Survey of the Aged," *Social Security Bulletin* 27 (1964):3-10.

10. Bernice L. Neugarten, "Age Groups in American Society and the Rise of the Young-Old," *Annals of the American Academy of Political and Social Science* 415 (1974):187-198.

11. Neal E. Cutler, "Generational Approaches to Political Socialization," *Youth and Society* 8 (1976):175-207.

12. Robin J. Walther and Neal E. Cutler, *Political and Economic Aspects of Age as a Social Issue* (Los Angeles: University of Southern California, Andrus Gerontology Center, Social Policy Laboratory, 1977).

13. James H. Schulz, *The Economics of Aging* (Belmont, California: Wadsworth, 1976).

14. As of this writing (December 1977), new Social Security financing legislation has just been signed into law by the president. That the new taxes and limits will substantially affect the financial integrity of the system is not yet predictable. That these changes are unlikely to silence debate on the issue is predictable.

15. William Petersen, "Population Policy and Age Structure," *Policy Studies Journal* 6, 2 (1977):146-155.

16. Robert H. Binstock, "Aging and the Future of American Politics," *Annals of the American Academy of Political and Social Science* 415 (1974):199-212.

17. Norval D. Glenn, "Aging, Disengagement, and Opinionation," *Public Opinion Quarterly* 33 (1969):17-33; Norval Glenn and Michael Grimes, "Aging, Voting, and Political Interest," *American Sociological Review* 33 (1968): 563-575; and Anne Foner, "The Polity," in Matilda White Riley, Marilyn Johnson, and Anne Foner, eds., *Aging and Society, Volume III: A Sociology of Age Stratification* (New York: Russell Sage, 1972), pp. 118-132.

18. Neal E. Cutler, *National Trends and Local Variations in the Older American Population: A Handbook for Students, Planners, and Service Providers* (Los Angeles: Social Policy Laboratory, Andrus Gerontology Center, University of Southern California, 1978), chapter 3.

19. Sidney Verba and Norman H. Nie, "Participation and the Life Cycle," in Sidney Verba and Norman H. Nie, *Participation in America: Political Democracy and Social Equality* (New York: Harper and Row, 1972), pp. 138-148.

20. E.M. Schreiber and Lorna R. Marsden, "Age and Opinions on a Government Program of Medical Aid," *Journal of Gerontology* 27 (1972):95-101; Neal E. Cutler and John R. Schmidhauser, "Age and Political Behavior," in Diana Woodruff and James Birren, eds., *Aging: Scientific Perspectives and Social Issues* (New York: Van Nostrand, 1975), pp. 376-406; and Jerry L. Weaver, "The Elderly as Political Community: The Case of National Health Policy," *Western Political Quarterly* 29 (1976):610-619.

21. Neal E. Cutler, "Resources for Senior Advocacy: Political Behavior and Partisan Flexibility," in Paul Kerschner, ed., *Advocacy and Age: Issues, Experiences, and Strategies* (Los Angeles: University of Southern California Press, 1976), pp. 23-40.

22. Henry J. Pratt, "Old Age Associations in National Politics," *Annals of*

the American Academy of Political and Social Science 415 (1974):106-119; and Henry J. Pratt, *The Gray Lobby* (Chicago: University of Chicago Press, 1976).

23. Neal E. Cutler, "Towards an Age-Appropriate Typology for the Analysis of Patterns of Membership in Voluntary Associations" (Paper presented at the Annual Meeting of the Gerontological Society, San Francisco, 1977); and Neal E. Cutler and Georgeana E. Mimms, "The Impact of Membership in Non-Political Voluntary Associations Upon Political Activity Among Older Persons" (Paper presented at the Annual Meeting of the American Political Science Association, Washington, D.C., 1977).

24. Matilda White Riley, "Social Gerontology and the Age Stratification of Society," *The Gerontologist* 11, part 1 (1971):79-87.

25. Neal E. Cutler, "The Effects of Subjective Age Identification Among the Old and Young: A Nation-wide Study of Political, Economic, and Social Attitudes," (Paper presented at the Annual Meeting of the Gerontological Society, Portland, 1974); and Neal E. Cutler, "Chronological Age, Subjective Age, and Social Welfare Orientations: The Organization of Attitudes Toward Society, Economics, and Politics," (Paper presented at the Tenth International Congress of Gerontology, Jerusalem, 1975).

4

Toward an Understanding of Population Policy in Industrialized Societies

Jason L. Finkle and
Alison McIntosh

Industrialized nations today are experiencing extremely low birthrates which, if sustained, will inevitably lead to zero population growth or even depopulation. Although many scholars and political elites in the industrialized world acknowledge that a stationary population is a desirable goal, the prospect of a cessation of population growth evokes a different reaction from governments. Already, six Eastern European countries have adopted population policies specifically designed to stimulate higher fertility, and a number of Western European countries seem to be moving in a similar direction. Low population growth and its consequences have worked their way onto the political agenda of almost all developed countries. Parliaments, government ministries, and the news media are devoting more attention to the implications of declining fertility, which some countries already see as a major social and economic problem. At the present time, the United States stands virtually alone among the industrialized nations in its reaction to low population growth but, as yet, no public official or interest group has—to the best of our knowledge—suggested that the United States government adopt a pronatalist policy to solve the problems associated with declining fertility and an aging population.

The purpose of the present paper is to suggest a framework by which to analyze the policy responses of industrialized nations to low fertility. In this effort we will try to indicate why the developed countries of Europe, notwithstanding variations in policy among them, have reacted to the phenomenon of low fertility differently from the United States. We hypothesized that what a government is likely to do, if anything, about demographic conditions will depend on three major factors: (1) how a society and its political elites perceive the relationship between population and national power; (2) how a society and its political elites perceive the relationship between population and the economy; and (3) the role of the state in that society, the extent to which government possesses the power, authority, and inclination to shape the structure of the society and the lives of its citizens.[1] This paper attempts to demonstrate that there is only a weak relationship between demographic variables and population policy. As in other areas of public policy, empirical realities do not determine

The present essay is a revised version of an earlier article by the authors entitled "Political Perceptions of Population Stabilization and Decline," published in the *Policy Studies Journal* 6, 2 (Winter 1977).

independently a government's course of action; rather, perceptions of these realities by the country's leaders and the importance attached to them shape governmental policy.

This observation may best explain why industrialized societies tend to look upon population stabilization and decline as conditions to be avoided. In almost all countries—developed as well as developing—there is a tendency for political elites to view population questions from an "Olympian" perspective which gives greater attention to the macro-effects of population trends than to their micro-consequences. Even though a strong case can be made that the individual in industrialized nations will fare better under conditions of population stabilization, political elites in these societies generally favor growth. Rather than concerning themselves with the effects of population change on family life, community environment, and personal income, political leaders are prone to focus their attention on the grand questions of national power, national culture, and national wealth.

The Demographic Context

An aversion to low or declining rates of population growth is not unique to twentieth century industrialized nations, but has been a reaction common to most societies throughout history. In contrast to the present era in which population stabilization is a concomitant of modernization and improved standards of living, in the past it was associated with famine, pestilence, and war. A stationary or declining population reminded a society of its vulnerability to natural disaster and invasion, and engendered fears of diminished national strength. States were often too weak to provide for the safety and welfare of their citizens, and populations had little protection from disease and famine, problems which became even more acute after the rise of the city. In the popular mind the failure of a population to grow signified stagnation and decay, whereas population growth was generally equated with progress and national vitality. Today, with the exception of heavy losses occasioned by warfare, high mortality is no longer a cause of low population growth in industrialized nations. Instead, population stabilization is the result of very low birth-rates, which in many countries are continuing to fall well below the level needed to replace the existing population.

Low population growth is confined at the present time to the industrialized segment of the world where income, education, and urbanization are highest. Of thirty-five countries classified by the Population Council as "more developed," all except Ireland experienced fertility decline between 1950 and 1975, and in several of these countries the declines were as large as 40 percent or more.[2] Seventeen of twenty-nine European countries already have replacement or subreplacement level fertility and five others are above that level only, it is thought, because of pronatalist policies adopted in the 1960s or before.[3] Five European countries—Austria, Luxembourg, both German republics, and Great Britain—have negative rates of natural increase;[4] for some years they have been experiencing more deaths than births. However, of these five countries, only East Germany is not gaining enough population through immigration to compensate for its negative rate of natural increase.

Replacement level fertility means that the parental generation is producing just enough children to replace itself. Under the conditions of very low mortality that prevail in all industrialized societies, replacement fertility indicates a completed family of approximately 2.11 children per woman on the average. A fertility level of replacement or below does not necessarily denote a stationary population; a society with many young people has a "growth momentum" built into its age-structure, and may continue to grow for as long as fifty to seventy years, even if birthrates remain at replacement level. Because of the length and intensity of the postwar baby boom in Canada and the United States, for example, it has been calculated that if replacement level had been reached between 1970 and 1975 and were maintained until the year 2050, Canada's population would grow by 43 percent and America's by 36 percent. In contrast, because of wartime losses and a weak, short-lived baby boom in the two German republics, the growth momentum inherent in their age-structures is only about 5 percent for the same period.[5]

While pronatalist policies are more likely to be adopted by low fertility societies and antinatalist policies tend to cluster in high fertility nations, demographic variables are nevertheless an unreliable indicator of a government's population policy. Among industrialized nations, pronatalist policies are found in those countries with relatively low fertility, but not always in the countries with the lowest fertility. The six Eastern European countries that adopted pronatalist policies during the 1960s did so at a time when their birthrates were considerable higher than birthrates in many Western countries that are still not overtly pronatalist today. France, the only Western European nation with an explicit pronatalist policy—which dates back to the Côde de la Famille of 1939—has expressed greater concern than any other country over its low birthrate, despite an unbroken record of above replacement fertility since 1941.[6] Further evidence of the weak relationship between fertility trends and public policy can be found in East Germany, the only European country in which the size of the population is actually declining. The German Democratic Republic is strongly pronatalist; yet it has found it necessary to bend to the wishes of its people by liberalizing abortion and making contraceptives more readily available, even though these measures are likely to further depress the birthrate.[7]

Determinants of Population Policy

The hypothesis that national power, the national economy, and the role of the state are crucial determinants of governmental responses to population stabilization and decline derives from a review of both the historical literature and contemporary documentation dealing with societal responses to low population growth.[8] In the following pages we will elaborate on these three determinants and, at the same time, attempt to show their interrelatedness.

Population and National Power

Statesmen as well as students of international relations have historically looked upon population as a basic element of national power. The larger the nation, the more soldiers it could mobilize for its armies; the larger the nation, the more workers to produce food and supplies for military needs. Although the calculus of power has become much more sophisticated in the modern era, taking into consideration a nation's technology, the health and education of its people, the organizational capacity of its leaders, its political legitimacy, stability, international moral standing, and structure of alliances, there is nevertheless a belief that population size is still of prime importance.[9] It is felt that although every large nation may not necessarily be a great power, every great power must be a relatively large nation. As recently as 1961, the authors of a volume on population and world power estimated that the minimum population for a great power was 45 million, and they postulated that the minimum size would increase as weapons systems and world trade became more sophisticated and costly, necessitating a larger tax base.[10] Even though there may not be a one-to-one correlation between population size and national power, China's population of 800 million makes it a powerful force in the international community, whereas Sweden, despite the quality of its population, its international moral standing, its technology, and its political stability and unity, is destined to be a far lesser influence on the world scene for no other reason than its small population size.

In many respects, France provides a classic illustration of the importance that a nation may attribute to population size and growth in its pursuit of national power. To appreciate the emphasis given by France to her demographic position, it is necessary to recall that in 1800 France was a preeminent international power whose wishes and counsel were heeded almost everywhere— an international position France has never again achieved. At the time of France's international supremacy, she had an appreciably larger population than any other European nation except Russia, which was still underdeveloped.[11] The comparative demographic advantage of France made possible the military exploits of Napoleon, who drew upon this large population base to build a mass army of conscripts that came close to overrunning all of Europe. By the time of the French defeat in the Franco-Prussian War of 1870-1871, however, Germany had not only surpassed France in population size but was growing at a more rapid rate. As Quincy Wright had noted, the French parliament began to make frequent allusion to the growing population differential between France and Germany, a development which was viewed by France as evidence of her increasing vulnerability.[12] From that time until the start of the second world war, French political leaders and intellectuals consistently forecast the decline of French diplomatic and cultural influence in world affairs because of what they considered to be her demographic weakness. They also feared that the low population density that was expected to result from low birthrates would encourage large numbers of alien immigrants who would "denationalize, deculturize and delanguagize" France, making her vulnerable to military penetration.[13]

French perceptions of population issues do not necessarily typify those held by the leaders of other developed societies. What is typical about France is that the views of its elites concerning the relationship between population and national power are intimately tied to the particular history and experience of the country. In the case of France, demographic factors have been used by French intellectuals and elites to rationalize the lack of success France has experienced in her wars in the nineteenth and twentieth centuries, as well as her reduced importance as an international power compared with the Napoleonic period. Even today there seems to be more discussion of "demographic deficiencies" among the French public than in any other European nation. Yet other European states, including Great Britain and Sweden, have expressed similar sentiments—albeit in milder form—as low fertility and the possibility of population decline raise doubts about their international influence, cultural identity, and "the maintenance and extension of Western values and culture."[14]

Population and the Economy

Notwithstanding an awareness of the social costs of continued population growth, politicians as well as professional economists in industrialized countries generally feel that population growth helps the economy. Uncertainty and disagreement over the precise relationship between population and economic growth still exist; yet, when birthrates fall to replacement level or below, there are signs of uneasiness in the highest echelons of government in socialist and nonsocialist societies alike. The belief that a steadily growing population is economically beneficial owes much to the observation that the period of most rapid population growth in Europe and European territories overseas, which started about 1750 and continued for upward of a century, was roughly coterminous with the period of greatest economic growth. Conversely, when fertility has been very low, as in the 1930s and today, the economies of much of the industrialized world have been in depression or recession.

Support for the view that population growth is important to the economy came from the research and writings of John Maynard Keynes, Alvin Hansen, and other "stagnation thesis" economists who analyzed the effects of declining fertility on the economy. Particularly influential were the views of Keynes, who maintained that the influence of a growing population in generating the enormous increase in capital during the nineteenth century and since has been given too little importance.[15] In looking at Britain in the period between 1860 and 1913, Keynes found that the major source of economic growth in those years was capital investment, which, in turn, was induced by an increasing population and technological change.[16] Hansen, building on the work of Keynes, saw the main implications of a declining rate of population growth as reducing the rate of investment and increasing the propensity to save, thus diminishing the volume oj both employment and income.[17] Kuznets, writing later, also found a positive relationship between population and economic growth in developed countries; however, he concluded that other factors, especially technological and social change, were more important to economic growth.[18] Still, the prevailing view is that declining fertility imposes a burden on the economic system and, in the judgment of one European economist, "the reassurances of those who believe that economic growth can still take place despite a low rate of population growth are certainly not yet sufficiently credible to convince the majority."[19]

Socialist political leaders and elites also see a positive correlation between population growth and economic prosperity, though they arrive at this judgment by a somewhat different route from their nonsocialist counterparts in Western Europe and North America. Socialist perceptions of the relationship between population and the economy start with Marx's views on population and his criticism of Malthus and other classical economists who were concerned about "overpopulation." Although Marx held that each historical mode of production has its own law of population valid within its own limits, he formulated only the capitalist law. Under capitalism, according to Marx, the laboring population produces, along with the accumulation of capital, the means by which itself is rendered superfluous and is turned into a relative surplus population. "This is the law of population peculiar to the capitalist mode of production."[20]

Marx's criticism of Malthus and his denunciation of capitalism endowed his followers with a sense of optimism about the ability of a socialist economy to absorb population growth. In the absence of an explicit formulation, it was assumed by many Marxists that the socialist law of population was the inverse of the capitalist law and that, in a socialist economy, a growing population would not lead to poverty and unemployment. "Relative overpopulation, therefore, does not exist and cannot exist under socialism. The growth of population accelerates the development of a socialist society, increases its power and strength."[21] In recent years, sharply declining fertility in the socialist states of Eastern Europe has forced economists, demographers, and government officials to reexamine some of their assumptions. The similarity of fertility behavior in Eastern and Western industrialized nations suggests to some population experts in Eastern Europe that population trends are affected by demographic factors that seem unrelated to either socialist or capitalist laws of population.[22] Committed to the belief that population is an economic asset, the majority of socialist governments have responded to the downturn in birthrates by adopting policies aimed at raising fertility.

Perhaps more important than ideology or theory in affecting the behavior of governments are some of the more down-to-earth problems caused by the impact of low population growth on the economy. Quite distinct from the large questions of savings and investment, capital formation, and national product, declining fertility introduces more immediate problems of accommodating to a lower—or zero—population growth rate and adjusting to an older population. As much of Europe has already learned, low fertility can mean severe labor shortages. With fewer young people entering the work force, manning new industries will require greater reliance on interoccupational mobility and the retraining and relocation of more established and possibly less flexible workers.[23] Many analysts fear that an aging population and labor force will be less creative and innovative than a younger one and that this may lead to a diminution of a nation's economic vitality.[24] As a result of changes in the age-structure, industrialized countries, which are already feeling strains in their social security systems, will have to bear heavier costs for pensions, and health and social services for the growing numbers and proportions of elderly dependents.[25]

Role of the State

While political elites may react to low population growth on the basis of their perceptions of its effect on national power and the economy, the policy options available to government are circumscribed by the legitimate role and function of the state in regulating society and the lives of its citizens. In some countries it is felt that government should be limited to maintaining the essentials for defense, security, and economic prosperity; it is believed that government has little if any role in influencing the private and personal behavior of individuals. Other governments hold to the view that society cannot function properly if individuals do not conform to the requirements of the larger community. In these latter countries, the fertility of a couple is seen as having consequences which are a proper concern of the state and which may warrant governmental intervention.

Of the seven European nations with pronatalist policies, six are Eastern European socialist countries where it is accepted that government has a legitimate interest in population questions, including fertility behavior. A hallmark of the socialist states is an ideological commitment to centralized planning as a means of laying the material and technical bases for communism. In these centrally planned economies, "demographic considerations play a role in formulating the strategy of development as well as in the preparation of plans."[26] Pronatalist policy, however, should not be identified exclusively with socialist planning. During the 1930s, the most comprehensive and systematically applied pronatalist policies were found in Nazi Germany and, to a lesser extent, in Mussolini's Italy. Even in historical times the most vigorous pronatalist policies were formulated in the centralized states of the Mercantilist period.

In the liberal democracies of Western Europe and North America there are distinct limits to how far government may go in attempting to influence fertility behavior. These more decentralized, pluralistic political systems must accommodate diverse groups and influences, making it difficult for them to formulate coherent and coordinated policies aimed at influencing levels of fertility. For example, while sentiment is growing in most industrialized societies that it is more important to encourage births than prevent them, there is still public pressure for governments to provide their citizens with family planning services, including abortion. Even France, the only nonsocialist country with an explicit pronatalist policy, has been forced to provide contraceptives under national health insurance and, more recently, to legalize abortion on demand during the first trimester of pregnancy.[27]

When Western European countries contemplate pronatalist strategies, they discover that the policy measures conducive to this end raise sensitive political questions involving the welfare responsibilities of society, the rights and equality of women, and the issue of governmental regulation itself. To encourage a higher birthrate, a government may attempt to restrict access to contraceptive services, to increase financial assistance to couples with children, and to reduce the conflict for women between participation in the labor force and motherhood—all of which engender varying degrees of public controversy. As a consequence, Western governments are hesitant to do those things that may be necessary to achieve a higher level of fertility even when political elites agree on goals. The socialist states, in part because of their greater political centralization, demonstrate more capacity to formulate and pursue pronatalist policies.

The American Reaction to Low Population Growth

At the beginning of this paper we observed that the United States is virtually alone among developed nations in its lack of concern over low fertility. An explanation for the different response of the United States is that most Americans do not see their national power and economic prosperity as dependent on a growing population. Furthermore, not only is the role of the state more circumscribed than in almost any other country, but political, ideological, and institutional factors also inhibit the United States from moving toward pronatalism even if birthrates were to decline still further.

While we have maintained that demographic variables do not determine population policy, there is little doubt that the way American society regards low population growth is influenced by the country's demographic history and contemporary demographic trends. In common with Canada, Australia, and New Zealand, the United States experienced a much more intense and prolonged baby boom after World War II than did any European country and, as a consequence, has a younger age-structure than most European countries. Notwithstanding subreplacement fertility, there will continue to be significant growth in the size of the American population for the foreseeable future.[28]

In addition to the effects of age-structure, American population growth is also affected by immigration, which at the present time accounts for nearly one-fourth of the annual population increase. This estimate does not take into account the contribution of illegal immigration to American growth. In the years between 1964 and 1975, the number of deportable immigrants located by the Immigration and Naturalization Service (INS) increased from 42,879 to 766,600, some 90 percent of whom were of Mexican origin.[29] According to the rough estimate of the INS Commissioner in January 1977, the number of illegal immigrants permanently resident in the United States was placed at around 6 million, most of whom have entered in the last decade.[30] There is evidence that American attitudes are hardening toward legal as well as illegal immigration. On the other hand, some ethnic groups and citizens committed to a generous immigration policy are exercising their influence to keep it relatively liberal.[31]

Population growth in the United States is destined to be considerably above the European average as a consequence of America's age-structure and the probable course of immigration policy. Therefore, it is not surprising that the United States has found no need to seriously consider adopting a pronatalist policy. Historically, there has been scant mention in the United States of population as a basis of national power. Rather, political leaders and scholars have tended to stress America's continental position, its dynamic economy, and the quality of its people as sources of national strength. The geographical isolation of the United States has served to protect its borders from direct attack. Furthermore, its neighbors on the American continent have been numerically, technologically and economically weaker and have posed no real threat. As the international commitments of the United States have begun to extend far beyond its borders, America's superior technology, natural resources, and system of alliances have loomed larger in its calculations of national power than population size.

There is little evidence at the present time that Americans or their leaders consider population growth as essential to the economic well-being of the country.[32] In the past, population growth and an adequate supply of labor were regarded as important in the economic development of the United States but, today, access to raw materials and world trade seem to be far more important than population growth in the minds of those who shape economic policy. Although many economists feel that population stabilization may mean a reduced rate of economic growth, there is no discernible sentiment in favor of stimulating a higher birthrate as a means of overcoming America's economic problems. An abundance of land and resources as well as a long history of prosperity unmarred by disastrous famines, epidemics, or breaches of territorial integrity seems to have given Americans a sense of confidence that they have control over the critical determinants of economic prosperity, and that population growth, while helpful, is of secondary importance.

Finally, the United States is not likely to follow other industrialized nations in adopting a pronatalist population policy because of the more circumscribed role of the state; no European country equals the United States in the limits it imposes on the functions and responsibilities of government. These limits are historical, ideological, and institutional in origin. As has become evident in political struggles over the issues of birth control and abortion, population questions are closely tied to religious attitudes, individual rights, and beliefs about the proper role of the state in a democratic society. The dominant view in the United States is that government should refrain from intervening in the private lives and decisions of citizens, especially in their fertility behavior—a principle emphasized by President Eisenhower when, referring to birth control, he asserted: "I cannot imagine anything more emphatically a subject that is not a proper political or governmental activity."[33] After leaving office, Eisenhower retracted this statement; nevertheless, his remarks symbolize the conflict in American life between a commitment to abstract principles and an adaptable approach to social problems—a conflict which is even more pronounced over issues of fertility and population.

The similarity between pronatalist and welfare measures creates an additional obstacle to the adoption of a policy explicitly intended to stimulate the birthrate in the United States. Those programs and measures which have been most efficacious in encouraging births in Europe are almost indistinguishable from a series of welfare measures which have not as yet been accepted by the American polity.[34] This is not to say that pronatalism, despite its necessitating an expansion of the welfare state, will remain unacceptable if low population growth is judged to constitute a social crisis. However, even though the population is failing to reproduce itself, is getting older, and seems headed for the cessation of growth, America's demographic situation is not perceived by its leaders or the public as a threat to the national interest. It may well turn out, as Norman Ryder recently remarked to the authors, that low fertility in America may be thrust onto the political agenda only when the newspaper headlines proclaim "American Deaths Exceed Births."

Summary and Conclusions

Some years ago, Kingsley Davis drew attention to the fact that governments do not adopt population policies to influence demographic trends *per se*, but do so to advance social, economic, and political objectives valued by the society and its leaders.[35] Consistent with Davis's observation, we have maintained that societies are prone to adopt population policies mainly to enhance national power and economic prosperity. However, as nations differ both in their culture and in their demographic and historical experiences, it follows that they will perceive the relationships between demographic trends and societal objectives differently. Thus, even when demographic conditions are similar, nations will not always react in the same way.

In this paper we have attempted to show that the prospect of a stationary or declining population generally induces a sense of unease or insecurity in a society. Despite a feeling that continued population growth threatens the environment and diminishes the quality of life, political elites as well as intellectuals seem to show greater concern over the prospect that their nation may experience population stabilization. We have held that this attitude among elites is rooted in their tendency to emphasize "the welfare of the nation" as they perceive it, often to the neglect of the individual and the family.

The paper maintains that the response of a government is not determined by the demographic situation alone, but is mainly dependent on the way a nation's political elites and other influentials interpret a country's population trends and their relevance to national power and the economy. Of perhaps greater importance in determining population policy is the role of the state in different societies. Although the power of the state has increased in all industrialized nations, there are nevertheless important differences among countries in what the state can and cannot do. The policy options available to a country's political leaders are in large measure defined by the role and responsibilities assumed by the state.

At the present time, France, West Germany, Great Britain, Austria, Luxembourg, and Sweden, among other countries, talk a good deal about low fertility and its deleterious impact on national power, prosperity, and cultural identity. Aside from France, however, only the socialist states of Eastern Europe are actually attempting to modify fertility behavior. The reason for this East-West split does not lie in differences in demographic conditions but in the way they are regarded by political leaders. The Eastern European socialist states begin with a Marxian bias in favor of population growth, have a tendency to attempt to manipulate birth rates in conjunction with economic planning, and feel less constrained than Western governments in undertaking interventions designed to influence personal behavior.

Whether the nations of Western Europe will follow the example of Eastern Europe and adopt pronatalist policies is difficult to predict. On the one hand, concern over low population growth is mounting and if replacement or subreplacement fertility continues for a sustained period, Western Europe's concern over low population growth may turn to alarm. Thus as astute an observer as Bernard Berelson of the Population Council has noted that, "while most of the developing world is after lower growth . . . the majority of these developed countries are seeking to move the other way."[3][6] On the other hand, the pluralistic political systems of Western Europe may find it nearly as difficult as the United States to achieve a political consensus that would enable them to undertake a coordinated campaign to stimulate fertility.

The United States is not immune to the influences that may lead governments throughout Europe to attempt to increase the birthrate; nevertheless, neither the American experience nor its present demographic condition point in that direction. The strength of the conservationist and environmental lobbies, the growing power of the women's movement, and a genuine feeling that the population is large enough, are factors that militate against the emergence of a pronatalist policy. At the same time, there are other features of American society and its political institutions that can also be expected to impede the adoption of an explicit pronatalist policy. Foremost among these is the probable difficulty of achieving a political consensus on an issue that would launch the country on a massive family welfare program. Yet as Europe is discovering, generous family allowances, maternity grants, more and better public housing, periods of extended and paid maternity leave for working mothers, and other welfare measures appear to be essential for encouraging larger families in highly industrialized societies. Additionally, the United States has less political capacity and inclination to undertake long-range social planning than most of the countries of both Eastern and Western Europe. In the long run the ability of the United States and Western European countries to manage without a pronatalist policy will depend on their ingenuity in coping with labor shortages, aging work forces and elderly dependents—that is, in devising public policies that satisfy societal needs which have hitherto been served by a growing population.

Notes

1. In a recent empirical study of perceptions of, and attitudes toward, population in Brazil, the responses of a broadly based sample of elites were classified in eight categories, all of which could be placed on our three dimensions of national power, national economy, and role of the state. See Peter McDonough and Amaury de Souza, "Brazilian Elites and Population Policy," *Population and Development Review* 3, 4 (December 1977):377-401.

2. W. Parker Mauldin, "Fertility Trends: 1950-1975," *Studies in Family Planning* 7, 9 (September 1976):243-44.

3. Pronatalist population policies are those explicitly intended to foster higher birthrates. Among European governments which can be described as pronatalist, the principal measures employed are: (1) financial inducements including family allowances which are progressive in amount for successive children; (2) increased child care facilities including extended postmaternity leave; and (3) restrictions on the availability of contraception and legal abortion.

The demographic effects of pronatalist policies in Eastern Europe have been evaluated by Jerzy Berent, "Fertility Trends and Policies in Eastern Europe in the 1970s" (Paper prepared for the Conference on Social, Economic and Health Aspects of Low Fertility convened by the Center for Population Research, National Institutes of Health, and the World Health Organization, Washington, D.C., March 7-11, 1977, publication in process). Gérard Calot and Jacqueline Hecht estimate that the stimulating effect of France's pronatalist policy on French fertility since 1935 may be in the region of 10 percent or 0.2 children per woman. See "Long Term Population Policies" (Paper prepared for the Council of Europe Seminar on the Implications of a Stationary or Declining Population in Europe, Strasbourg, September 6-10, 1976, p. 15).

4. For Austria, Luxembourg, and the German republics see United Nations *Demographic Yearbook*, 1975 (New York: United Nations, 1976) table 22. The information that Great Britain has had a negative rate of national increase since December 1976 was given to the authors by Dr. David E.C. Eversley.

5. Michael S. Teitelbaum, "U.S. Population Growth in International Perspective," in Charles F. Westoff, ed., *Toward the End of Growth.* (Englewood Cliffs, N.J.: Prentice-Hall, Inc., 1973), pp. 76-78.

6. United Nations, *Demographic Yearbook*, 1954, table 21; 1965, table 30; 1969, table 31; 1975, table 22.

7. Arno Donda, Head of the Delegation of the German Democratic Republic, Statement before the Plenary Session of the World Population Conference, Bucharest, 23 August 1974, p. 5.

8. Among the best of the many historical accounts of population policy are: Charles Emil Strangeland, *Pre-Malthusian Doctrines of Population*, Studies in History, Economics and Public Law, vol. 21, no. 3 (New York: Columbia University Press, 1904); Hugh Last, "The Social Policy of Augustus," in *The Cambridge Ancient History*, vol. 10 (Cambridge, England: The University Press, 1934), pp. 441-55. For twentieth century responses, see David V. Glass, *Population: Policies and Movements in Europe* (London: Frank Cass and Co., 1940); Alva Myrdal, *Nation and Family* (New York: Harper and Brothers, 1941); Gunnar Myrdal, *Population: A Problem for Democracy* (Cambridge, Mass.: Harvard University Press, 1940); Bernard Berelson, ed., *Population Policy in Developed Countries* (New York: McGraw Hill, 1974); Maurice Kirk, Massimo Livi-Bacci and Egon Szabady, eds., *Law and Fertility in Europe* (Dolhain, Belgium: Ordina Editions, 1976); Robert J. McIntyre, "Pronatalist Programs in Eastern Europe," *Soviet Studies* 27, 3 (July 1975):366-80. Both historical and twentieth century policies are discussed in Joseph J. Spengler, *France Faces Depopulation* (Durham, N.C.: Duke University Press, 1938).

9. The role of population size and change in the calculus of national power is discussed by Quincy Wright, *The Study of International Relations* (New York: Appleton-Century-Crofts, 1955), p. 362; A.F.K. Organski, Bruce B.

des Mesquita and Allen Lamborn, "The Effective Population in International Politics," U.S. Commission on Population Growth and the American Future, Research Reports, vol. 4, *Governance and Population* (Washington, D.C.: U.S. Government Printing Office, 1972), pp. 235-50; Hans J. Morgenthau, *Politics Among Nations*, 5th ed. (New York: Alfred A. Knopf, 1973), p. 126; Ray S. Cline, *World Power Assessment: A Calculus of Strategic Drift* (Boulder, Colo.: Westview Press, 1975).

10. Katherine Organski and A.F.K. Organski, *Population and World Power* (New York: Alfred A. Knopf, 1961), p. 13.

11. Philip Hauser, *Population and World Politics* (Glencoe, Illinois: The Free Press, 1958), p. 17.

12. Quincy Wright, *A Study of War* (Chicago: University of Chicago Press, 2 vols., 1942), p. 1136.

13. Spengler, *France Faces Depopulation*, p. 132, esp. n. 40.

14. United Kingdom, Royal Commission on Population, *Report* (London: H.M.S.O., 1949), p. 226; Alva Myrdal, *Nation and Family*, pp. 104-5.

15. John Maynard Keynes, "Some Economic Consequences of a Declining Population," *Eugenics Review* 29 (April 1937), p. 14.

16. V.J. Tarascio, "Keynes on the Sources of Economic Growth," *The Journal of Economic History* 31, 2 (June 1971), p. 432.

17. Alvin H. Hansen, "Economic Progress and Declining Population Growth," *The American Economic Review* 29 (March 1939):1-15.

18. Simon Kuznets, *Modern Economic Growth* (New Haven: Yale University Press, 1966), pp. 8-16, 63-85.

19. Denis Maillat, "Population Growth and Economic Growth" (Paper presented at the Council of Europe Seminar on the Implications of a Stationary or Declining Population in Europe, Strasbourg, September 6-10, 1976), p. 1.

20. Karl Marx, *Capital*, vol. 1, Trans. S. Moore and Edward Aveling, (Chicago, London, 1909). Cited in Mandell M. Bober, *Karl Marx's Interpretation of History* (Cambridge, Mass.: Harvard University Press, 1927), p. 230.

21. A.Y. Popov, Sovremennoe Mal'tusianstvo—*Chelovekonenavistnichev-skaya ideologiia imperialistov* (Moscow, 1953). Cited in William Petersen, *Population*, 2nd ed. (New York: Macmillan, 1969), p. 635.

22. See, for example, V. Srb, "On the Issue of Population Laws of Socialism and Communism." Paper prepared for the International Demographic Symposium, Zakopane, 1964 (Warsaw: Panstwowe Wydawnictwo Naukowe, 1966), pp. 51-56; Egon Szabady, "Interdependence Between Fertility Changes and Socio-Economic Development in Eastern European Countries," *Population Review* 16, 1 and 2 (January-December 1972):9-17. A number of economists and demographers in the USSR are also calling for the adoption of pronatalist policies similar to those of other Eastern European countries. See, for example, the citations in David M. Heer, "The New Direction of Soviet Population Policy" (Paper delivered at the Annual Meetings of the Population Association of America, St. Louis, April 21-23, 1977).

23. See, for example, Gunnar Myrdal, *Population*, pp. 168-71; W.B. Reddaway, *The Economics of a Declining Population* (London: George Allen and Unwin Ltd., 1939), pp. 59-63; Joseph J. Spengler, *Declining Population Growth Revisited*, Carolina Population Center, Monograph 14 (Chapel Hill, N.C.: University of North Carolina, 1971), pp. 31-34.

24. Gunnar Myrdal, *Population*, pp. 160-161; Ansley J. Coale, "Should the United States Start A Campaign For Fewer Births?" *Population Index* 34, 4 (October-December 1968), p. 471.

25. See, for example, David E.C. Eversley, "Social Implications of Low Fertility" (Paper presented at the Conference on the Social, Economic and Health Aspects of Low Fertility convened by the Center for Population Research, National Institutes of Health and the World Health Organization, Washington, D.C.: March 7-11, publication in process); Martin Feldstein, "Facing the Social Security Crisis," *The Public Interest* 47 (Spring 1977):88-100; *New York Times*, 17 May 1971, p. 1. See also the papers by William Petersen and Neal Cutler in this volume.

26. United Nations, *Determinants and Consequences of Population Trends* (New York: United Nations, 1973), p. 595.

27. Paul Paillat and Jacques Houdaille, "France," in Maurice Kirk et al., *Law and Fertility in Europe*, vol. 1, pp. 249-51.

28. Some demographers believe that fertility will remain very low, though with fluctuations up and down (e.g., Nathan Keyfitz, "On Future Population," *Journal of the American Statistical Association* 67, 38 (June 1972), p. 361; Norman Ryder, "The Family in Developed Countries," *Scientific American* 231, 3 (September 1974):123-32. Other demographers give more emphasis to the predicted upturn in the late 1970s and 1980s (see June Sklar and Judith Berkov, "The American Birth Rate, 1975: Evidences of a Coming Rise," *Science* 189 (August 1975):693-700. Recently, three different economic-demographic analyses based on the Easterlin Hypothesis predicted a marked upturn of fertility starting in 5-10 years. (Ronald D. Lee, "Demographic Forecasting and the Easterlin Hypothesis," *Population and Development Review* 2, 3-4 (September-December 1976):459-68.)

29. United States Immigration and Naturalization Service, *Annual Report*, 1972, 1975, table 27B.

30. *Los Angeles Times*, 9 January 1977, p. 3.

31. See, for example, the report of class actions brought by a number of immigrant aid organizations on behalf of ethnic groups denied permission to enter the United States, *New York Times*, 24 June 1977, p. 8. See also the article by David North in this volume.

32. The clearest indication of the equanimity with which America views the prospect of population stabilization is found in the Report of the United States Commission on Population Growth and the American Future (Washington, D.C.: U.S. Government Printing Office, 1972). The words and tone of the report bear a close resemblance to those of the National Resources Committee which was set

up to explore the consequences of the low fertility of the 1930s. See *The Problems of a Changing Population* (Washington, D.C.: U.S. Government Printing Office, 1938).

33. *New York Times*, 3 December 1959, p. 18.

34. For a discussion of these measures see Jason L. Finkle and Alison McIntosh, "Policy Responses to Population Stagnation in Developed Societies" (Paper presented at the Conference on the Social, Economic and Health Aspects of Low Fertility, sponsored by the Center for Population Research, National Institutes of Health, and the World Health Organization, Washington, D.C., March 7-11, 1977, publication in process.

35. Kingsley Davis, "The Nature and Purpose of Population Policy," in Kingsley Davis and Frederick G. Styles, eds., *California's Twenty Million*, Population Monograph Series, no. 10 (Berkeley, Calif.: University of California, 1971), p. 6.

36. Berelson, *Population Policy*, p. 773.

Part II
Population Policy:
National Perspectives

5 Procedural and Substantive Unorthodoxies on the Population Commission's Agenda

A.E.Keir Nash

Most commentaries on presidential commissions satirize or bemoan their fate in the federal policy process.[1] Often, it is said, their recommendations are honored only in the breach. From this perspective, it is a fault of the American political process that it does not take commissions seriously. A minority view is that most commissions fare better in long-run influence upon policy making than they are usually given credit for.[2]

I wish to suggest a third view. It's a good thing that their advice is not usually taken all that seriously. Most commission critics err in their initial assumption about commissions. They assume that the primary commission product is useful policy advice that should be acted upon by the president and by Congress. But is that so?

A good analytic starting point is examining the policy formulation processes of the Commission on Population Growth and the American Future. Created by Congress pursuant to a July 1969 presidential message, few commissions have been asked to wrestle with weightier issues than was the Population Commission in the two years of its legislated existence, March 1970 to March 1972. Concerned with the prospect of accommodating a third 100 million Americans between then and the century's end, President Nixon called for a commission to explore the impact of population growth and migration up to the year 2000 on the American economy and polity. Pressed by the population lobby, Congress added two further tasks to the commission's agenda—assessing the impact of population change on natural resources and environmental policies, stipulating, however, that such policies would have to be consonant with American ethical values. Few commissions received as much limelighting. Yet, those who have written about it, despite varying greatly in their analyses, err equally on a critical count—what actually happened.

The Population Commission's Modus Operandi—Two Views

Two discussions of the commission's structure and policy formulation processes adequately illustrate the variance: those by the commission's executive director, Charles Westoff, and political scientists Peter Bachrach and Elihu Bergman.[3] There is little to take exception to in what Westoff *does* say. The commission

55

originated in "pressures brought to bear . . . from the environmental concerns of the day, which had reached a shrill level in 1969 and 1970," and in "the persistence of John D. Rockefeller 3rd."[4] "Conservative by college students' standards, liberal by national and White House standards,"[5] the commissioners spent the first nine months hearing expert presentations on the fundamentals of population studies, deciding what issues to tackle, and issuing in March 1971, an Interim Report that was politically "extremely successful" and that "undoubtedly contributed to enhancing"[6] the commission's cohesiveness as a working group. During its second and final year, getting down to the brass tacks of formulating policy positions threatened this cohesiveness chiefly over: (a) the issue of abortion; (b) whether to recommend a more restrictive immigration policy; and (c) most basic of all, the scope and sweep of the final report's analysis of the "population problem" and of its policy recommendations. As Westoff put it, "The basic problem was the intrinsically diffuse nature of population effects."[7] One *could* make policy proposals about almost anything that affected people.

There developed on the commission three basic positions: (1) the "unwanted fertility" view that saw the population problem "mostly as the consequence of the lack of control of fertility . . . to be solved by promoting equal access to the means of control";[8] (2) the ecological view that argued for "nothing less than a different set of values toward nature, the transcendence of a laissez-faire market system, a redefinition of human identity . . . and a radical change . . . of the growth ethic";[9] and (3) the "social justice view," which simply did not place population "high on the agenda of priorities," regarded the unwanted fertility solution as a poor substitute for redistribution of income and real equality of opportunity, and "found the anti-establishment views of the ecological minority at least superficially compatible."[10] Yet for Westoff, despite the "frequently acrimonious debates," there were "few consequences for the final policy recommendations."[11] Settling the immigration issue in favor of recommending no significant change, and agreeing to disagree over abortion, the commission was aware that its chances for effectiveness depended on maximizing unity. Though recommending population stabilization as a national goal, the commission determined to stress the unwanted fertility solution and derivative proposals. Such a solution "had everything" going politically for it—low cost, no radical changes, and advocating what people wanted to do anyhow.[12] Though chagrined with the White House's reaction (damning the abortion and "contraceptives for minors" proposals, while ignoring everything else), the commission disbanded, on balance well-pleased with its work. Confident that the enormous amount of population research contracted for and published would have an indirect long-term effect on policy, making plans for a "citizens' commission" to influence public opinion, the commission believed that, if nothing else came to pass, the report would be influential in other countries with more acute population problems.

Standing outside the fast-closed door of commission deliberations, Bachrach and Bergman reached a different verdict. Applying the Bachrach-Baratz "non-decision-making" model, Bachrach and Bergman judged the commission's work "an opportunity forfeited" to take up the full range of population issues.[13] Although the commission did not avoid controversy with respect to abortion and sex education, these were well-worn issues in the family-planning dialogue. "In the work of the commission we see a bias favoring the familiar and the traditional, and a resistance to venturing further afield, despite substantial justification for so doing."[14] The commission "resisted what could have been a fruitful encounter with . . . controversial substance."[15] This would have required exploring thoroughly, inter alia, "the potentially explosive controversies involved in . . . interlocks among resources, affluence, population, and technology as a major cause of environmental deterioration."[16] And it would have required grappling with, rather than merely assuming, the political and social values entailed in the unwanted fertility school's "freedom of choice solution," especially as it related: (a) to the redistributive wants of the poor and minorities, and (b) to the effects on the environment of increasing per capita affluence even if ZPG were achieved. Taking a basically "non-political 'within system' approach,"[17] the commission reached specific recommendations in respect to contraceptive technology and availability. But, "although . . . condemning widespread institutional racism . . . the related commission recommendations" were strikingly nebulous in the contrast.[18] The commission, in short, "consciously or unconsciously engaged in nondecision-making by constructing a policy making agenda within a limited and familiar range, and by simultaneously limiting the scope of controversy that might enlarge it."[19]

Not for Bachrach and Bergman was the reason for all this "non-decision-making" hard to find. It lay in the composition of the commission. Although in a superficial sense containing "a broad representation from the public and private sectors,"[20] eight of the original twenty-four members came from the "family-planning establishment." Neither leading demographic critics of that position (for example, Judith Blake and Kingsley Davis), nor leading ecological critics (such as Barry Commoner, Paul Ehrlich, and Garrett Hardin) were appointed. Further, although there were women appointed, "not one . . . was poor."[21] Nor were the black appointees. *Q.E.D.* Rather a different version of what happened from Westoff's. Which is right?

A Third View

My difficulty with both is that they avoid equally the most conspicuous feature of commission policy formulation—how little went off according to Hoyle, whether the rule-book be Westoff's pluralistic Hoyle or Bachrach and Bergman's antipluralist edition.

This can be clearly seen by focusing on four points: (1) the commission's composition; (2) its authority and communication structures; (3) in consequence, what did and did not get onto its policy agenda, and (4) what very nearly came to pass by way of policy recommendation.

In my judgment the most distinctive features of the commission's composition were quite different from what Bachrach and Bergman imply. True, there were no Hardins or Ehrlichs on the commission. But I think that less interesting than two other circumstances. One is the extent to which the makeup of the commission was not "White House dictated" but rather more broadly representative and more academic than customary. Not many commissions, after all, draw 45 percent of their membership from primarily academic backgrounds. The other was the role of chance or, if you prefer, of imperfect "background checking" in the appointment process. There were at least two instances of this.

In one instance the White House appointment managers doubtless thought they were getting a moderate Republican inasmuch as the youthful appointee had worked for a senatorial candidate from that party. They erred. In the other instance, the White House presumably thought it had an even better bet—a student at a leading law school who had a solid right-wing background in Young Americans for Freedom and who had penned a letter to Nixon congratulating him just after his 1968 election. (The letter presumably was duly filed away as an entry on the short roster of "young Republican talent.") Imagine the surprise when said appointee turned up at his first commission meeting in "hippie regalia"—long hair, jeans, buckskin jacket, and boots. During the eighteen months between the election and the commission's formation the commissioner had, unbeknownst to the White House talent scouts, undergone a "theopolitical" conversion to the cause of "ecologism." Thus, quite by mistake, the Ehrlich-Hardin viewpoint found itself vocally represented for the life of the commission—with a touch of populist radicalism thrown in too. The most picturesque of the instances, it illustrates a more pervasive characteristic of the commission's composition. The viewpoints that many commissioners came to express could not have been predicted from the appointment process or from their backgrounds.

The second important organizational factor affecting the commission's policy agenda was its communication and authority structure. Consider for a moment the orthodox textbook version of commission-staff linkage: a full-time GS-18 executive director, typically a Washington lawyer or other capital city knowledgeable whose expertise is primarily political, who is preeminently an expediter of conflict-resolution. Through him flow communications between commission and staff. He and his deputy alone among the staff have the general "right of the floor" during commission meetings.

None of these orthodoxies characterized the Population Commission. Quite contrary to the enabling legislation's anticipation of a full-time GS-18 equivalent executive director, the commission chairman agreed to a two-thirds-time executive director who commuted from a distinguished university some 200 miles away. This decision had numerous consequences.

One consequence was exacerbation of the usual commission problems of assembling an able and committed staff on brief notice. To simplify a bit, the result was a staff very unequal in abilities and background, whose capacities and achievements bore fitful relationship to the inchoate staff hierarchy within which they were placed, whose abilities bore equally fitful relationship to the demographic knowledge that the executive director considered pivotal, and whose aims, both personal and ideological, varied enormously.

A second consequence stemmed from the circumstance that the two-thirds-appointment worked out in practice to an executive directorial staff-controlling presence running only from Tuesday lunchtimes through Thursday midafter-noons. There was no regularized structure of staff meetings to work out responses to commission needs or to iron out intrastaff differences.

A third consequence was a pronounced tendency among the staff to follow the well-known precept for mice's recreation when the cat's away.

Absent from normal internal mechanisms of conflict-resolution, the "less loyalist" staff turned to a device that was to prove as fruitful to the commission agenda's openness as the happenstance appointment of some of the commissioners. The opportunity for that device resulted from two curious circumstances. One was the commission chairman's sustaining injuries that prevented his chairing one commission hearing. The other (what this proves about either elitist or non-decision-making models I shall not seek to divine) was the fluke that a former prep-school roommate of one staff member knew well one of the two vice-chairmen. Not to belabor the details, the result was a successful move during the meeting chaired by this vice-chairman to extend the right of the floor to all professional staff. Later "conservative" attempts to rescind this grant did not long succeed against the participatory mode of the day.

A further consequence of this unsettling of hierarchy was that staff persons and dissident commissioners began, by the devices of individual staff member to individual commissioner letters and phone calls (and vice versa), to circumvent the normal "hourglassing" of communications through the executive director. This became a fairly common practice.

The combined result of these procedural and structural unorthodoxies was substantial in terms of what issues got onto the policy agenda and how they were resolved. In general, one may summarize what happened as follows:

(1) More or less anything that two commissioners, or one commissioner and one staffer, wished on the agenda, got there. That pretty much covered the field.

(2) If one is to speak at all of commission deliberations in the Bachrachian mode of mobilization of bias, one would properly have to speak in the plural, of mobilizations of biases. To the extent that one group pushed for a limited "unwanted fertility" agenda, other groups pushed for broader views.

(3) Although the problem analyses and policy recommendations in the final

report were chiefly of the limited sort, that outcome by no means stemmed from the executive director or the chairman keeping ironclad control over the terms of the debate. It is not even evident that they wished to. Certainly it would not have been feasible. Instead, the outcome is more accurately attributed to four factors.

The first was the way in which the commission's agenda was temporally (*not* substantively) structured. The first year and a half of the commission's deliberations were mainly a series of expert presentations on more or less every conceivable aspect of the population problem. The consequence was a veritable parade of witnesses giving out informative knowledge, educating the commission, but leaving little time for debate among the commissioners. Indeed, many commissioners objected to this procedure from time to time, but with only modest success—in part because they had agreed to it early on, and in part because such procedure did have a certain academic logic to it. Its costs only became clear to most much later.

The second sprang from the natural advantage which accrued to those on the commission and on the staff who preferred the more limited approach. It is always easier to resolve in favor of a little than a lot.

The third is closely related. The commission was acutely aware of the desirability of presenting a solid front. That surely affected the outcome. Yet it is important to distinguish between keeping something off the agenda and a prudent preference for half a loaf of accomplishment in affecting public and legislative disposition of recommendations.

The fourth boils down to different levels of skill and time-input among the commissioners and staff. Space does not permit a detailed justification of this judgment. Let me therefore rest with the following observations. Notwithstanding minority grievance-raising about the professional staff appointment pattern, the primary problem lay elsewhere for the "social justice" proponents. It was not that the professional staff was lily white. That was true but less important. It was rather, to be blunt, that with the notable exception of the Chicano vice-chairwoman, the minority spokesmen simply did not make their cases as well as they might have. To a considerably lesser extent, the same judgment is warranted of the "ecological view" proponents. As I reread the commission's internal minutes,[a] what sticks out are intermittent objections to the commission's trend of decision making coupled with a failure adequately to follow through. How so? The point is worth pausing over.

By the summer of 1971, the minority "social justice" commissioners numbered four, the "ecologically oriented," three. At least two others inclined toward an expansive reading of the commission's mandate, but nevertheless did not fall clearly into either of the other two groups. They were, so to speak, "macro" in their approach to the commission agenda without being committed to a particular set of solutions. In addition, at least two more were *sotto voce*

[a]Editor's note: Nash served as staff director of political research.

unenthusiastic about the manner of execution of the two primary leadership roles. Moreover, given the customary nonattendance rate of four or five out of twenty-four members (the number increased as the commission's life wore on), at most meetings the foregoing groups had a latent majority. Certainly they had sufficient strength to control to a considerable degree the agenda's structure and problem-resolutions. They could, had they chosen, have attempted at least two types of concerted tactics with a high probability of success.

First, while they might well have lost an open-ballot motion of no confidence in the executive director, more oblique tactics would probably have carried, including: (a) a motion that the commission's timetable was falling sufficiently behind to require returning to the enabling legislation's prescription of a full-time director; or (b) channelling a heated discussion (there were enough of those) towards a motion of confidence by a member of the "unwanted fertility" group, which (with appropriately timed questions about the possibilities of abstaining and secret balloting) would probably have resulted in at most an affirmative plurality. Either result would have put them in a very strong position.

Second, they could have made a joint behind-the-scenes approach to the commission chairman, indicating that unless X, Y, and Z changes were made in commission procedures, they would propose a motion of no confidence at the next meeting or resign from the commission, announcing their resignations at an appropriate press conference. Given the chairman's premium on harmony, the second, less drastic type of tactic would probably have succeeded without recourse to the first, assuming of course that X, Y, and Z were not wholly unreasonable.

Why did the dissident commissioners not try these tactics? This is not the place for attempting a definitive reconstruction. Suffice it to state that the answer is traceable to four factors. To name the two less important first, they were: inadequate communication among the dissident commissioners; and lack of combinatory and parliamentary-tactical homework. Behind these stood two more critical factors.

One is perhaps best put as an American preference for relegating showdowns to the celluloid of High Noon regardless of whether the real world's political corral is OK, or not. The American tendency to give primacy to pleasantness of interpersonal relations over the nastiness of genuine solution-reaching came importantly, and predictably, into play. To avoid a possible confusion, made endemic by the almost endless chain of books since Bryce's day that lump together an Anglo-American political culture, let me signal plainly that I am not here referring to a dichotomy of "civility of fair procedure" versus "ideological passion," that dichotomy so often used to contrast the Anglo-American and continental political traditions. What I am referring to is different—the English insistence upon procedural weaponry as a means to set up and defeat the opposition in a substantive policy debate versus a more typically American proclivity for *"Gemutlichkeit* of proceduralism" in order *not* to reach a substantive debate, to avoid precisely the nastiness of defeating an opposition. The latter, I submit, was at the core of the dissident commissioners' inability to capitalize. Such capitalizing would have been "not nice."

The other critical factor was simply a natural tendency among volunteer organizations that meet occasionally to put up with managerial frustrations on the boundaries of the members' lives, that they would not have accepted had those frustrations occurred in the "existential center." To put it differently, the pleasures of being a commissioner outweighed the dissonances contained in the once-a-month sense that the wrong Commission course was being taken. Had the commission dissenters really been before the mast, they might well have mutinied. Residing two or three days a month on a movable-feast-like poop-deck (now in the great hall of the New Executive Office Building in Washington, now at Antoine's in New Orleans, now in the pleasant reconstructions of Williamsburg), even the most critical commissioners preferred to "go along," limiting their criticism to a concerned letter here and there.

To say this about the commission's modus operandi is to indicate some of the grounds for my view that it is just as well that commission's policy proposals are not always taken too seriously by the White House or by Congress. Yet it is what nearly happened that most strongly sustains the view, even as it undercuts the implication of the Bachrach and Bergman perspective, that the policy recommendations were foreordained to come out wearing a pluralist hue. Such was not quite so. To illustrate, it is necessary to recapitulate the major substantive differences that emerged during the commission's second and final year of existence.

By July 1971, commissioner dissatisfaction with the staff's management was more than marginal. Although concentrated among the "social justice" and "environmentalist" commissioners, the dissatisfaction extended, on occasion, further. For example, at the July meeting the commission chairman (in a moment of surprisingly untypical directiveness) found himself insisting that the chief of staff might very well have to interrupt his vacation in order to arrange and attend an August retreat designed to get matters back on course. The need for such a demand seemingly puzzled both parties—though not quite for the same reasons, it is fair to opine.

What was going on? The minutes for a meeting of May 1971 provide, with their Donald-Barthelme-like quality, half the clue, the organizational half. Commissioner A "suggested adding a . . . session." ". . . There was some resistance to adding a session for discussing issues in such an unstructured manner." Commissioner B "suggested that perhaps the remaining time could be used more efficiently if the . . . educational materials were sent to the commissioners long enough before the meetings so that members would have sufficient time to read them." Commissioner C "added that no more than 1/2 day per 2 day session should be spent listening to experts' lectures . . . the Commissioners should spend the remaining time in discussion led by the staff."

The other half of the clue, the substantive half, surfaced when the August 1971 retreat occasioned the penning of a document designed to serve as a preamble to, and to determine the content of, the final report. The document attacked the nation's growth ethic straight on. Venturing further, its author urged that "the Commission should try to suggest a new ethic," one that rejected the philosophy of voluntarism theretofore dominant on the commission. In the author's view it was "idle to pretend there is freedom of choice in a situation where any one person acting irresponsibly can destroy freedom for the whole." So was the issue joined. The doctrine espoused was of course flatly repugnant to the voluntarist "unwanted fertility" view espoused by the commission's executive director. Yet what gave the document its intragroup strength was the circumstance that its author was not one of the commission's "young Ehrlichites" but rather its academically most prominent member.

During the meetings of fall 1971, the substantive division slowly deepened, albeit in a fashion that for the most part was submerged. Then quite abruptly, at a Williamsburg meeting, November 29-December 1, matters came to a head. The staff produced a draft of the report's introductory chapter that was rejected by the majority of commissioners precisely on the ground that it was too voluntaristic and insufficiently "ecological." The commission directed a consultant, who was present to report on the "population ethics task-force" he had led, to take over the staff's job and produce an introduction that put squarely the divergent opinions. Working swiftly, he did so overnight. "After extended discussion, it was agreed that his paper would become the basic working document for the Introduction of the Report." The vote was 8-4.

On December 15 and 16, at its next meeting, the commission resumed the dispute—on this occasion with respect to the draft final report's section on "Government and Population." Faced with two explicitly competing drafts, one designated pluralist and the other designated post-pluralist, the commission had an even starker choice. Where the competing introductions differed primarily with respect to future "ifs," the section on government and population contained some quite far-reaching "indictments" of the American polity in its post-pluralist version.

A few examples comparing the language of the two drafts will suffice to illustrate. In each example the pluralist phraseology is in parentheses.

There is (*is no*) good reason to doubt the capacity of the American governmental systems to accommodate a third 100,000,000 citizens in the final decades of the twentieth century. There are (*are no*) strong grounds for doubting the ability of the government . . . to attain social justice.

Optimal population policy making is hindered by the very failure of the government thus far to provide leadership adequate to the late twentieth century. A century after the passage of the XIVth amendment, the equal protection and due process clauses remain largely empty promises for millions of Americans. . . . Due process means no lynching anymore: equal protection means equal protection in poverty. This constitutes the first failure of American government.... The second failure ... is the failure to shift governmental actions, and the norms underlying ... to make them appropriate to the increasingly crowded world in which we live.... Such ... are the two main·themes which run through the whole history of this country: increasing environmental fragility and increasing ... demands upon government. Precious little in the structure of American governmental decision making indicates a serious realization that this is so.... Policy-making continues to be based upon logrolling and incremental solutions to problems in the society and the economy which are not genuine solutions at all.

The public good too rarely emerges (*emerges*) from present patterns of interest group representation (*representation*) in legislatures, executives, and court systems.

The real question before Americans ... is: Would population stabilization enhance the likelihood that the American governmental system will gain a capacity for governance equal to the tasks which confront it between now and the year 2000? (*Would the governmental benefits outweigh the governmental costs of population stabilization?*)

The December 16, 1971 vote on these two drafts may come as a surprise to those convinced that "mobilization of bias" and "non-decision-making" prevent the full airing of issues on the governmental policy agenda. By a vote of six to four the Population Commission endorsed the post-pluralist version, and instructed that its content become part of the final report.

Yet, a month later things changed again. With a slightly different group of commissioners present, the commission reversed itself, opting for the pluralist version. And from that point forth, a drift began back toward the voluntarism with respect to human reproduction that had been defeated at the Williamsburg meeting. The precise points along the way can be less readily demarked inasmuch as no quite so dramatic reversal took place. The result was the somewhat uneasy variance in tone and substance reflected in the dominantly voluntaristic "unwanted fertility" makeup of the actual final report that a retrospective rereading discloses.

In conclusion, two points of interest about the American policy-making process and the role of commissions emerge. One is, of course, the closeness of the pluralist and voluntarist outcome. But here that is of lesser interest than the second, than the way in which the policy advice came to pass. On this showing, whether the "right view" did or did not emerge is not the important thing. I have my views on this, though, influenced by the demographic course of the past five years, they are not exactly what they were at the time. Yet, is not the substantive verdict less important than the procedural one? That is, whatever the commission's policy judgments were, or might have been, were they judgments reached in a fashion such that they warranted the uncritical deferrence of Congress or White House? I think not.

Notes

1. Elizabeth B. Drew, "On Giving Oneself a Hotfoot: Government by Commission," *Atlantic Monthly* (May 1968):221-229. Michael Lipsky and David J. Olson, "On the Politics of Riot Commissions" (Paper presented at the 1968 Annual Meeting of the American Political Science Association). See also Michael Lipsky and David J. Olson, *Commission Politics: The Processing of Racial Crisis in America* (New Brunswick, N.J.: Transaction Books, 1976).

2. Thomas R. Wolanin, *Presidential Advisory Commissions: Truman to Nixon* (Madison, Wisc.: University of Wisconsin Press, 1975).

3. Charles F. Westoff, "The Commission on Population Growth and the American Future: Its Origins, Operations, and Aftermath," *Population Index* 39 (1973):491-502. Compare Peter Bachrach and Elihu Bergman, *Power and Choice: The Formulation of American Population Policy* (Lexington, Mass.: Lexington Books, D.C. Heath and Co., 1973).

4. Westoff, "Commission on Population Growth," p. 491.

5. Ibid., p. 494.

6. Ibid., p. 496.

7. Ibid.

8. Ibid., p. 497.

9. Ibid.

10. Ibid.

11. Ibid.

12. Ibid., p. 499.

13. Bachrach and Bergman, *Power and Choice*, p. 26.

14. Ibid., p. 27.

15. Ibid., p. 26.

16. Ibid., p. 28.

17. Ibid., p. 30.

18. Ibid.

19. Ibid., p. 31.

20. Ibid., p. 60.

21. Ibid., pp. 61-62.

6

A Comparison of Policy-Making Capacity in the United States and Five European Countries: The Case of Population Distribution

James L. Sundquist

The structural differences between the policy-making institutions of the countries of Western Europe and those of the United States are well known. The purpose of this paper is to try to determine which of those differences, if any, were significant in bringing about markedly different policy outcomes in a particular case.

The case selected is called regional policy in Europe and usually national growth policy in the United States. A more definitive term is population distribution, or population dispersal, policy. In any case, it refers to national policies and programs for the distribution, among regions, of economic activity and hence of people.[a]

The Difference in Policy Outcomes

The analysis that follows is based upon a comparative study of the regional policies of the United States and of five countries of Western Europe—Britain, France, Italy, the Netherlands, and Sweden. The five European countries are among the nations of the world having the most comprehensive and ambitious policies to influence the distribution of their populations on a national scale. Each has adopted explicit programs to stabilize the economies of declining regions, retard the growth of the most prosperous regions, and thus reduce internal migration with its attendant waste and hardship. Several of the countries have set quite specific, quantitative goals for the distribution of economic and population growth by region, province, or county.[1]

In Britain, the aim has been to stem what is called the "drift to the South"—the movement of people from older, declining industrial areas of Scotland, Wales, and northern England to the overcrowded London region and

This chapter is based on a paper delivered at the Congress of the International Political Science Association, Edinburgh, Scotland, August 1976. The author has benefited from the comments of readers of that paper, particularly those of Arnold J. Heidenheimer.

[a]This is distinct from policies for distribution *within* regions, which is often also embraced within the definitions of some of the above terms.

the Midlands. The object of French policy has been to reduce the dominance of Paris in every aspect of national life by building effective competitive centers in the hinterland and particularly by developing the underdeveloped rural areas of southern and western France. In Italy, the aim has been to develop the economy of the South—or Mezzogiorno—so that the people of that region who have been emigrating for decades will not inundate the cities of northern Italy. In the Netherlands, the purpose has been to stabilize the population in the eastern part of the country, so that no unnecessary migrants will be added to the densely settled "Randstad," the ring-shaped conurbation that links Amsterdam, the Hague, Rotterdam, and Utrecht and surrounds a prized—but threatened—"green heart" of canals, fields, and pasture. And in Sweden, as in Britain, the policy goal is to stop the drift to the south that has been gradually depopulating most of the land area of the country—the northern regions which begin a little north of Stockholm and extend beyond the Arctic Circle.

The five countries implement their growth policies through a combination of specific measures. Most important are incentives for private investment in the declining areas designated for development. These take the form, primarily, of a cash grant to the investor, usually in the range of 15-25 percent of the cost of the investment, sometimes supplemented by tax concessions and favorable credit terms. Complementing the incentives are disincentives to investment in the regions of too-rapid growth, such as those centering on London, Paris, Rotterdam, and Milan. To locate in one of these areas, designated types of enterprises must obtain government permission based on a showing of necessity; in some cases special taxes are an additional, or alternative, form of restraint. The central governments have also made extraordinary expenditures to improve transportation and other public facilities in the development areas, channeled the investment of state-controlled industries to those areas, and decentralized the central administrative operations of the national governments themselves.

The policy measures, steadily strengthened over the years, have proved effective. In four of the five countries, population flows have been reversed. The regions centered on London, Paris, Stockholm, and the Randstad have experienced net outmigration—undoubtedly, in every case, for the first time in history—and in the fifth country, Italy, south-north migration has unquestionably been slowed. Although other factors may have contributed to the turnaround, the impact of governmental policies seems clearly to have been the strongest influence. Sophisticated economic analyses credit regional policy with reducing unemployment significantly, increasing the gross national product, and easing inflationary pressures by "taking the work to the workers" rather than forcing workers to relocate.

The costs, of course, are substantial, but in every country the political judgment is that the benefits outweigh the costs. In each of the countries, every major political party accepts population distribution policy as a necessary and proper function of government, and the debate centers on the details of policy, not on the principle itself.

Although there are differences in program measures among the European countries, these differences are relatively minor compared to the gulf that separates any of their policies from those of the United States. This country has no policy of active intervention in regard to population distribution, and its programs are for practical purposes limited to the third of the above four categories—infrastructure development. And even the infrastructure measures, such as the Appalachian Regional Development Program, are conceived within a context of unemployment relief rather than population distribution planning. (The European programs began as relief measures, too, but were within a few years brought into the broader context of national planning.)

The Comparability of the Input into the Policy-Making System

The first question, of course, is whether the difference in policy outcomes between the United States and Europe can be attributed in whole or in large part to differences in the character and functioning of the policy-making institutions, or whether it is attributable simply to differences in the nature of the problem, or in the way in which it was perceived at the time the institutions went to work on it, or in the intensity of interest and support in the general environment within which they worked. In other words, is the contrast in what came out of the respective policy-making systems due to differences in what went into the black boxes, or due to differences in wiring inside?

My conclusion is that while there are inevitable differences in what went in, these are by no means sufficient to account for the divergence in policy outcome. Some indeterminate, but nevertheless large, share of that divergence is attributable to differences in the ability of the policy-making institutions to respond to a not dissimilar set of external circumstances creating comparable policy demands—not identical circumstances or demands, of course, but comparable enough.

Granted, the patterns of internal migration have been more complex in the United States. They have been multidirectional rather than unidirectional; there has been no single magnet of unequaled drawing power, as in Britain or France, but several—the Atlantic seaboard megalopolis, the shores of the Great Lakes, California, Florida. But this is a difference of degree, not of kind. The fundamentals are the same: population draining out of some areas and piling up in others, with consequent maladjustments at both ends of the migration stream—underemployment, poverty, demoralization, malaise at the losing end; high costs in infrastructure development, social disruption, and individual and family hardship at the receiving end. Although it is difficult to measure the relative intensities of these maladjustments among countries, the rates of metropolitan population gain and rural population loss appear to have been no less in the United States than in Europe during the first couple of decades after World War II.

Granted, the United States has a tradition of hostility to governmental intervention and governmental planning that is probably more pronounced than that of any other country in the world. The United States, therefore, tends to be slower than are European countries, when they face comparable social problems, to arrive at a broad political consensus favoring governmental intervention. But that does not mean the United States always fails to reach that broad consensus. It often does reach it. It did in this case, albeit somewhat later than four of our five European countries. If Britain undertook its first significant programs to assist its depressed areas in the 1930s, and France, Italy, and the Netherlands in the early 1950s, the United States entered the field in 1961, a few years earlier than Sweden. And if it took from two to half a dozen years in each of the European countries to reach the realization, through experience, that piecemeal measures were not enough and a bold and comprehensive program was required, it took only a few years longer in the United States. By 1968, or at the latest 1970, a consensus was reached in the United States that a clear national policy, and broad new measures to implement that policy, needed to be established. Rural areas had long been clamoring for measures to stem out-migration, and the urban riots of 1965-1968 in the cities had persuaded urban politicians and opinion leaders that internal migration was undesirable for the receiving areas as well; the cities seemed ungovernable, and the continued influx of population only added to the tension.

There could hardly have been a greater degree of unanimity. Both major political parties recognized the problem of internal migration and unbalanced growth in their 1968 platforms and promised to develop and carry out measures to deal with it. President Nixon, speaking for the Republicans, emphasized the objective in his 1970 State of the Union message. He called for development of "a national growth policy" that would "not only stem the migration to urban centers, but reverse it" and would "make the 1970s an historic period when by conscious choice we transformed our land into what we want it to become." For the next eighteen months or so, he reiterated this theme in speeches and messages; in all, between February 1969 and July 1971, he made more than a dozen statements on the subject, some in formal messages to the Congress, some in emphatic, even passionate, extemporaneous speeches to various gatherings. In 1970, the Congress, with its Democratic majority, committed the country in two different acts to adoption of a national growth policy that would retard internal migration.[2] The consensus also included the National Governors' Conference, the National League of Cities, the organized counties and city mayors, and the Advisory Commission on Intergovernmental Relations. No national political body of any kind stood outside that general consensus.

And granted, finally, the United States is a federal system, while four of the five European countries are unitary and the fifth (Italy) was unitary at the time its major regional policies and programs were adopted. But the consensus in the United States related to national action; the alternative conclusion, that population distribution is a matter to be left to the states, was discarded in the process of consensus formulation. The existence of our federal system, then, would account only for differences in the character of the national policies and programs to be developed, not for their absence altogether.

In summary, once the political consensus was reached in Europe, the plans were drawn up and adopted and the national program measures passed. Facing a comparable problem and operating in a climate of public and political opinion no less favorable, the institutional structure in the United States did not respond to the political directives. The fault, it seems clear, should be looked for *inside* the black box.

The Short Circuit in the U.S. Black Box

What happened in response to the consensus in the United States can be sketched quickly. President Nixon, upon his inauguration in January 1969, established as his first official act an Urban Affairs Council, consisting mainly of the Cabinet members heading domestic departments. That Council created a subcommittee on internal migration as one of nine such bodies. Career civil servants, principally from the Department of Agriculture, began assembling demographic information on urban growth and rural decline. Meanwhile, the policy staff attached to the Council and its committees, consisting of political appointees of the new president on the White House staff and at the top levels of the departments, began considering this policy problem along with the many others confronting the country at the time. They developed the language that went into President Nixon's 1970 State of the Union message and other documents, they brought in experts from outside the government for two days of conferences with the president on growth policy in April of that year, and they organized a presidential meeting on the subject in July with governors of the northern plains states, one of the regions suffering heavy out-migration. When the Domestic Council superseded the Urban Affairs Council in July 1970, it created a committee on national growth, made up of Cabinet members and staffed again from the corps of policy advisers recruited by the new administration to man the White House and the top levels of the departments. The president continued to advocate in speeches and measures the growth policies he had laid out in his State of the Union message, and he signed the two measures passed by the Congress committing the country to develop such policies. From time to time, according to one of the key men assigned to growth policy planning, the president made inquiries as to their progress, and expressed impatience.

Meanwhile, however, the president was pushing more vigorously another policy line, which was the devolution of governmental power to the states—known as the New Federalism—and this brought about a split within his group of staff policy advisers. While one group was going ahead to try to define a specific national growth policy, at least some of those developing specific proposals to implement the New Federalism concluded that the initiation of new programs at the federal level to influence internal migration and population distribution would be philosophically in conflict with their devolutionary objective.

There is no indication, however, that they brought the supposed conflicts into focus for the president to force him to choose between the objectives or reconcile them–at least for the first two and a half years of his administration. He continued to advocate the concepts of a growth policy along with the New Federalism in speeches during the first half of 1971, and as late as February 1972 he signed his name to a report that still endorsed the basic objective.[3] But the report, reflecting the negative view of what was by then a majority of his policy advisers, contained no specific proposals to that end. That 1972 report was the last that was heard of the idea in the Republican administration, despite the mandate of the statutes that Nixon himself had signed into law. As the urban riots had receded into the past, public interest in growth policy had slackened. The president lost interest, too, or he was persuaded by his New Federalist advisers that he should drop the subject, or both.

The Institutional Causes of the Output Difference

The comparative analysis of institutions could perhaps end right here if we could ascribe the difference between the U.S. and European policy-making outcomes simply to the fact that the president of the United States exercised the perfectly human prerogative to change his mind. But we cannot. In the first place, he held to his position consistently for somewhat more than three years, even though his enthusiasm appeared to flag toward the end of that period. In each of the European countries, three years was far more than ample time to enable governmental planning groups to devise policies to implement a political directive on this subject; they usually did the job in a matter of weeks, or at most months. Moreover, if the president changes his mind, that too may reflect a difference in institutions. So we still have to look for institutional causes for the failure of the staff to respond to the political leadership in the United States. I find four such causes.

Cause Number 1: Differential Levels of
Bureaucratic Capability

The first of the institutional differences that appears to have significance in this case is the composition of the policy staffs that were available to advise and assist the responsible political officials. In a typical European country, when the appropriate cabinet minister undertook to develop specific legislation to implement the regional policy objective established by the governing party, or coalition of parties, the task of analysis and of making recommendations was assigned to a planning group made up predominantly or wholly of career civil servants. Those planners usually had long experience in government. They were a cohesive group. If they were assembled from different departments, they had probably worked together before. They were familiar with the data that formed the basis of their analysis, and had probably analyzed it for policy-making purposes on other occasions.

When President Nixon undertook to develop legislation to effectuate his objective, and that of his party, the assignment did not fall into the hands of a comparable group. The Urban Affairs Council and the later Domestic Council were staffed not by civil servants but by political appointees, and in 1969, because there had been a turnover of partisan control, they were almost entirely new to Washington. A few had had experience in the Eisenhower administration eight years earlier, and one or two had actually served in the Kennedy-Johnson period, but for the most part they had won their jobs by virtue of their service to the candidate and his party in the 1968 campaign. They were suspicious of the civil servants they inherited from the preceding Democratic administrations. So there was a gulf between the career bureaucracy, which was familiar with the data and had some degree of competence to analyze it, and the staff advisers who had responsibility for developing policy recommendations. The kind of individual who was the typical participant in the development of regional policies in Europe—that is, who was at the same time the long-time career civil servant and the respected policy adviser—hardly exists in large areas of the United States government. No such individual had important responsibility in this particular case of policy making in the United States.

The United States has always had a much higher proportion of political appointees at the policy-making levels than has the typical European country, but in recent years the proportion has been gradually increasing, in a process that in the Washington vernacular came to be called "politicization." The politicization inevitably results in a depletion of talent in the civil service, as many of the most competent and ambitious of the career officials—the kind that rise to the top in European civil services—find themselves excluded from the inner policy-making circles, or subordinated to younger, less experienced political appointees, and so depart. The capability of the career service is reduced, which leads to pressures for further politicization, in a vicious circle. The whole process was accelerated in the Nixon administration, partly because of a conviction on the part of many of the incoming Republicans that much of the senior civil service—having been recruited during the two decades of Democratic control from 1932 to 1952—would at best be unresponsive to the new Republican leadership, and at worst be bent on sabotage. For this and other reasons, policy making was centered to a much greater degree than ever before in the White House itself, where it could be wholly in the hands of Nixon loyalists.

As this case shows, "politicization" often means "amateurization"—which can mean, to coin a less charitable term, "incompetization." This is not to suggest that the new political appointees were not highly intelligent and able. Person for person, they were surely as bright as the civil service planning groups in Europe, with the added advantage of being fresh and eager and innovative, unbound by traditional ways of doing things. Nevertheless, when political newcomers were assigned a task as complex and vaguely defined as the development of national growth policy, the first few months at least could be little beyond a learning period. A new and inexperienced policy-making establishment was at that time overloaded with questions to be resolved; it could master a few of the top priority problems that were thrown at it in 1969, but not all of them.

Moreover, the newcomers in a change of administration are not always able to concentrate upon mastering a complex subject. They often take office without clear and fixed assignments, they are ambitious and eager, they are jockeying for position, and they are mobile. So the membership of planning groups shifts. And it takes time for the members of these fluid groupings to get acquainted with one another—to "get on the same wave length," as the saying goes—and this is a particular problem when the new appointees come from different wings of an ideologically divided party, as was the case in 1969. The congeniality, cohesion, and common outlook that make for quick creativity in a planning group do not spring from a common loyalty to the man in the White House as surely as they arise from years of collegial association in a European career civil service.

Cause Number 2: Differential Degrees of Bureaucratic Discipline

As mentioned earlier, the policy-development staff serving President Nixon fell into ideological disagreement, and the staff wing opposed to the president's declared objective—which, to repeat, was also the Republican party's official position as well as the law of the land—prevailed. In other words, the very kind of unresponsiveness, or "sabotage," that the incoming administration feared from the career civil servants was inflicted on the president by his own political appointees. From all the evidence, it was the dominant group of staff policy advisers who changed their minds first; the president changed his later. Whether the president underwent an intellectual conversion at the hands of his staff, or became preoccupied with other matters and simply gave up when his staff failed to produce the detailed program recommendations that he sought, is not clear. Nevertheless, in the corresponding situation in Europe, planning groups assembled from the career civil service did not undertake to reverse the policies pronounced by their political superiors.

It is anomalous that politicization of the civil service, defended in the United States as the means to give the president a greater degree of control over governmental policy, actually resulted, in this case at least, in less control. What seems to develop at the political level in the United States during some periods is a kind of policy entrepreneurship, in which a proportion of political appointees—many of whom come to Washington for an intellectual fling and some excitement, with no intention of staying for long—feel their mission during their temporary service is to promote their own ideology and represent the policy views of their own branch of the party, their own sponsors, or their own outside supporters where these may conflict with the expressed objectives of their political superiors. Civil servants of the European tradition, in contrast, subordinate their own policy preferences once a decision is made at the political level.

Cause Number 3: Differences in the Institutional
Environment of Planning

The uniquely pluralized structure of the American system, with its separation of powers—to which many policy failures in the United States can be traced—cannot be blamed in this case, because no program proposals ever came out of the executive branch. Nevertheless, the pluralized system does appear to have had an indirect influence. It provided an institutional environment for the planners' work distinctly less favorable than the environment in Europe.

The differences in institutional environment can be expressed in terms of the distance between the bureaucracy's plan and the policy decision. In Europe, the distance tends to be short, in America, long. Or it can be put in terms of the size of the policy-making circle. In Europe, the circle is often relatively small and intimate, which provides for the planner a secure and comfortable environment; in the United States, it is always large, which makes for discomfort and insecurity.

In a European government, when the planning task force dealing with regional policy finally threshed out the points at issue and reached agreement, it had only to convince, basically, a single individual—the responsible cabinet minister. He in turn had only to convince the rest of the cabinet. There might be some give and take at that point, but the discussion was among friendly colleagues, either of the same party or of collaborating parties, and usually through a kind of logrolling and mutual deference the responsible minister won his point. When the cabinet decision was reached, it was normally confirmed by the parliament without significant alteration, or—as in France—enacted by decree. During the decades that regional policies had been evolving (up to 1973) in the five European countries studied, only in one instance was a government forced by legislative criticism to substantially modify its proposals—in the Netherlands in 1972-1973. Under these circumstances, the bureaucrat-planner possesses genuine authority.

In the United States, on the other hand, a planning group assigned to draft program proposals knows that even if its members reach full agreement, not much will have been settled. They may be able to convince the appropriate cabinet member, and he in turn the president—or if they are working directly in the White House, they may convince the president at first hand. But whereas in Europe that stage normally marks the end of the struggle, in the United States it is only the beginning, for the executive branch in America is not "the government." Each policy issue settled within the administration must be reviewed, and agreement reached all over again, in the Congress. And this is a very public process, with governors, mayors, and private organizations of all kinds, both national and regional, making their influence felt. Here, the views of the executive branch as expressed by the president do count for more than those of a business or labor organization, say, but sometimes they do not count for very much more. That is especially the case when the Congress is controlled by the party opposite to that of the president, as it was in the period we are reviewing in the United States.

In the legislative process, too, the rationality of the planners' original product is likely to be overwhelmed by the multiple pressures originating from interest groups affected—the most important in the case of population distribution policy being state and city governments and other spokesmen for localities and regions. There are many examples of how rational schemes for depressed areas have been distorted to spread the benefits to more constituencies, but one that will make the point is the 1961 amendment that required each state to have one depressed area, whether there was any basis for the designation or not! In a European country, where the distance from the planners' judgment to the ultimate decision may be as short as the single step from the planners to the minister in charge, the rationality of the plan has a chance of being preserved. An American has to be impressed by the way the planners in a European country can look at local and regional interests in a detached and objective way, subordinate them to a concept of the optimum settlement pattern for the nation, and get away with it—finally seeing their product emerge in law unscathed, or almost so. The Second Report on Regional Planning in the Netherlands comes to mind, or the point system by which the *métropoles d'équilibre* were chosen in France's Fifth Plan.

The American planning group can anticipate that no matter how thorough its analysis, no matter how great the degree of unity achieved, its work will be torn apart during the legislative process. Every difference that may have surfaced and been resolved in its own deliberations will be reopened and magnified into a major public issue. Around those issues, interest groups will mobilize themselves, legislators essentially independent of party discipline will balance pressures, and the equity and internal consistency of the plan will be impaired. The planners will be thrown on the defensive. Flaws in their reasoning may be seized upon and ridiculed in public hearings. Anything less than perfection will not be acceptable, yet nothing will be seen as acceptable by all 535 members of the Congress.

This wide open process is not, of course, without some benefit. Presumably, if there is any nonsense in the planners' scheme, it will be knocked out somewhere along the way. The breadth of participation may be reflected in a breadth of acceptance of the policy that finally emerges—if it emerges at all. But the process can inhibit the bureaucrats' best efforts, too, as it seemed to do in this case. If the members of an American task force are writing drafts rather than final products, why should they beat their brains out trying to draft the perfect plan and reach agreement on it? Moreover, if the probability on most controversial legislative issues is that no legislation at all will pass (because of the multiple points of veto in the decentralized processes of the American Congress) what is the reward for even the most diligent labors?

In this hostile environment, it is easy for planners to get discouraged, to decide that the problem is too difficult, to conclude that it is a matter for the states, to simply make no recommendations, or very general ones, and pass the buck to Congress. It takes a sense of authority to beget a sense of responsibility at any administrative level.

Finally, if one were to choose a field of policy that especially taxes the ability of the American policy-making system to produce, one might well select growth policy. The political consensus of 1970 was on the principle, not on the particulars, and it is the latter that define winners and losers in the geographic redistribution of opportunity and income that is the meaning of growth policy. Such redistributions are especially difficult to come by in a Congress whose members represent not national parties but individual local constituencies. The prospect that a key committee-chairman might happen to be from a district that might not be designated for favorable treatment in a national growth policy—and would be in a position to bring all the efforts of the planners to naught—was a factor in 1969 and 1970 tending to discourage the expenditure of effort by the American planning group.

All this has a bearing upon the problem of bureaucratic competence, discussed earlier. The policy planner in the executive branch of the United States government—far from being part of a tiny elite policy-making circle as can be the case in Europe—is reduced to the level of just another consultant making recommendations. His success score is not likely to be high, especially when the government is politically divided, as it was during fourteen of the twenty-two years between 1955 and 1976. If that is all the status he has, then he may just as well set up shop as a private consultant outside the government, where he will have more freedom and probably make more money while being just about as influential, and that is where much of the finest bureaucratic talent in America has wound up. And as talent dwindles, status declines further—the vicious circle once again.

Cause Number 4: Differences in the Stability and
Authority of Party Programs

American political parties do adopt platforms every four years, but even when they are quite specific—as was the Republican platform in 1968 in setting the objective of stemming the rural-urban migration flow—they are not taken seriously as pledges. The people, the media, and even the party faithful look to the candidate for president, and to the president after he is elected, to state the party policy. But when he does, his policies are not really thought of any longer as *party* policies, in the European sense, but rather as *administration* policies. They are only recommended to the coequal members of the president's own party in the Congress, who do not feel necessarily bound by his suggestions. So the party as such really has no policy. As for the president's policy, since it is his he can change it at will.

So President Nixon felt free to abandon his party platform position on growth policy—and, for that matter, his own even stronger position—and no one inside or outside his party took him to task for it. It was considered his prerogative, right, proper, and normal.

This may not sound entirely different from the practice in European countries, for party manifestos there also may consist of generalities, and governments may change their minds about the pledges on which they were elected. Nevertheless, of the score or so of parties that have endorsed strong regional policies in the five countries studied, not a single one has ever withdrawn from that position (although there have been the inevitable ups and downs in enforcement of declared policies, as governments and economic conditions change and as the policies themselves succeed or fail).

This seems to reflect what is usually recognized as the greater stability, generally, in the policy positions of the "responsible" European parties (as we in America like to call them), which appears in turn to have its roots in an institutional factor—the collective nature of the party policy-making machinery. France may be a partial exception, but elsewhere major policy positions are normally not taken unilaterally by the head of the party in power, even if that person be the prime minister, but by a collective cabinet. And when a governing party relinquishes power, it continues much the same kind of formal and collective policy-making apparatus—unlike an American party, which when it goes out of power disbands in everything but name, with no leader, no authoritative spokesman, and with the policy commitments in its latest platform becoming instantly obsolete. European parties, therefore, to a greater degree than American parties, are programmatic—identified with, and known for, their programs, more loyal to those programs, and compelled to regard changes in their policy positions as a serious matter to be approached deliberately, formally, and collectively.

Had President Nixon operated within such a structure of collective party policy determination, before taking his forceful position of 1969 and 1970 amplifying the platform declaration of 1968, he would have gotten the advance concurrence of his party colleagues (which presumably would have been obtained readily enough, given the consensus in the party and the country at the time). The decision would then have been binding upon the whole executive branch until it had been reconsidered by the same collective process and reversed or modified. The policy entrepreneurship of a part of the executive branch in opposition to its political leadership would not have been permissible. The task force of planners assigned to devise the program would have had more authoritative support in the bureaucratic infighting. And the president's position would probably have remained stable for at least a somewhat longer period—perhaps long enough for his inexperienced planning group to struggle their way through the complexities of the problem to produce the specific measures he desired.

Conclusion

One case is always a narrow base on which to rest generalizations. To determine the extent to which these institutional differences may have wider consequences, affecting other areas of policy, would of course require the examination of other cases, including some from the same period—like welfare reform, where President Nixon did put forward a bold scheme that was defeated in the Senate.

But comparative analyses in a wide range of fields would, I think, confirm this generalization: Because the institutional structure of policy making in the United States is more complex and pluralized than those of the other industrial democracies of the Atlantic community, because the policy-making circle is broader and more amateur and less disciplined, public participation more intense, and the points of potential veto of policy innovation more numerous, and because political parties are weaker as integrating mechanisms, a higher degree of national consensus and a more intense commitment of political leadership are necessary before new departures can be developed and approved, and a narrower range of innovation can be successfully attempted at any one time.

These analyses would suggest, I suspect, that American and foreign scholars alike have been too prone to attribute the relative conservatism of American social and economic policies to certain aspects of our history, such as our individualistic conquest of the frontier, and to the special traits of the American character that are the supposed outgrowth of that history—our reputed individualism and antipathy to government. It may well be that *institutional* differences that have evolved quite accidentally are more important than differences in geography or resources or ideology in making the United States stand out among those industrial democracies as the one with by far the most conservative domestic policies.

Notes

1. The nature, evolution, and accomplishments of the policy measures in the five countries are set forth in detail in my book, *Dispersing Population: What America Can Learn from Europe* (Washington, D.C.: Brookings Institution, 1975).

2. The Urban Growth and New Community Development Act of 1970 (P.L. 91-609); and the Agricultural Act of 1970 (P.L. 91-524).

3. *Report on National Growth*, 1972, the first biennial report on the subject, as required by the Urban Growth and New Community Development Act of 1970.

7 The Growing Importance of Immigration to Population Policy

David S. North

During the decade of 1901-1910, the number of immigrants admitted to the nation was more than 8,700,000; this total represented more than 55 percent of the nation's population growth during that decade, which was a little under 16,000,000. During the 1930s, the number of immigrants to this nation totaled a little more than 500,000, while the population increased by close to 9,000,000; the former was about 6 percent of the latter.

Given the migrant-discouraging events of the 1920s, 1930s, and 1940s, respectively, the ethnocentric country-of-origin immigration acts of 1921 and 1924, the depression, and the war, flows of immigrants slowed considerably, and the stock of foreign born (the accumulation of past migration) declined relatively and, since 1930, absolutely with each new census (see table 7-1).

There are strong signs, however, that we have entered a new phase, and that immigration, after playing a declining role in the growth of the U.S. population, has started to play a more important one. As table 7-2 indicates, immigration in the first eight years of full operation of our current immigration policy, that shaped by the 1965 Amendments to the Immigration and Nationality Act, is now making a contribution to population growth that has moved beyond the 25 percent mark—a considerable change from the 1930s, but still well below the level experienced at the turn of the century.

Assuming as I do that immigration is a vital part of our heritage, and, simultaneously, that the nation's finite resource base is one of the considerations that should be borne in mind as our population (and immigration) policies are examined, I will discuss the currently visible future trends of immigration to the United States, the two sets of policies (de facto and de jure) which relate to it, and the domination of both sets of policies by private, rather than communal or national, interests.

Future Trends

One of the principal difficulties in discussing either immigration or the policies which are supposed to govern it is the shoddy state of the data on the subject. There are four components of population change: births, deaths, immigration, and emigration. In this, as in most civilized countries, relatively good records are kept on births and deaths; but, unlike most immigrant-receiving nations, our

81

Table 7-1
Number and Percentage of Foreign Born in U.S. Population: 1910-1970

Census	Number of Foreign Born	Percent of Total Population
1910	13,516,000	14.6
1920	13,921,000	13.2
1930	14,204,000	11.6
1940	11,595,000	8.8
1950	10,347,000	6.9
1960	9,738,000	5.4
1970	9,619,000	4.7

Source: Data for 1920-1970 are taken from U.S. Bureau of the Census, *Statistical Abstract of the U.S.*, table 40; data for 1910 are taken from U.S. Bureau of the Census, *Historical Statistics of the U.S.*, series A29-42 and A105-118.

data on the other two variables are sadly deficient. Imagine a system (a demographer's nightmare, if you will) in which only legitimate births are recorded, and deaths are never noted; that is essentially the state of immigration statistics.[1] Only legitimate arrivals of immigrants are recorded in the U.S. system, and no departures (emigration) are ever recorded. It can be argued, of course, that illegal immigration, like other illegal activities, is hard to measure, but the sad fact is that the government—though expressing profound interest in this challenging subject—has not yet secured even a plausible set of estimates of the flows or stocks of illegal immigrants. As for emigration, perhaps we do not want to admit that there may be substantial numbers of our citizens—or disappointed immigrants—who opt to leave the nation; while the number of emigrants has been estimated in the annual neighborhood of 150,000,[2] the annual movements of emigrants are probably outnumbered by those of the illegal immigrants by ratios of three to six to one. The portion of annual total population growth attributable to immigration, and shown in table 7-2, takes no account of either emigration or illegal immigration, and thus the rising percentages noted there can only be understatements, substantial understatements, of the significance of international migration to population growth.

The principal change in the impact of immigration on population growth, comparing the thirties to the seventies, is the expanded size of the annual cohorts of immigrants, from an average of about 50,000 in the earlier decade to about 400,000 currently. Even if legal immigration remains constant, however, it would play an increasingly important role in population growth, if the number of live births continues to decline as it has for the last two decades. (In 1976, there were some 3,165,000 live births, an absolute decline of more than a million from the baby boom peak of 4,255,000 in 1957.)

Table 7-2
Immigrants to the U.S.: Their Number and Percentage of Population Growth, FY 1969-1975

Fiscal Year	Net Increase in U.S. Population[a] (A)	Immigrants Admitted to the U.S. (B)	Percentage of Population Growth (C)
1969	1,970,000	358,579	18.2
1970	2,200,000	373,326	17.0
1971	2,180,000	370,478	17.0
1972	1,790,000	384,685	21.5
1973	1,560,000	400,063	25.6
1974	1,480,000	394,861	26.7
1975	1,650,000	386,194	23.5
1976	1,580,000	398,613[b]	25.2
Total	14,410,000	3,066,799	21.3

Source: Column A computed from U.S. Bureau of the Census, *Statistical Abstract of the U.S.: 1975*, table 2 for the years 1969-1974; estimates for 1975 and 1976 were derived by phone from the Population Division, U.S. Bureau of the Census. Column B figures from *INS Annual Report, 1975*, table 10 for 1969-1975, and for 1976 by phone from Statistics Branch, INS. Column C is the percentage of Column B to Column A.

Note: There is no allowance for the arrivals of illegal aliens or the emigration of permanent resident aliens in this table; hence it tends to understate the demographic significance of migration.

[a]Population estimates are for the total U.S. population (including armed forces abroad) as of July 1 for each year; figures have been rounded to the nearest 10,000.

[b]Excludes transitional quarter.

Legal immigration, however, in the near future is likely to increase. Since the passage of the 1965 amendments, legal immigration has been stabilized at just short of 400,000 a year. This is the case because more immigrants want to come to the United States than we will accept, and the 120,000 limit for the Western Hemisphere and the 170,000 one for the Eastern Hemisphere are always met; the additional 100,000 or so immigrants admitted outside these hemispheric ceilings are a tightly defined group of persons (mostly immediate relatives of U.S. citizens) whose numbers do not vary much from year to year.

The 400,000-a-year pattern is about to be broken, however, by two governmental decisions, one generated by the executive branch, and the other, by the judicial branch. The more visible of the two decisions was that of the executive to admit 160,000 Indochinese refugees, a number which has been increased by additional thousands of the "boat people." These refugees, though physically in the country, will not be counted in formal immigration statistics until their status can be changed from that of parolee to that of immigrant, which will happen in the next year or two.

A second decision now emerging from the courts will have a similar impact—about 145,000 aliens are involved, all from the Western Hemisphere. In a class action suit, attorneys for non-Cuban Western Hemisphere aliens, who are on waiting lists for immigrant visas, challenged the government's practice of using numerically limited Western Hemisphere visas for Cuban refugees; they argued that the practice was contrary to the intention of Congress, and that their clients were, in fact, entitled to visas which had gone to Cubans. (The Cubans are not adversely affected; the contention is not that they should be denied the visas, but that the visas should have been issued outside the numerical limits.) In a preliminary ruling, the U.S. district court in Chicago ruled that petitioners now in the country (presumably largely illegally) should be granted a stay of deportation until the issue can be resolved;[3] the Justice Department has decided, as a matter of policy, to allow those granted the stays to work legally. The prevalent speculation among immigration lawyers at this writing is that the courts will rule in favor of the petitioners.

These two additions to the flow of legal immigrants, more than 300,000 persons spread over two or three years, are likely to be overshadowed by still a third group of aliens admitted outside current patterns. This group consists of those illegal aliens now in the nation who would be covered by the Carter Administration's two-level amnesty program, should it be enacted by Congress.

The administration has proposed, as part of a larger package, that those illegal aliens who have been in the nation since January 1, 1970, be granted permanent resident alien status; they would be issued the symbolic green card and be treated like other legal immigrants.[4] There are probably no more than two to three hundred thousand eligibles in this category; few illegals have been in the nation that long, and of those who were here and were interested in regularizing their status, many have already taken steps to secure the green card by taking advantage of one of the pronatal elements of the immigration law (i.e. by marrying a legal resident or becoming the parent of a U.S. citizen baby).

The administration proposal, which is likely to have a much greater impact than the full amnesty for a few described above, if enacted, is the granting of half-an-amnesty to a much larger group of illegal aliens, those who can trace their arrival to the period January 1, 1970 to January 1, 1977. The number of potential "temporary resident aliens," the status that the administration proposes for this group, is clearly in the millions.

This new class of aliens can be viewed, cheerfully, as a cleaned-up, semilegalized group of persons, previously an underclass beyond the law; or it can be viewed, with less optimism, as an additional, statutorily created and substantially disadvantaged sector of the population. The administration proposes that for a five-year period these aliens be allowed to work and to cross the country's borders, but that they not be allowed to receive social service benefits or to bring their relatives to this country. Let us assume for the moment that some such class is created, and that substantial numbers of eligible aliens come forward and seek this status, what happens at the end of five years? Will they then be deported? It seems highly unlikely; conversion of their status to that of permanent resident aliens, or possibly a prolongation of the temporary status, would appear to be more in keeping with American tradition. In sum, half-an-amnesty is likely, over time, to legalize millions of additions to the nation's population and to its labor force.

It is interesting to note that legal immigration is making a rather smaller contribution to the increase in the labor force, in recent years, than it is to the increase in the population. (Note we are only referring to legal immigration here.) Although the labor participation rates of immigrants appear to be roughly comparable to those of the host population, when the variables of sex and age are held constant,[5] the 90 million plus U.S. civilian labor force has been growing at extraordinary rates in recent years because of the increasing rates of female labor market participation, and because the babies of the baby boom years are now going to work. Within a few years, with the numbers of teenagers entering the labor force declining each year, the percentage of labor force growth attributable to immigration will increase, even though immigration remains at a steady level.

There are various ways of measuring the extent to which immigrants contribute to labor force growth, none of them totally satisfactory. A traditional technique has been to note the number of arriving immigrants who indicate that they have an occupation when they fill out their visa application; and then compare that total to the increase in the civilian labor force. In the most recent period for which we have data (mid-1968 through mid-1976), there was, on average, a growth of 2,000,000 a year in the labor force, and an average of about 154,000 immigrants with stated occupations; thus only about 7.7 percent of the increase could be attributed to immigration.[6]

Subsequently we worked out a more comprehensive estimation technique which took into account a variety of other factors, principally the fact that many adult immigrants, who report no occupation on their visa application, are hard at work a few years later; further, children arriving as immigrants grow up and join the labor force. On the other hand, immigrants, just like other workers, die, retire or emigrate. Using a technique described elsewhere,[7] and assuming a steady flow of immigrants at the 400,000 a year level, we estimated that in the period mid-1972 through mid-1985 that the *net* increase in the labor force attributable to immigration would average about 222,000 a year, thus comprising about 13 percent of the projected increase in the labor force in that time period.

More significant than the exact numbers of arriving alien workers are the terms and conditions under which they work. It is clear that the wages and working conditions experienced by legal immigrants are quite different from those experienced by illegal aliens. Chiswick has pointed out in his retrospective analysis of 1970 census data, that white male immigrants gain earnings parity with their native peers within thirteen years of their arrival, and subsequently surpass the earnings of these peers.[8] In work now nearing completion for the U.S. Department of Labor, we have found that, similarly, immigrant women surpass the earnings of their native peers after only a few years in the nation.

Illegal aliens, on the other hand, according to all reports known to us, are paid considerably less than their native peers, and in many cases are paid less than the minimum wage.[9] Although the arguments on the subject are vigorous, it is our contention that the principal impact of illegal aliens in the labor market, at a time of high unemployment, is to depress wages of all workers in the affected labor markets, and to displace some domestic workers from their jobs.[10]

The Nation's Two Immigration Policies

The impact of illegal aliens on the nation's labor markets was one of the concerns which caused the Carter administration in the summer of 1977 to offer its package of proposals on the subject. In addition to the amnesty provisions discussed, and references to aiding economic development in the nations which export the undocumented workers, the administration also proposed fines for employers who hired such workers, and more funds for the border patrol. (The lack of proposals regarding the issuance of nonimmigrant visas, or tighter inspection procedures at ports of entry, or a work permit system were as interesting as that which was proposed.)

Whether or not the administration's proposals are adopted by Congress and whether or not they represent a sound approach to the problem, they do represent the first significant effort in our recent history to create a single immigration policy for the United States, and that is highly commendable.

Since 1921, when we first set numerical limits on some classes of immigrants (those from the Eastern Hemisphere), we have essentially had two immigration policies. Our de jure policy is restrictive, highly legalistic, and displays concern for the rights of those admitted through its processes; our de facto policy, on the other hand, is nonrestrictive, operates outside the law, and is neutral to callous (depending on the specific circumstances) regarding the postadmission rights of the migrants whose entrance it tolerates.

The de jure policy, ensconced in law, enforced by the State Department's consular corps and the Justice Department's Immigration and Naturalization Service calls for both quantitative and qualitative screening procedures. In 1921, when the post-World War I rush of conservatism was at its peak, the Congress decided (and President Harding agreed) to impose numerical limits on what was then the major migration stream, that from the Eastern Hemisphere. These limits, which ultimately worked out to about 150,000 a year, were subdivided among the nations of the world, with the quotas allocated to the blue-eyed, blonde-haired parts of Europe the most generous and those for Southern and Eastern Europe considerably less generous; Asians were virtually excluded. The de jure policy was adopted, despite the opposition of employers who knew that a continuing flow of fresh immigrants would help fill their needs for workers; it was, as one historian put it, "a triumph of bigotry over greed."[11]

Subsequently, there have been two significant changes in the de jure immigration policy, both included in the 1965 amendments. The first was the deletion, after decades of debate, of the country-of-origin quota system, a major victory for the liberals, which came at a time of other major victories, such as the various Civil Rights Acts, and the launching of the War on Poverty. The second principal change (something of a tradeoff for the first) must be characterized differently. It was the extension of the concept of numerical limitations to immigration from the Western Hemisphere. Previously, all immigration from that part of the world had been unlimited, although each would-be immigrant was examined to make sure that he or she was not excludable under the law. Congress has over the years worked out an elaborate qualitative screening process for immigrants, to keep out classes it finds objectionable, such as criminals and Communists, polygamists and prostitutes.

An immigrant admitted through the workings of the de jure immigration process becomes a permanent resident alien, with many (but not all) of the rights of a citizen; after a few years, the alien can apply for citizenship. Once such an alien has been admitted to the nation, it is possible to eject him only after substantial due process.

While the nation's de jure immigration policy faced East and concerned itself primarily with immigration from the Old World, the nation's de facto policy faced South, and dealt primarily with migration from Latin America, particularly from Mexico. The thrust of this policy has been to meet the needs of U.S. employers, to bring them cheap labor when they need it, and to send it home when the need had been satisfied. The policy has taken many forms over the years, but the underlying thrust has remained constant—as has the tacit approval of the Mexican government, which has an enormous stake in the continuation of this policy. Poverty-stricken Mexicans, who remove their unemployment from Mexico, convert it to employment in the United States, and send home remittances, remove substantial potential pressures on the Mexican establishment, which might otherwise be pressed towards painful policies, such as devoting resources to labor-intensive economic development in the countryside, working out a more equitable distribution of national income, or creating an effective rural birth-control program. A similar situation prevails, although the numbers are smaller, in many other nations around the Caribbean rim.

The de facto immigration policy was substantially aided for decades by the lack of numerical limits on Western Hemisphere immigration; Latin Americans who could meet the sometimes casual and sometimes rigorous standards of the consuls could secure immigrant visas and settle in the United States. But the more significant migrations were not of legal immigrants; they were of either illegal entrants or legal nonimmigrant workers (in our West, they were called braceros, the strong-armed ones; in Western Europe, they are guestworkers). Nonimmigrants are admitted temporarily to a nation, for a specific purpose; when that purpose has been accomplished, they are expected to leave.

During World War I, we imported nonimmigrant Mexican workers for the farms, ranches, and railroads; during the twenties, many Mexican nationals drifted into the booming Southwest with and without papers; when the depression arrived, hundreds of thousands of Mexicans, some of them legally resident in the United States, including some U.S. citizens, were driven back to Mexico, to keep them out of the U.S. job market and off the U.S. welfare rolls. During the forties, they were welcome again, this time as braceros, whose function was to harvest the crops; again some stayed beyond their time, and illegal entries were made as well. Again, the tide turned, the economy slackened, and the Eisenhower Administration mounted "Operation Wetback," which, on close to two million occasions during a two-year period, threw Mexican nationals back across the border.

The mid-sixties was an interesting time for our de facto immigration policy. A series of secretaries of labor—James Mitchell, Arthur Goldberg, and particularly, Willard Wirtz—pressed for better wages and working conditions in the bracero program, so that it would be less likely to depress working conditions for competing U.S. workers. Eventually, the secretaries, supported by church, labor, and some Chicano groups, were able to terminate the bracero program. The de facto immigration policy seemed to have lost a major round, but only temporarily, for while the forces which had killed the bracero program had triumphed in the arena where they had assembled (within Congress and in the Labor Department), they had not paid sufficient attention to the possibility of a revived flow of illegal immigration. The possibility soon became a reality, and illegal immigration increased steadily following the termination of the bracero program; one makes that statement assuming that the increasing apprehensions of illegal aliens reflect primarily an increase in traffic, rather than an increase in the manpower of the border patrol, which is only marginally larger now than it was in 1965. Apprehensions of illegal aliens increased from 110,371 in that fiscal year to more than a million in fiscal 1977. In short, the de facto immigration policy had emerged in still another form.

This de facto policy is not expressed positively in laws, regulations, forms or procedures; it is expressed negatively through these channels:

- there is no law on the books making it illegal for an employer to hire an illegal alien;
- the State Department has been given neither the resources nor a firm set of instructions to cut back the number of visas it grants to those who are likely to become illegal aliens;

- the Immigration and Naturalization Service has not been given the funds (or the laws) needed to effectively limit illegal immigration.

The de facto policy is a highly effective one; apparently millions of illegals (I prefer a three to six million range) are present in the nation, simultaneously deflating the wages of disadvantaged U.S. workers and inflating the size of the population.

Private Interests

Both the de jure and de facto immigration policies of the nation are dominated by private interests, to an extent unknown in other immigrant-receiving democracies (such as Israel, Australia, New Zealand, and Canada).

It is not generally recognized that our de jure immigration policy is essentially one of nepotism; three-quarters of those admitted annually to the nation are not admitted because a determination has been made that they might be useful to the nation in some way, politically, culturally, or economically; they are simply admitted because a legal resident of the United States has requested their admission. It does not matter whether the U.S. resident has even *met* the alien in question, the crucial act is the signing of a petition seeking the alien's admission. The very complicated immigration law, for example, makes an allocation of 24 percent of the much-demanded numerically controlled immigrant visas for the brothers and sisters of U.S. citizens, *and their dependents*. Thus a U.S. citizen who has not seen her sister for forty years, and who has never met her brother-in-law or any of the nieces or nephews, can secure immigrant visas *for all of them* by filing a petition with INS.

This is not an obscure, little-utilized portion of the immigration law; in 1976, an estimated 31,000 such dependents from the Eastern Hemisphere secured immigration visas—issued to them not because they were a relative of a U.S. citizen, but because they were a relative of a relative of a U.S. citizen. In that year, we admitted more of these Eastern Hemisphere relatives of brothers and sisters of U.S. citizens (just one of the relative categories) than we admitted needed workers from all over the world; the 31,000 in this special category almost equaled the number of refugees we admitted that year, 39,000.[12]

An immigrant visa is a governmentally created good; more of them might be used to admit refugees (including refugees from right-wing dictatorships, a step rarely taken), and more of them might be used to attract some of the world's restless talent to our shores, rather than simply distributing them (in an often pronatal way) to the relatives of resident aliens and U.S. citizens.

While the de jure immigration system produces relatives, the de facto system produces self-selected, largely disadvantaged workers for U.S. employers. These workers, from all accounts, are highly motivated, are eager to please their employers, but (at least the ones from Mexico) come with very low levels of education.

We have only to look over a border, the one to the north, to learn that a more rational immigration policy *is* possible in a democracy. The Canadian system is a highly flexible one, which produces more immigrants in good times than in bad (because the government wills it), and which is operated through a points system. Immediate relatives of Canadian citizens are admitted outside the point system, but all other immigrants are covered by it; it simply awards points for qualities regarded as useful to the country, ability to speak one of the nation's two languages, skills in need, education, youth, and willingness to settle in a part of the nation which is not overpopulated or where unemployment is not rife.

Conclusion

Immigration is good for the United States at numerical limits at or somewhat above the current limits; it makes the nation a more interesting one, and it keeps us in touch with the rest of the world; it is an honorable part of our tradition. What we need, however, is a more rational immigrant-selection process, which makes more of its decisions on the needs of society as a whole, rather than the desires of some individual members of it. And then we need to enforce that policy, to keep some grip on the size of our population. Similarly, we must make sure that we are not creating an alien underclass who will do the nation's dirty work cheaply for the benefit of a privileged class of citizen employers and workers—that is a form of exploitation which should be rejected, out of hand, by an egalitarian society.

Notes

1. For a more extensive treatment of this subject, see S.M. Tomasi and C.B. Keely, *Whom Have We Welcomed? The Adequacy and Quality of United States Immigration Data for Policy Analysis and Evaluation* (Staten Island, N.Y.: Center for Migration Studies, 1975), pp. 57-72; and Robert Warren, "Recent Immigration and Current Data Collection," *Monthly Labor Review* (October 1977).

2. This estimate is based on an estimate of 110,000 annual alien emigrants from Robert Warren and Jennifer Peck, "Emigration from the United States: 1960 to 1970" (Paper presented at the annual meeting of the Population Association of America, Seattle, Washington, April 17-19, 1975), and our estimate of 40,000 annual U.S. citizen emigrants. For more information on the subject of citizen emigrants, see Ada Finifter, "Emigration from the United States, an Exploratory Analysis" (Paper prepared for the Conference on Public Support for the Political System, University of Wisconsin-Madison, August 13-17, 1973).

3. See *Silva* v. *Levi*, U.S.D.C., N.D. Ill., No. 76 C 4268, and, for a commentary, see Maurice A. Roberts, ed., *Interpreter Releases* 54, 14 (New York: American Council for Nationalities Service, April 12, 1977.

4. Office of the White House Press Secretary, "Undocumented Aliens Fact Sheet, Summary of the President's Proposals," August 4, 1977.

5. U.S. Bureau of the Census, *1970 Census of Population, Subject Reports: National Origin and Language* (Washington, D.C.: U.S. Government Printing Office, 1973), tables 6 and 13.

6. Immigrant data from *INS Annual Reports*, 1968-1976, table 8A; U.S. labor force data for 1968 from Bureau of Labor statistics, *Handbook of Labor Statistics, 1975*, table 1 (noninstitutional population, civilian labor force sixteen years of age and over); comparable data for 1976 secured by telephone from BLS.

7. See David S. North and Allen LeBel, *Manpower Policy and Immigration Policy in the United States: An Analysis of a Nonrelationship* (Washington, D.C.: National Commission for Manpower Policy, forthcoming), chapter IV and appendix B.

8. Barry R. Chiswick, "The Effect of Americanization on the Earnings of Foreign Born Men," Hoover Institution, Stanford University, mimeo, June 1977).

9. David S. North and Marion F. Houstoun, *The Characteristics and Role of Illegal Aliens in the U.S. Labor Market: An Exploratory Study* (U.S. Department of Labor, March 1976), pp. 128-131; and Julian Samora, *Los Mojados: The Wetback Story* (Notre Dame, Ind.: University of Notre Dame Press, 1971), pp. 98-105.

10. For the opposite point of view, see Michael Piore, "The 'New Immigration' and Presumptions of Social Policy" (Paper presented at a meeting of the Industrial Relations Research Association, December 29, 1974), and subsequently condensed in *The New Republic* 22 (February 1975).

11. Robert A. Divine, *American Immigration Policy: 1924-1952* (New Haven, Conn.: Yale University Press, 1957).

12. The group of 31,000 relatives of arriving immigrants who are siblings of citizens are, in the eyes of the immigration law, secondary fifth preference beneficiaries; the estimate is derived from *INS Annual Report*, table 4, which reported 52,660 fifth preference admissions of all kinds, and from reports of the Visa Office, 1969-1975, which provides data on the proportion of visas issued in those years to primary fifth preference beneficiaries (the siblings of citizens) and to secondary beneficiaries (the relatives of the primary beneficiaries). It is assumed that the 1969-1975 primary-secondary ratio persisted in 1976.

8 Abortion and American Population Politics

John M. Ostheimer

The conservative spokesman, M. Stanton Evans, recently noted a "growing indifference toward the value of human life . . . hostility not only to personal freedom but to the very concept of life itself."[1] Evans' criticism of what are derogatorily called "antilife" policies was, typically, based on individual-level criteria. For example, his attack on abortion argues that a fetus is a human life, and an abortionist is, therefore, a murderer.

One sometimes hears permissive abortion decried because of its relationship to broader, demographic impacts. For example, Evans connects such dangerous liberal policies to what he calls the population "scare." He argues, "our population phobia has powerfully spurred the recent movement toward demographic controls. The crusade for elective abortion has been greatly aided by population fears, while a national campaign for euthanasia . . . is also taking form and drawing strength from similar apprehensions."[2] In this passage, however, Evans has overstated the *political* connection between the abortion issue and demography.

No one would deny the strong theoretical relationship between population growth levels and abortion.[3] Furthermore, research has shown that induced abortions have actually played an important role in the population programs of less-developed countries,[4] as well as in other industrialized countries.[5] The Commission on Population Growth and the American Future observed, though cautiously because of the inadequacies of available data, that the relationship also exists for the United States. Though legal abortion would lower the maternal and neonatal (birth to twenty-eight days) death rates, "there is little doubt . . . that legal and illegal abortions exert a downward influence on the United States birthrate."[6] The commission predicted that a decline of 1.5 per 1000 in the birthrate would result from liberalized national abortion laws during the first year.

Nevertheless, abortion is not perceived by the general public as a population issue. Nor, for the most part, has it been fought as one. The fundamental dissimilarity between demographic questions and the abortion issue is emotional content. India may be different, but in this country there is a detached, ethereal quality to the warnings made by Zero Population Growth, Inc.[7] Contradictory warnings, that the declining birthrate will cost the United States its position as a leading world power, seem equally detached from personal concerns.[8]

"Doubling times" and "age cohorts" lend an air of cold science to the

The author is indebted to the Transition Foundation of Los Angeles for research support.

population debate, but the abortion issue is totally different. Brought home by personal experience, the issue deeply concerns millions of Americans, the vast majority of whom connect it to individual rights and responsibilities. This paper will provide some description of abortion as a political issue, of its relationship to population questions, and of the difficulties it presents the American system in formulating appropriate policies.

The Nature of the Abortion Issue

Lowi developed a typology with three major categories which represent a scale of importance various types of political issues have for the society as a whole.[9] *Distributive*, or pork barrel issues, represent the lowest significant level. Such issues may be economically significant within a region, but they do not have general national importance, other than serving as evidence of the priorities that determine resource allocation.

Abortion seems to fit best Lowi's second level of significance, *regulative* issues, which do represent important philosophical choices for society. For example, no distributive issue could have caused the type of debate that abortion has stimulated in journals that straddle the interface between philosophy, medicine, and the social and policy sciences.[10] Regulative issues such as abortion can be generalized across the society.

Income tax and welfare are examples of the third and highest level, *redistributive* issues. These are the most politicized; interest group peak associations and political parties will have long-standing and well-articulated positions on redistributive issues, but one can also expect these organizations to have comparatively well-developed positions even for middle-level regulative issues such as abortion. Nevertheless, the abortion issue has not stimulated a full complement of formally-stated positions by representative political organizations. It is relatively "undeveloped" in this sense. A broad variety of interest groups should have articulated viewpoints. Individuals should, by now, be viewing the abortion issue in partisan and ideological terms, as they do other regulative issues. Americans widely identify certain issues and constituencies as "Republican" or "Democratic." Abortion has been a national debate for over a decade, and political parties and candidates should be making known their positions. To be sure, the issue has provided sufficient excitement, but the closer one gets to the center of American decision making, the more vague become the stands taken by leaders. The 1977 congressional battle over Medicaid abortions verified this; Democratic congressional leaders, in a year which found them flexing their muscles vis-à-vis the president as well as their own party caucuses on most issues, demonstrated very weak leadership on the abortion fight. One explanation is that the emotional and moralistic nature of the issue intimidates most officials.

While many influential people avoid the issue of abortion, other Americans pursue it precisely because of its high emotionalism. They view its effects as tremendously important. Proabortion groups cover a range of interest group types. The most significant single-issue organizations—The Association for the Study of Abortion and the National Association for the Repeal of Abortion Laws, recently renamed the National Abortion Rights Action League—have been joined by a few multi-issue groups. Of these, most important have been the Women's Lobby and N.O.W., and the American Civil Liberties Union. Certain Protestant denominational organizations, representing Methodists and Presbyterians, have also been active. Among demographically-oriented groups, Planned Parenthood and the Population Council have consistently stressed the contribution that liberal abortion policies can make to population control.[11] But these groups seem less in the political forefront since abortion's legalization in 1973. They have concentrated on increasing access to abortions for less advantaged people, and are not currently very vocal allies in the political battle to protect the legality of abortion. Of course, as the enemies of abortion continue to show successes in pecking away at liberalized policies, these groups will have to become active once again.

The range of active groups seems quite narrow compared with other major issues. Abortion law reformers argue that liberalization aids many sectors of society, but interest groups from those sectors, such as organized labor, have shunned the issue; their members are disproportionately Catholic and are among the more morally conservative elements of society.

More conspicuous since the 1973 Supreme Court ruling that legalized abortion for virtually any reason during a pregnancy's first three months have been those organizations which oppose liberalization. These have been headed by single-issue groups, particularly the National Right-to-Life Committee, the Alliance Against Abortion, the Human Life Foundation, and Birthright. As with the proabortion side, multi-issue groups have tended not to become involved, with key exceptions being certain religious organizations such as the National Council of (Catholic) Bishops, the Salvation Army, and the Mormon Church.

Proabortion activists have not been numerous, considering the large numbers affected by the issue. The few activists are disproportionately well educated and from professional occupations. Perhaps this reflects the technical complexity of the issue. Another cause may be the natural reticence of those who have firsthand experience with abortion. Lingering traditional values do not make such experience the sort of thing most women wish to advertise. From the beginning, abortion liberalization was an elite issue, but a curious one; masses of women from every economic and social group were having abortions, but the leadership, laced with intellectual "humanists" (atheists and agnostics) and feminists were, ironically, those who could have most easily continued to make use of the relative secrecy and expensiveness of the prelegalization world.[12] On the antiabortion side, the political activists seem more representative of the mass viewpoint they are expressing.

Neither pro- nor antiabortion camps have been successful in stirring the broader public to firm convictions. The abortion issue does not rank on the pollsters' monthly list of "most important" issues. This is also true for population control as a political issue, but for very different reasons. For abortion, one reason for public hesitation is what Hardin called the lingering "taboo"; many people consider abortion wholly inappropriate as a political concern.[13] The liberalizers advocate private choice through the elimination of antiabortion laws. Antiabortionists agree that the issue belongs "outside politics," but wish to ban the practice through constitutional amendment. Both sides would prefer a short political life for the issue, as long as the result goes their way.

The public has views, but has not developed the widespread salience levels required to force politicians to announce the clearcut positions. A second reason for this developmental sluggishness of attitudes on abortion is the issue's tremendous complexity for anyone attempting to be objective. It is technically difficult to determine when human life begins, for example. Should conception, movement in the womb, or birth be the moment a human has emerged with full rights? Such snags invite extreme positions among activists, confusion among the masses, and obfuscation by politicians.

Although intensity of abortion attitudes appears low for most Americans, public opinion has certainly shown the effects of events of the past two decades. By the mid-1960s, few Americans had "no opinion" when asked whether abortions were justified. Until recently, directional changes in those attitudes were striking. The first scientific polls showed extensive hostility towards abortion. By the early 1970s, however, half the public favored legal status for abortions justified only by discretionary reasons, while 90 percent were in favor if the mother's health was threatened. The great increase in acceptance occurred before the Supreme Court's 1973 rulings. Since then, attitudes have been quite stable.[14] As the Congress voted to restrict Medicaid abortions in late 1977, polls indicated that two-thirds of Americans still believed in a woman's right to have an abortion if she desired one. In sum, the American public discriminates between reasons for abortions, but generally approves of the current legal status for the practice during the first trimester. However, it has also become clear that a majority of the public does *not* condone use of public funds for abortions save for cases of extreme medical need, rape, or incest.

Peoples' reactions to abortion differ according to standard background variables. Higher socioeconomic status correlates strongly with permissiveness. Religion also emerges in the literature as consistently indicative of abortion attitudes.[15] The Catholic masses are relatively antiabortion, though far less so, particularly for medical justifications, than are the Catholic hierarchy. Furthermore, fundamentalist Protestants are as antiabortion as are Catholics.[16] Not surprisingly, Hertel, et al. argue that degree of religiosity relates strongly to abortion attitudes.[17] But Renzi found ideal family size intervening between religion and abortion attitudes; Protestants favored abortion *because* they favored smaller families.[18] More research needs to be done to clear up the lingering confusion over how abortion attitudes relate to background variables.

More important to this analysis are findings on the relationships between abortion attitudes and ideological-political variables. Current research results are harmonious; the abortion issue has not yet come of age, politically speaking. People are aware of most of the pros and cons usually offered regarding abortion, but the issue has not leavened into mass partisan or ideological identity.[19] A logical connection has been shown to exist between abortion legalization and liberal political ideology.[20] The less religion-bound "left" was more likely to favor maximizing rights and equalities for *existing* humans, and to point out the social and economic injustices of the old abortion laws.

Reactions of contemporary journals of known ideological orientation have been predictable. Readers of *The New Republic*, for example, have no trouble finding support for their convictions on the issue. These journals are also predictable on population control issues, with conservative writing hostile to such concepts, at least as applied to our own country. But the major organizations that relate these viewpoints on abortion and population to the process of policy making have not followed through. The abortion issue was not added to the shopping list of demands voiced by the clearly defined politico-ideological camps; it fits clearly neither the cultural liberalism nexus (environmentalism, consumerism) nor the bread-and-butter issue group. Some liberals have argued that abortion represents a redistributive issue; society can choose to pay now for abortions for the needy or later (and more) for medical care of septic abortions and social care for unwanted children. For example, a Planned Parenthood leader cited a 1974 H.E.W. report which observed that a return to illegal abortions would result in 25,000 hospitalizations for septic abortions, and in some $500 million for medical care and public assistance in the first year after birth. These costs were compared to $50 million annually for medicaid abortions.[21]

Proabortion groups might expect support in promoting reform from people, including relatively poor racial minorities, who would benefit from redistributive policies. The abortion and population issues are closely related on this point. Failure to provide adequate subsidized facilities penalizes the black and the poor.[22] But many black spokesmen have disavowed interest, or even condemned family planning practices directed at them as "genocide."[23] Thus, the legalization movement resides by default in the hands of cultural-issue liberals, with only a fragmentary political base among the masses.

The Abortion Issue in the Policy Arena

In spite of their success in keeping the abortion issue in the news, interest groups on both sides of the question have failed to establish a consistent perspective among decision-makers. Bachrach and Bergman wrote of a "mobilization of bias" which prevents significant viewpoints on population control issues from reaching decision makers.[24] The dominant moral and religious elements of society may have had a similar issue-suppressing impact on abortion politics. Also, as stated above, the highly emotional and sensitive nature of the issues has contributed to denial of systematic treatment within the policy-making process.

By 1973, state abortion laws varied greatly, as did interpretations by state and federal courts.[25] Spurred by the thalidomide and rubella cases,[26] and by events in other countries, particularly Britain's 1967 abortion reform law, a few state legislatures had amended their laws. Disparities widened between "reformed" states, such as California and New York, and those which stayed with traditional laws. *Roe* v. *Wade*, in January 1973,[27] had the effect of pulling the many traditional states into line with the reformed. In fact, the Court's action went further; most new state laws had not permitted social justifications, while *Roe* allowed virtual abortion-on-demand during the first trimester. By 1976, however, counter-pressures from antiabortion lobbyists were beginning to force specific revisions in the structure of permissive, post-1973, abortion law.

Once in the federal policy arena, the abortion issue has proven resistant to compromise and resolution. Congressional debate, especially during 1977, leaves the impression that the issue is used for ideological reconfirmation by legislators who were chosen primarily for their ideological credentials, or that it is used for building political support in constituencies whose religious makeup invites such cultivation. Unless the apparent national preference for liberal abortion policies can be joined with high issue salience to ensure that legislators will pay attention to public preferences, no more than piecemeal policies will emerge from Congress. Since 1973, Congress has rejected any constitutional amendment that would, in effect, sacrifice its further power to make abortion policy. Antiabortionists are attempting to circumvent this rejection. As of June 1977, nine states had called for a convention that would write an antiabortion amendment into the federal Constituion. Meanwhile, antiabortion forces have also pressured Congress to ban use of Medicaid funds to pay for abortions for the needy, who will, presumably, be returning in thousands to the back street butchers because they cannot afford the $200 legal operation. By December 1977, the continued failure of House and Senate conferees to resolve the issue of restrictions on medicaid abortions threatened the entire operation of the Department of Health, Education and Welfare.[28] Finally, a "compromise" was reached which prohibited Medicaid abortions unless (1) the woman's life was endangered; (2) two doctors attest that she may suffer "severe and long lasting health damage" from pregnancy; or (3) rape or incest, promptly reported to authorities, caused the pregnancy.

Executive branch leadership has been as cautious as Congress. President Nixon's hostility to legalized abortion became known through his disapproval of the liberalizing policies recommended by the Commission on Population Growth and the American Future. But, even without Watergate, it is unlikely that Nixon's antiabortion position, used in political wars against Rockefeller and McGovern, would ever have led to an active role vis-à-vis Congress. Of course, a president has some latitude to act in such matters, as Nixon showed prior to 1973 by ordering federal government medical facilities *not* to follow the reforms of certain states. President Ford preferred a constitutional amendment that would return control to the states, and presided over a federal administration that preferred sterilization to abortion as an "approved means" of family planning. President Carter seems content with the current legal situation, but shares the view of HEW Secretary Califano that abortion is "personally unacceptable." In their first HEW appropriations package, Carter and Califano put their views into practice with provisions against Medicaid abortions. Critics charge that such executive branch initiatives, coupled with those of anti-medi-caid-abortion legislators, are, essentially, clever ways to dodge the political issue. The *Roe* doctrine of legal abortion remains intact, and middle class Americans can make use of it while salving their consciences with the knowledge that they are at least not subsidizing the promiscuity of the poor! Indeed, for poor people, conditions are virtually returning to pre-*Roe*; initiatives during 1978 by the antiabortion lobby will undoubtedly add more states to the current 60 percent which deny public funding for abortions.

By default, the main features of current abortion policy were decided by the courts. Since *Roe*, the courts have continued to be the determining factor. In 1976, Federal district judges invalidated the Hyde amendment banning medicaid payments for all "discretionary" abortions. Then, in a 1977 decision, the Supreme Court reversed that ruling by allowing state and local governments to decide whether such abortions should be publicly financed.[29] Spousal and parental rights to participate in the abortion decision were protected until 1976, when they were declared unconstitutional.[30] This heavy judicial role supports the view that the abortion issue resembles the experience of population politics as described by Bachrach and Bergman. Society's moral fabric was propped up by traditionalistic state laws whose vagueness (Pennsylvania's banned, but failed to define, "unlawful" abortions) allowed dominant moral values to control undesirable behavior or ideas.

The key question becomes: how can the political system be maneuvered to expose hidden moral issues festering below the surface, and then to resolve them through public policies? Though the diversity of contest arenas assures that the public will see such issues argued out, most features of the American system discourage policy resolution. The strong judicial system has intervened to ensure some form of national policy that corresponds to the majority's wishes. Once again in the postwar era, liberals ironically find their cause supported by the structure in which, logically, they have least faith.

Administrative performance on abortion is weak, befitting the lack of political issue resolution in the executive and legislative branches. Though legalization was imposed by the Supreme Court, subsequent weak administrative policies have reflected the desire of the other two branches to avoid the issue's political volatility. Administrative practices since *Roe* also reflect regional differences, as well as dissatisfaction within the professions most affected. Methods of enforcing provision of abortion facilities, a potential Fourteenth Amendment problem, have been inadequate to ensure availability during the first trimester. These delays force the woman into the later periods of pregnancy, during which *Roe* allowed state infringements.

Conclusion

Demographic concerns can, and do, lead to suggestions of abortion as a possible means of controlling population growth. While the relationship between abortion policies and birthrates is not fully understood, one can at least estimate the consequences of recent restrictions. In the first year after *Roe*, between 20 and 30 percent of abortions performed could be attributed to legalization, either at the federal or state levels.[31] Perhaps as many as 300,000 births did *not* occur as a result of such legalization. With between 250,000 and 300,000 abortions a year financed by Medicaid funds, one can anticipate a substantial increase in the birthrate following Congress' restrictions of December 1977, even if the exact number of "additional" births cannot be predicted.

Apart from these relationships, however, the abortion issue really operates on a different wavelength from the politics of population. That difference may make the issue hard for demographers and population activists to understand. Moreover, the highly moralistic, emotional nature of the abortion issue will continue to render resolution difficult regardless of who the issue activists are.

Notes

1. M. Stanton Evans, *Clear and Present Dangers* (New York: Harcourt Brace Jovanovich, 1975), p. 362.

2. Ibid., p. 219.

3. Stephen J. Williams and Thomas W. Pullam, "Effectiveness of Abortion as Birth Control," *Social Biology* 22, no. 1 (1975):23-33.

4. C. Djerassi, "Fertility Control through Abortion: Assessment of the Period 1950-1980," *Bulletin of the Atomic Scientists* 28, no. 1 (January 1972):9-14, 41-45.

5. James W. Brackett, "The Demographic Consequences of Legal Abortion," in Sidney H. Newman, Mildred B. Beck, and Sarah Lewit, eds., *Abortions, Obtained and Denied* (New York: The Population Council, 1971). For further background, see also the special issue on abortion and fertility control in *Studies in Family Planning* 7, no. 8 (1976).

6. *Population and the American Future* (New York: New American Library, 1972), p. 176.

7. Zero Population Growth, Inc., "A U.S. Population Policy: ZPG's Recommendations" (Washington, D.C., 1976).

8. Colin Clark, "World Power and Population," *National Review* 21, no. 19 (May 20, 1969):481-84.

9. Theodore J. Lowi, "American Business, Public Policy, Case Studies and Political Theory," *World Politics* 16, no. 4 (1964):677-715.

10. John M. Ostheimer, "Induced Abortion Policies in Britain and the United States" (Paper presented at the Annual Meeting of the American Political Science Association, Washington, D.C., September 1977), pp. 6-9.

11. For example, Ronald Freedman and Bernard Berelson, "The Record of Family Planning Programs," *Studies in Family Planning* 7, no. 1 (1976).

12. Robert E. Hall, ed., *Abortion in a Changing World* (New York: Columbia University Press, 1970).

13. Garrett Hardin, *Stalking the Wild Taboos* (Los Altos, Calif.: William Kaufman, Inc., 1973).

14. John M. Ostheimer and James L. Regens, "Continuity and Change in Public Opinion Concerning Abortion" (Paper presented at Western Political Science Association Annual Meeting, Phoenix, April, 1977).

15. Judith Blake, "Abortion and Public Opinion: The 1960-1970 Decade," *Science* 171, no. 3971 (February 12, 1971):540-59.

16. John M. Ostheimer and Leonard G. Ritt, "Life and Death: Current Public Attitudes," in Nancy C. Ostheimer and John M. Ostheimer, eds., *Life or Death—Who Controls?* (New York: Springer, 1976), pp. 286-93; James T. Richardson and Sandie W. Fox, "A Longitudinal Study of the Influence of Selected Variables on Legislator's Voting Behavior on Abortion Reform Legislation," *Journal for the Scientific Study of Religion* 14, no. 2 (1975):159-64.

17. Bradley Hertel, Gerry E. Hendershot, and James W. Grimm, "Religion and Attitudes toward Abortion: A Study of Nurses and Social Workers," *Journal for the Scientific Study of Religion* 13, no. 1 (1974):23-35.

18. Mario Renzi, "Ideal Family Size as an Intervening Variable between Religion and Attitudes towards Abortion," *Journal for the Scientific Study of Religion* 14, no. 1 (1975):23-28.

19. American Institute of Public Opinion. "Social Issues/Behavior," *Gallup Opinion Index* 113 (1975):17-18.

20. Hans J. Eysenck, "Primary Social Attitudes: A Comparison of Attitudes Patterns in England, Germany, and Sweden," *Journal of Abnormal and Social Psychology* 48, no. 4 (1953):563-68.

21. Werner Fornos, letter to the *New York Times* (20 March 1975).

22. Betty Sarvis and Hyman Rodman, *The Abortion Controversy* (New York: Columbia University Press, 1973), chapters 8, 9; Arthur J. Dyke, "Procreative Rights and Population Policy," *Hastings Center Studies* 1 (1973):74-82.

23. Dick Gregory, "My Answer to Genocide," *Ebony* (October 1971), pp. 66-72; Ralph Hallow, "The Blacks Cry Genocide," *The Nation* 208, no. 17 (April 28, 1969), pp. 535-37; and E. Patricia McCormick, *Attitudes Toward Abortion* (Lexington, Mass.: Lexington Books, D.C. Heath and Co., 1975), pp. 8, 21.

24. Peter Bachrach and Elihu Bergman, *Power and Choice: The Formulation of American Population Policy* (Lexington, Mass.: Lexington Books, D.C. Heath and Co., 1973).

25. Mary S. Calderone, ed., *Abortion in the United States* (New York: Hoeber-Harper, 1958); Russell B. Shaw, *Abortion on Trial* (London: Robert Hale, 1969).

26. Kenneth J. Ryan, "Humane Abortion Laws and the Health Needs of America," in David T. Smith, ed., *Abortion and the Law* (Cleveland: Case Western Reserve Press, 1967).

27. *Roe* v. *Wade* 410 U.S. 113 (1973).

28. Mary E. Eccles, "Conferees Inch toward Abortion Agreement," *Congressional Quarterly Weekly Report*, 1 October 1977, pp. 2084-85.

29. *Beal* v. *Doe* 97 S. Ct. 2366 (1977).

30. *Planned Parenthood of Missouri* v. *Danforth* 428 U.S. 52 (1976).

31. Christopher Tietze, "The Effect of Legalization of Abortion on Population Growth and Public Health," *Family Planning Perspectives* 7, 3 (May/June 1975):123-27.

Family Policy and Fertility in the United States

Dorothy M. Stetson

The term population policy brings to mind government incentives or disincentives to increase or decrease fertility rates.[1] Discussion among American population policy makers has focused almost exclusively on policies that will directly manipulate fertility.[2] They assume that since many couples have more children than they believe desirable, optimum fertility levels will be reached if adequate contraception is available. The foundation of fertility policy is the Family Planning and Population Research Act of 1970, providing contraceptive services through grants to states for clinics. The purpose of these services is to influence aggregate childbearing behavior by allowing couples to reach their individual reproductive goals more effectively.

Despite recent attention to population policy, there is scant evidence that these government programs have much direct impact on fertility in the United States. The family planning services have coincided with increased use of contraceptives by women in public clinics, but not an increase in the overall contraceptive use, since these women would very likely have received these services through private sources anyway.[3] In other words, the programs have changed the pattern of distribution between public and private services, rather than increasing the overall use of contraceptives and reducing fertility.

This narrow approach to population policy-making has made it difficult to determine and evaluate the impact of government action on fertility. First, it ignores the fact that many government actions may affect childbearing behavior without being specifically directed toward fertility. One such area of policy is family policy, which although not aimed explicitly at population goals, involves the government in important population processes. Sometimes people forget that the United States has a family policy because it is not as explicit as those in some of the European countries. For example, Sweden and France have adopted comprehensive family policies in order to increase fertility.[4] Others, such as Britain and Canada, provide family allowances and maternity services as part of a general policy of social services. It is true that while the United States has not developed policies to subsidize family formation and child rearing along the lines of many European countries, there are a number of federal and state policies that regulate and provide services to families. Such actions are likely to affect childbearing and should be included in the study of policies affecting fertility.

A second problem with the current approach to population policy is the official view of the object of policy, that is, individual fertility behavior.

103

Knowledge, Attitude and Practice surveys seem to indicate that couples set reproductive goals and are likely to make conscious decisions to reach those goals. If so, there appears to be little need to deal with the problem of changing individual reproductive goals since providing the means for individuals to achieve existing goals will be sufficient. These assumptions are too narrow in several respects. They depend on safe, foolproof contraceptive devices which technology has not yet provided. They pertain only to a portion of adults, those who actually do plan their families, and do not take into account the growing problem of unplanned teenage pregnancies. Further, they ignore the wide range of psychological, social, and economic variables that are pertinent to the decision to give birth to a child.

The object of this paper is to introduce a conceptual framework for analyzing population policy which allows for a more realistic approach to determining and evaluating the fertility effects of government actions. It focuses on the wide range of government actions regarding families and the influence of such policy on the complex environment surrounding individual childbearing decisions. The framework will be applied to a number of U.S. family policies as they relate to childbearing, including family formation, dissolution, pregnancy, taxes, Aid to Families with Dependent Children, child care, and abortion. In the United States, these policies which regulate families and provide services to them are not aimed at any specific population goals, yet they represent implicit official values about children. The application of this framework will have two purposes: (1) to suggest studies of the impact of family policy on childbearing behavior and fertility that will be useful in policy making with respect to population goals; and (2) to encourage the evaluation of family policy, especially the pattern of benefits and burdens family policies distribute to citizens in relation to the dominant social norms about childbearing and family life.

The Framework

The number and spacing of children in a family can be accounted for only by examining a complex set of personal norms and life experiences.[5] Parents learn norms and information about family life from their ethnic, religious, economic, and cultural groups. They may want children for their personal fulfillment, destiny, status, affectional ties, or security in old age. At the same time, children mean costs to parents, both financial and psychological. Parents bear children in this environment of group norms, personal values, and relative costs. Public policy makes a contribution to this environment by increasing or decreasing the psychological and material costs of children. Policies can thus be classified according to their contribution to this cost environment. Policies which reduce the costs of having children are *pronatalist* and those which add to the costs are *antinatalist*. The relative significance of these government inputs may vary according to the economic and social circumstances, personal values, and personalities of the parents.

Specific policies will be described in this paper according to content, target, cost, implementation, type, and strength: (1) *Policy content* includes those aspects of a law or program which pertain to various childbearing activities, such as family formation, conception, pregnancy, childbirth, child support, and care; (2) *Target of policy* focuses on the particular group in society that is the object of government action, such as poor mothers, couples wishing to marry, or employees; (3) *Cost of policy* means the nature and direction of financial or psychological cost which the policy, if fully implemented, contributes to the childbearing environment; (4) *Policy implementation* estimates the extent to which the policy is carried out; (5) *Classification of policy* indicates whether it is pronatalist or antinatalist according to type of cost; (6) *Strength of policy* combines estimates of the amount of financial or psychological cost and the extent of implementation to determine if the policy is limited, moderate, or extensive to the target group. The result of applying this framework to a number of family policies will be to place them in one of six categories: limited pronatalist, moderate pronatalist, extensive pronatalist, limited antinatalist, moderate antinatalist, extensive antinatalist.

Family Formation

State marriage and illegitimacy laws regulate the establishment of families. Marriage laws vary, but most set minimum age requirements, require seriological tests, and impose a waiting period.[6] They pertain to any couple who wish to establish a family legally. The laws represent some minimal financial costs for licenses and tests. For those under the legal age, the law sets additional barriers by requiring them to obtain parental consent to marry. Marriage laws are implemented widely, since the states have a monopoly on definitions of legal marriage and couples must comply with the requirements of the legal procedure if they wish to marry.

Couples can avoid the slight costs of marriage by having children out of wedlock. However, state policies based on common law penalize illegitimate children and their mothers by denying them rights to support or inheritance from their fathers. Thus, avoiding the costs of legal marriage often leads to increased costs of illegitimacy. In the past few years, some states have reformed laws to make the legal rights and status of illegitimate children nearer those of legal marriages, especially in the areas of support and inheritance. Government regulations about family formation are becoming more uniform whether or not a couple seeks a legal marriage.

The government imposes a few limits on the freedom of people to form families through legal marriage. Illegitimacy laws may mean greater financial costs to a mother who has her child out of wedlock. Marriage laws are a limited antinatalist policy and illegitimacy laws are moderately antinatalist. How these costs affect childbearing behavior depends on other values and norms, for example, how important legal marriage is to parents in forming a family.

Family Dissolution

The government steps in to regulate the breakup of families through divorce laws. Traditionally, states have wanted to make divorce difficult to encourage family stability. Under strict fault laws, an unhappy couple who has a child may find it less costly to continue the marriage. In the past decade most states have reformed their laws to make divorce more accessible. Over half the states have incorporated marital breakdown provisions which often allow divorce on the petition of just one spouse. Divorce laws which affect unhappy couples facilitate marriage breakup. These laws increase fertility costs. When divorce is difficult, a woman can have another child and the law protects her against the loss of support for that child. Easier divorce laws add to the cost of having a child in a troubled marriage especially if the child is born after the parents break up. As such, easy divorce laws are antinatalist but their effect is limited to couples who have a child after the marriage has broken down. The burden of these laws on such couples may be reduced by other reforms which facilitate remarriage. Former prohibitions on the remarriage of guilty spouses and lengthy waiting periods between filing and receiving decrees have been removed in many states. For those spouses who have found new partners, the law reduces the costs of family reformation. Divorce and remarriage laws can be limited pronatalist policies by reducing costs to a few couples.

Pregnancy and Employment

Federal policies have evolved in the last decade to provide guidelines for regulations affecting pregnancy and employment. However, these policies have developed in two conflicting directions. Equal Employment Opportunity Commission (EEOC) guidelines for Title VII of the Civil Rights Act of 1964, amended in 1972, treat pregnancy as a temporary disability. Pregnant employees with companies covered by Title VII have the right to maternity leave without loss of salary or job status for a specified period to receive benefits that may accrue from disability insurance. Otherwise, they are treated like other employees and not specially penalized for pregnancy. This policy affects working women, by reducing the financial and psychological costs of bearing children. It protects the jobs, status, and pay and delivers whatever disability benefits are available. EEOC pregnancy policies are pronatalist. Enforcement of these guidelines is a piecemeal affair. Those companies that have adopted approved equal employment policies have such provisions. This includes major industrial firms and many educational institutions. Thus, one type of government policy about pregnancy and employment is moderately pronatalist.

On the other hand, the Supreme Court has put forth an alternate doctrine regarding the constitutional and statutory protections available to pregnant employees. The Supreme Court has ruled that pregnancy is a problem only to pregnant women.[7] Although it is illegal under Title VII to discriminate in employment on the basis of sex, the Court argues that pregnancy is a condition only of some women, not all women, and thus policies that treat pregnant women differently from other employees do not violate bans on sex discrimination. Under these guidelines, an employed woman who becomes pregnant and bears a child may be fired or denied disability benefits and unemployment insurance. Such a policy, if implemented, increases both the financial and psychological costs of having a child to a working mother. Thus far, the courts have applied it to disability insurance programs where cost is considered a major factor in denying benefits. The policy is classified as moderately antinatalist.

Taxes

Since the 1940s, federal income tax law has given a deduction to parents with minor children.[8] This deduction reduces the cost of children. The size of the reduction is small compared with the average actual cost of child support ($750 compared with average cost estimated at nearly $3000 per year).[9] The relative importance of this cost reduction varies according to the income and size of the family. The $750 reduction in taxable income may represent a considerable saving in larger families with smaller incomes.

The 1976 Tax Reform Act repealed previous limited deductions for child care and substituted a tax credit for child care and related dependency expenses. Parents who, because of part-time or full-time employment or disability, must pay someone to care for their dependent children may claim 20 percent of their expenses. The credit allowed is up to $2000 for one child and $4000 for two or more. This reform reduces the cost of children to a large number of parents, but unlike the tax deduction, it benefits smaller families. As the number of children in care increases the reduction from the tax credit remains the same. Federal tax policies apply extensively in society, but the size of the cost reduction is limited. Therefore they are classified as moderately pronatalist.

AFDC

The major federal/state program providing income to poor families is Aid to Families with Dependent Children (AFDC) established under the Social Security

Act. AFDC provides cash payments to low income or indigent women with minor children. AFDC is jointly funded by state and national governments, but implementation of federal guidelines is decentralized and rules and regulations may vary among the states. The two aspects of this program which seem to pertain most directly to childbearing decisions are "suitable home" provisions and "work incentive" programs.

A basic purpose of the AFDC program from the beginning has been to subsidize husbandless mothers to enable them to bring up their children in a morally and materially adequate environment. Thus, funds may be restricted to those mothers with good moral character who maintain suitable homes. States may cut off aid to a mother who has an illegitimate child while receiving AFDC payments. Suitable home regulations increase financial costs of bearing a child to poor mothers who depend on welfare. As such they are antinatalist. Enforcement of suitable income provisions has been sketchy.[10]

The work incentive programs of AFDC have been developed to encourage welfare mothers to seek employment. Under these programs, mothers can earn income and still receive additional benefits for each child. For low income working mothers, work incentive programs reduce the cost of bearing another child. Thus, they represent a pronatalist aspect of AFDC policies. Studies show that pronatalist work/welfare policies are extensively implemented among the poor, while antinatalist suitable home provisions are more limited.[11] However, under current guidelines a state might emphasize either approach.

Child Care

Funds to subsidize child care are available under the Social Security Act, the work incentive programs, and the Equal Opportunity Act. These public services have been directed toward low income families and are part of a program of incentives to mothers to find permanent employment and eventually get off welfare. However, if their income rises enough they may become ineligible for these child care services. Child care is not fully implemented and coverage is inadequate to handle the demand.[12] Thus, although the policy is pronatalist, limited coverage reduces its overall benefits to working parents.

Abortion Services

Since 1973, the Supreme Court has upheld the right to abortion in the first six months of pregnancy.[13] However, the Court has since confirmed the right of states not to pay for abortions for indigent women which are medically unnecessary.[14] The Court majority maintained that while it was true that *Roe* v. *Wade* had established a constitutional right for a woman to seek an abortion, that decision did not set limits "on the authority of the state to make a value judgment favoring childbirth over abortion, and to implement that judgment by the allocation of public funds."

Congress has also tended to restrict financial support for abortion services in the last five years. Antiabortion amendments have been included in foreign aid and legal services legislation. The 1976 HEW appropriations bill contained an amendment prohibiting funds for abortions except to save the life of the mother. The major program affected was Medicaid, which provides medical service to poor women receiving AFDC. Federal courts threw out the abortion ban but the government appealed to the Supreme Court. The U.S. Department of Justice lawyers argued that: (1) women have a constitutional right to seek an abortion, but not necessarily to get one; and (2) further, that the government had no constitutional responsibility to relieve all burdens of poverty, such as the burden of unwanted pregnancy. The Supreme Court agreed with the federal government and in the summer of 1977 reinstituted the ban on the use of Medicaid funds for abortions except to save the mother's life. The 1978 appropriations bill relaxed the prohibition slightly to include payment for abortions that resulted from rape or incest and in cases where continuation of the pregnancy will greatly endanger the physical health of the mother. These restrictions on abortion services are tied to the annual HEW appropriation and it is likely that some sort of restriction on Medicaid funds for abortions will continue in the future.

As a result of the cutoff of federal funds, few states will be able financially or politically to continue to subsidize abortions for poor women. For most of the poor, the costs of terminating an unwanted pregnancy have increased as a result of the government's actions, thereby reducing the relative cost of continuing the pregnancy to term. The federal government and most states, by denying subsidies for abortions, impose compulsory pregnancy on poor women. The U.S. abortion services policy has become pronatalist and extensively implemented to the target group.

Policy Proposals

Since 1976, leaders of the federal executive have been interested in developing new policies affecting the family. The secretary of HEW has proposed to pay maternity benefits to pregnant women who agree to put their children up for adoption. This policy would encourage women to find alternatives to abortion for unwanted pregnancies.

Then, after months of study the president proposed a reform of welfare policy that would simplify the income supplement programs for the poor. The proposal includes cash payments to single parents with young children, not unlike the existing AFDC program. There would be incentives for work, and government payments would be partially reduced for each dollar earned. The goals of the program would be to raise the income of single-parent families above the poverty level.

Congress has been considering a bill prompted by court decisions exempting pregnancy costs from disability programs in companies subject to civil rights regulations. The proposed amendment to Title VII expands the definition of sex discrimination to include discrimination on the basis of pregnancy, childbirth, and related conditions. The proposal is supported by both feminists and antibortionists, although the latter group wishes to have abortions specifically excluded. Opposition comes from industry and insurance companies who fear increased costs to companies and consumers.

These various family policy proposals, similar to current federal policies, would reduce the cost of bearing children and are therefore pronatalist. Welfare reform proposals continue the pattern of previous AFDC policy in reducing the costs of children to single parents. If implemented, these proposals would distribute government benefits for having children to a larger group of mothers than currently. Proposals to make company rules that discriminate against pregnant women illegal would affect most women in the work force. According to the discussions, Congress and the executive intend these policies to be pro-child. There is little indication, however, that they have considered their effects on fertility and population growth.

Summary and Conclusion

Family policies regulate the family and provide services. States regulate families with limited antinatalist policies which impose small costs on couples wishing to form families. The costs are less for legal marriage than illegal but the gap between rights of legitimate and illegitimate children is narrowing. Divorce is becoming more accessible and this may increase the costs of having a child in a troubled marriage. These costs can be balanced in specific cases by the ease of remarrying and forming new families.

Federal regulative policies, on the other hand, tend to be moderately pronatalist. Tax policy reduces costs by providing tax deductions for child support and credits for child care expenses while EEOC guidelines require companies to limit penalties imposed on pregnant employees. However, the Constitution does not guarantee the rights of pregnant employees and judicial interpretation has allowed discrimination against them. This policy is moderately antinatalist and it increases costs of having children to working women. If Congress passes the proposed amendment to Title VII protecting pregnant employees, all federal regulative policies will be pronatalist.

Policies providing services to family members are made at the national level, administered by state and local government, and directed toward low-income families. Work incentives, abortion services, and child care programs are all pronatalist in content. Limited funding and variable implementation reduces the coverage of these programs. One aspect of the AFDC, the suitable home provision, is antinatalist in that it cuts off assistance to mothers who have children after receiving welfare. However, suitable home provisions are not widely enforced.

Public policies regulating the family and providing services may have an effect on fertility in two ways. First, they may change childbearing patterns. To determine such impact, studies should focus on comparing the fertility in groups subject to a policy with those which are not, taking into account social, economic, and cultural variables. Second, policies may affect the consequences of childbearing for couples. In this regard attention should focus on how the benefits and costs of government policies are distributed to different social groups and on whether these outcomes represent a desired use of government powers.

The application of this classification scheme clearly indicates that research on the impact of policy should be small in scale. A number of small-scale studies of specific groups and subgroups is preferable to grand studies because policies are directed toward target groups rather than the entire population and there is wide variation in administration. In addition, the significance of government-imposed costs to parents varies according to other costs, group norms, and personal values. A research agenda consisting of small-scale studies should also include plans for longitudinal analyses. Childbearing behavior spans twenty to thirty years in a woman's life. As parents grow older, values about children and social and economic circumstances change and thus the relative importance of government-imposed costs changes. It may take several years before a government program, such as child care, is felt by individual parents.

A good example of the type of research proposed here is suggested by Presser and Salsberg.[15] They have tried to determine the effect of public assistance programs on fertility. They point out that in examining welfare, it is unrealistic to study women in a large group because of the changes in childbearing that occur during life as well as the variation in welfare status. They studied the family-size goals of young women who had just had their first babies, comparing attitudes of those on welfare with those who were not. In general, welfare recipients desired smaller families than nonrecipients. On the other hand, more nonrecipients planned their first babies. Most of those on welfare were there as a result of their babies. According to Presser and Salsberg, welfare policy reduces the cost of childbearing for the poor but such cost reduction is a consequence of having a child, rather than an incentive.

Following are a few research questions and hypotheses about the impact of policy on fertility behavior that may be explored by a number of such small range studies:

1. What has been the effect of reducing legal costs of illegitimacy on family formation?
   a. Reducing costs of illegitimacy has increased the number of illegitimate children.
   b. Reducing costs of illegitimacy has reduced shotgun marriages.
   c. Reducing costs of illegitimacy has had no effect; laws have changed because people have decided to have children despite marriage.
2. What are work/childbearing patterns of women employed in Company A where pregnancy is treated as a temporary disability compared with those employed in Company B where there is no job protection for pregnancy?
   a. Women in A have fewer children than in B because they can continue working.
   b. Women in A have more children than in B because the overall cost is reduced.
   c. Women in B have fewer children than in A in order to continue working.
   d. Women in B have more children than in A because they are not able to continue steady work.
3. What is the effect of antinatalist suitable home provisions on the family size of welfare mothers?
   a. Suitable home policies decrease the number of children over time because mothers do not want to lose welfare benefits.
   b. Suitable home policies increase the number of children because welfare mothers are more vulnerable without the security of financial assistance.
4. What is the effect of increasing the cost of abortion to low income women?
   a. Without abortion poor women will have more children because they will carry an unwanted child to term.
   b. Without abortion services poor women will be more likely to use contraceptives.
   c. Without abortion services poor mothers will have illegal abortions.

The classification of policies also suggests the consequences of government actions for society and social norms. For some groups in society, costs of childbearing are increased or decreased by these policies. Tax policy reduces cost for all parents. Working women gain assistance from EEOC in being able to continue jobs and receive disability benefits. Other working mothers are penalized by government for having children. The low-income mothers, however, many of whom are not working, receive the most help from the government in the form of services that are largely pronatalist. These pronatalist policies seem to make it easier for poor women to have children than not to have them. How do these policies relate to concerns about population growth among the poor? Can we reconcile prochild values with values of limited population growth and reproductive choice?

Any discussion of the values underlying public policy leads the policy analyst to seek reasons for a particular policy decision. How did these various pro- and antinatalist policies develop? Why are some values promoted rather than others? Why are the prochild policies for poor people and working women so poorly funded and inadequately implemented? Are fertility variables taken into account during policy making? These questions are especially timely when the federal government and many states are focusing on family policies. To answer these questions requires analysis of the policy process and the development and change of policy over time. As fertility norms and values change, costs imposed by policy may seem excessive, deficient, or unrealistic. Demands for change in policy may be expressed in a number of ways by parents and interest groups. Groups pressure Congress to amend laws as in the case of pregnancy and welfare reform. Or, parents may seek to reduce the impact of undesirable laws, for example, by getting out-of-state divorces or back-street abortions. Eventually the study of population policy must complete the links between policy output and impact, on the one hand and the policy formulation process, on the other.

Notes

1. R.J. Cook, "Formulating Population Policy: A Case Study of the United States," in *Population Policymaking in the American States*, Elihu Bergman et al., eds. (Lexington, Mass.: Lexington Books, D.C. Heath and Co., 1974), pp. 15-42.

2. Peter Bachrach and Elihu Bergman, *Power and Choice: The Formulation of American Population Policy* (Lexington, Mass.: Lexington Books, D.C. Heath and Co., 1973).

3. J. Richard Udry, Karl E. Bauman, and Naomi Morris, "The Effect of Subsidized Family Planning Services on Reproductive Behavior in the United States," *Demography* 13 (November 1976):463-478.

4. William Petersen, "On the Relation between Family Policy and Population Policy," *International Journal of Comparative Sociology* 16 (September-December 1975):246-259; Alva Myrdal, *Nation and Family: The Swedish Experiment in Democratic Family and Population Policy* (London: Kegan Paul, 1947).

5. E. Pohlman, *Psychology of Birth Planning* (Cambridge, Mass.: Schenkman, 1969).

6. Council of State Governments, *Book of the States*, vol. 21, 1976-1977.

7. *General Electric* v. *Gilbert* 429 U.S. 125 (1976); *Geduldig* v. *Aiello* 417 U.S. 484 (1974).

8. Harold Graves, "Issues in Taxation of the Family," *Brookings Papers on Public Policy* (Washington, D.C.: Brookings Institution, 1965), pp. 113-120.

9. T.J. Espenshade, *The Cost of Children in the United States* (Berkeley: University of California Press, 1973).

10. Winifred Bell, *Aid to Dependent Children* (New York: Columbia University Press, 1965); Joel Handler, *Reforming the Poor* (New York: Basic Books, 1972).

11. Mildred Rein, *Work or Welfare?* (New York: Praeger, 1974).

12. Sheila Kamerman and Alfred Kahn, *Social Services in the United States* (Philadelphia: Temple University Press, 1976); Dennis Young and Richard Nelson, *Public Policy in the Day Care of Young Children* (Lexington, Mass.: Lexington Books, D.C. Heath and Co., 1973).

13. *Roe* v. *Wade* 410 U.S. 113 (1973).

14. *Beal* v. *Doe* 97 S.Ct. 2366 (1977).

15. Harriet Presser and Linda Salsberg, "Public Assistance and Early Family Formation: Is There a Pro-Natalist Effect?" *Social Problems* 23 (December 1975):226-241.

10 Policies for the Resolution of Commons Dilemmas in Population

R. Kenneth Godwin and
W. Bruce Shepard

Collective decisions on public policy issues involve different types of situations. In one type of situation the affected parties have common, or complementary, objectives, but are unable to reach their goals because of information and organization costs. In other situations the persons involved have competing goals or objectives. This essay demonstrates an approach to public policy analysis in which identification of types of collective decision situations is based on game theory. The initial step in this approach is to identify the winners and losers under both existing institutional arrangements and possible alternative arrangements. In an earlier article for the *Policy Studies Journal* we indicated that many population-related policy issues have been depicted as intractable because they have been incorrectly classified as commons dilemmas rather than as situations in which some policy alternatives benefit at least some people without necessarily increasing costs to others (i.e., Pareto efficient situations).[1] We illustrated this error by an analysis of fertility issues. The analysis was based on Garrett Hardin's famous article, "The Tragedy of the Commons."[2] In the current chapter we extend our original argument to include mortality and mobility and examine the distributional impacts of resolving commons dilemmas in a purely cooperative manner.

Commons Dilemmas

Overpopulation, pollution, urban sprawl, and other population-related issues have been characterized as commons dilemmas. If an issue is, in fact, a commons dilemma, it has several characteristics that make it unsolvable at the individual level and quite difficult to solve satisfactorily through collective action. The "dilemma" involves use of a collective good (such as air, water, or collectively owned grazing lands). The dilemma results from an incentive structure in which the benefits to an individual who increases his use of the resource exceed the costs to him even though the sum of the benefits of the action to all users is less than the sum of the costs to all users. In such situations, behavior based on what is rational for individuals leads to harmful, perhaps even disastrous, consequences for the entire group of resource-users.[3]

As Dawes, Delay, and Chaplin have shown, the commons dilemma is equivalent to the Prisoner's Dilemma Game (PDG).[4] (See figure 10-1 for an example of a PDG payoff matrix.) Commons dilemmas are also closely related to common pool resource problems often studied in resource economics.[5] In PDGs and common pool resource issues the collective decision situation is neither purely cooperative nor purely competitive; these situations have thus been described as "mixed-motive." In the absence of binding agreements, the persons involved will be forced into an outcome that is undesirable from the perspective of the entire group. The persons "caught" in the dilemma can escape it only by collective action that changes the incentive structure of individuals.

Was "The Tragedy of the Commons" a Commons Dilemma?

In "The Tragedy of the Commons" Hardin cites the historical example of the English Commons lands. He attributes the deterioration of these lands to overgrazing caused by an incentive structure that allowed individuals to obtain the full benefits of adding an additional sheep to the Commons while the cost was distributed among the entire set of users. He argues that this example provides a useful analogy to overpopulation where parents receive the benefits of each child they bear while the costs of the environmental damage and resource depletion to which the child contributes are distributed across the entire population of the earth. Hardin proposes to resolve this contemporary commons dilemma through "mutual coercion mutually agreed upon."

Player II

	Player I		A	B
Where: $w > x > z > y$		A	x, x	y, w
and $2x > w + y$		B	w, y	z, z

Example:

Player II

Player I		A	B
	A	3, 3	1, 4
	B	4, 1	2, 2

Note: The payoff is determined as follows: If Player I chooses A and Player II chooses A, the payoff for both players is 3; if Player I chooses A and Player II chooses B, the payoff for I is 1 and the payoff for II is 4. If I chooses B and II chooses A, I receives 4 and II receives 1; and, if I chooses B and II chooses B, each player receives 2.

Figure 10-1. A Prisoner's Dilemma Game

In addition to the historical inaccuracies in Hardin's essay,[6] we believe his failure to distinguish between those users of the common pool resource who are capable of increasing the demand on the resource (for instance, adding sheep or children) and those users who are not capable of this behavior is a serious analytical error. Analysis of commons dilemmas requires this distinction because of the likelihood of spillovers between the two groups.

Discussions of commons dilemmas typically assume as does Hardin, either that all users are capable of increasing the demand on the resource or that there are no spillovers between those who can increase the demand and those who cannot. However, if the policy analyst is to identify the character of a collective decision situation it becomes essential to determine whether this assumption is valid. Logically there can be positive, negative, or no spillovers. (An illustration of positive spillovers in a commons dilemma would be capitalism and its invisible hand. The market works because the rationality of defection reduces the probability of collusion. Producers are trapped in a PDG where their collective benefits would be maximized by collusion, but individual rationality leads to defection (competition). This creates positive spillovers to nonproducers who try to assure that producers do not escape the PDG by mutual coercion mutually agreed upon, often called "price fixing" by nonproducers.) As we will illustrate, to reduce the current fertility rate in a purely cooperative manner requires an explicit realization that even though everyone is a user of the common pool resource only those who are fecund can increase the demand. The fecund can create negative spillovers to the nonfecund. The importance of this essential difference between the two groups suggests that the nonfecund may be willing to pay to change the behavior of the fecund. Once the incentive structure of the two sets of individuals is identified, it may be possible, via collective action, to escape the commons dilemma and move to a purely cooperative situation. To illustrate this process we will use a hypothetical example concerning fertility rate and unwanted pregnancies.

Ineffective Decision Making

If there is an ideal situation for the politician it is a purely cooperative game—i.e. there are no conflicts. One might expect that these situations would rarely require government action to resolve because presumably they would be settled quickly by the persons involved. Such situations do occur, however, when decision and information costs make it impossible to realize substantial individual improvement in the absence of collective action.[7]

Let us assume, with Hardin, that the citizens of the United States and the world would benefit from a reduction in birthrates. Also assume that some couples do experience unintended and unwanted births in the United States (we refer to this group as those at risk). If the unwanted births could be avoided, all would benefit from the reduced fertility rate. Unwanted pregnancies typically result from factors that interfere with an individual's ability to make effective decisions, namely decisions that would increase the probability of the preferred outcome—no birth. The ineffective decisions leading to the unwanted birth can be caused by inaccurate information, weak decision-making skills, or situational factors that make effective decision making exceedingly difficult such as laws that limit the accessibility to contraceptives. Ineffective decision making meets Hardin's criteria for a commons dilemma if ineffective decisions can be reduced at a cost to society that is less than the cost to society of the pregnancies and childbirths that would have resulted had the ineffective decisions not been reduced.

To further simplify our discussion we will assume that the information, decision skills, and changes in situational factors necessary to make ineffective decision makers at risk into effective decision makers are pure public goods, i.e., that once supplied they are available to all and one person's use of the good does not decrease the supply to others. When the expected benefits of these goods are summed over all members of the set of persons at risk (those persons who are fecund but do not intend to have an additional child at this time), the benefits are greater than the expected cost. The cost of supplying the public goods is, however, greater than the benefit to any one member in the set. Therefore, the persons at risk are not likely to achieve the collective action necessary to provide the public goods; it will be individually rational for each individual to avoid paying his share of the cost.[8]

Given the size, geographic distribution, and heterogeneity of the above-described set of persons, the achievement of mutual coercion mutually agreed upon through private contracts is not a reasonable alternative. Even if the national government were utilized to enforce such an agreement, it is unlikely that a solution involving only persons at risk could be achieved. The reason for this difficulty is that many persons of reproductive age (15-45) are not at risk because they are not fecund or because they have not yet completed their desired family size. It is unlikely that a solution coercing only those at risk could be achieved, since it would be individually rational for those who are at risk to claim they are not at risk and thereby become free riders.

Escaping the Commons Dilemma

The crucial element in this situation, the element allowing for the "escape" from the dilemma, is the fact that ineffective decisions by those who are at risk create negative spillovers (for example, congestion, high dependency ratios, pollution, resource scarcities, and so forth) for the members of the society not at risk. Because of these spillovers, those not at risk have an incentive to reduce the number of ineffective decisions in order to realize opportunities for less congestion, lower dependency ratios, cleaner air, and other expected benefits.

We now have two, interrelated PDGs! The first is among those at risk, and concerns the production of the public goods necessary to reduce ineffective decisions. The second PDG involves all members of society and concerns avoidance of the negative effects of high fertility rates. However, the two commons dilemmas are interconnected as the play of the first PDG affects the second. Once these interconnections are recognized, it can be seen that those persons at risk and those who are not are in a collective situation analogous to a two-person cooperative game. The payoff matrix would be like that in figure 10-2, and cooperation is the dominant strategy for both players. In this situation members of society, as represented by their governmental institutions, would benefit from having public resources spent to reduce ineffective decisions up to an amount equal to the smaller of $(w-y)$ or $(y-z)$. This means that it is not necessary to identify who is at risk and who is not. All solutions to the game are Pareto-efficient to d,z and the optimum combination would be a,w.

Limitations on Cooperation

Actually in situations such as those described above, "society" is "playing" not with a single individual but with all individuals subject to making a particular ineffective decision. Therefore, the payoff for society is the sum of the payoffs from all such decisions. Similarly, the choices available to society are not simply to spend or not to spend. If it chooses to spend, it then must decide how much. An additional qualification of the matrix in figure 10-2 concerns the probable differences among individuals at risk in the level of resources necessary for them to achieve an effective decision. Effective decision making for one individual might be achieved by supplying accurate information on the probability of a pregnancy; for a second individual this information plus a less costly contraceptive may be required; while for a third individual the information, the contraceptive, and extensive counseling to develop decision skills might be necessary.

A third factor influencing policies for ineffective decisions is that for most

Where:		Player 2	
Individual payoff	$a > b > c \geqslant d$		
Society payoff	$w > y > x \geqslant z$	Society	
		Cooperate	Defect
Player 1	Cooperate	a, w	b, x
Individual at Risk	Defect	c, y	d, z

Figure 10-2. Cooperative Decision Situation

issues society's benefits are subject to diminishing marginal returns. For example, it might be that a 50 percent reduction in unwanted births would achieve the socially optimal fertility rate. More than a 50 percent reduction may not yield additional benefits to society greater than the costs of the additional reduction and could conceivably create some harm. If the level of resources needed to correct the ineffective decision varies across individuals, and society is indifferent as to which births are avoided, then society would utilize policies that affect individuals who require fewer resources to decide effectively. Figure 10-3 demonstrates how society could determine its spending level. In this diagram society should be willing to spend resources up to an amount equal to OCBX with a net social "profit" of ABC.

This solution also avoids the problems of unrevealed preferences and free riders. Because all members of society are negatively affected by unwanted pregnancies and the benefits of the reduction in births are greater than the costs for both those who are at risk and those who are not, it is not necessary to determine who belongs in which set.

It might be argued that we have not met the criteria for a purely cooperative game or for Pareto-efficiency in a strict sense, as the damages caused by the spillovers are not as great for some individuals as their expected share of the cost of the policy. The damage to the commons is largely in the future and will be heavily discounted by those who do not anticipate any utility in that future.

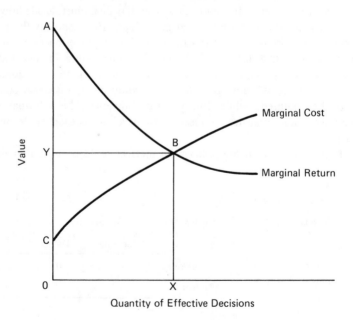

Figure 10-3. The Social Utility of Decreasing Ineffective Decisions

However, if the decision was reached through a previously agreed upon decision rule, and it is recognized that collective choice is a continuous process where votes are traded over time, then it seems that *within the limits of collective decision making under uncertainty* the criteria are met.[9]

The reader may at this point feel that he has been tricked and that we have "solved" the dilemma by the *deus ex machina* of a "social contract." The reader is, of course, correct in that we have assumed that a government and a set of decision-rules exist. The trick we hoped to accomplish, however, was to show that many population and environmental dilemmas can be solved through policy actions similar to the provision of public education, postal service, national defense, and a host of other issues for which "solutions" have been found.

An Example from Mortality

The example concerning fertility illustrates how the recognition of spillovers from one group to another may justify the allocation of resources from the general fund to specific groups. As such, the policies adopted would be quite similar to Lowi's or Salisbury and Heinz' category of distributive policies.[10] As Lowi has previously shown, distributive policies are typically justified on the basis of their value to the entire population rather than their value to the specific group involved. Nevertheless, the incidence of ineffective decisions can be reduced not only by allocating resources to improve individual decisions but also through the manipulation of the environment. In fact, it may be significantly less costly to society to change the environment. An example of such a change was the requirement of safety caps on poisons and medications to prevent their accidental use by children. This measure would be classified by the Lowi typologies as regulatory.[11] As we will attempt to demonstrate, however, the situation is directly analogous to the previous fertility example. The difference in policies is that the resource provided by society in the safety cap case is the giving up of certain individual rights rather than material goods.

Prior to the regulations requiring safety caps, a massive informational program was used to inform persons of the dangers of accidental poisoning (a self-regulatory policy by Salisbury-Heinz classification). Ineffective decisions were being made, at least part of the time, by persons who regularly or only occasionally had small children in their homes. To remove, or at least reduce the risk, these persons had to "childproof" their homes and remember after using a potentially dangerous substance to place it out of harm's way. Each decision point had, therefore, some probability greater than zero of leading to an accidental poisoning. Although not all members of society were "at risk," the remaining members of society can reasonably be said to experience negative spillovers from ineffective decisions. These costs were mainly nonmonetary (for instance, the psychological costs of knowing that a child had died) but also included the loss of certain material goods (such as, medical care and other investments in the child, the cost of which were partially paid for by society).

As with the fertility example, the expected benefits to any one individual would not be equal to the cost of designing and preparing safety caps for all the substances that would need them. The problem of unrevealed preferences (knowing who was at risk) and charging only them could be avoided so long as the benefits from the reduction of negative spillovers to those not at risk was greater than the cost of the regulations requiring safety caps. If this condition is met, everyone benefits from the regulatory policy. Again we have two interdependent PDGs which, when combined, result in a purely cooperative game.

Examples from Mobility

There appears to be a growing sentiment—particularly among relatively affluent citizens—favoring limitations on the sizes of the communities in which they live. In practice, these sentiments are expressed in forms ranging from mild taxes on new housing to highly restrictive limitations on the rate at which new building permits can be issued. Petaluma—a city thirty miles north of San Francisco—is one of the better-known examples of a city attempting to stringently limit future population growth. Petaluma's policies have been challenged in court. In a brief filed against Petaluma, plaintiffs argued that there was a commons dilemma; if all communities were to limit growth then the collectivity of all communities would suffer many costs resulting from restricted residential mobility. These costs range from declines in economic efficiency created by impediments to labor mobility to reductions in opportunities for upward status mobility, especially for minorities.[12]

In this section, we analyze the commons dilemma just described, beginning with a simple example and then working through increasingly complicated dilemmas. As we proceed along this path we at times find that the dilemma is easily solved; hence, there is no tragedy. For other cases, we conclude that while there may be a tragedy, the tragedy does not result from a commons dilemma; hence, policies which assume the problem is in a form of a commons dilemma may fail to alleviate the tragedy or may even compound it.

To begin analysis of the growth limitation dilemma, we start with a very simple game. Imagine a metropolitan area consisting of only two communities, say Petaluma and Palo Alto. We assume—as was argued in the suit against Petaluma—that the growth limitation problem involves a commons dilemma.[13] This dilemma can be viewed in two ways. A community which allows growth pays all the costs of that growth but part of the benefits are shared by neighboring communities in such forms as expanded employment, recreation, shopping, and migration opportunities. Looked at differently, a community which limits growth receives the benefits of that limitation while costs such as restricted housing and employment opportunities are shared with neighboring communities.

If the above dilemma is indeed a tragedy, we must assume that a community ideally would like to receive the benefits of limiting its growth while still having the opportunity to take advantage of the mobility allowed by the neighboring community. However, if the neighboring community has already limited growth, we assume that the benefits to the first community of limiting its growth are greater than the net benefits of receiving all future growth in the area. Finally, we assume that if both communities limit growth, then they are each worse off—for reasons mentioned above—than if there had been no growth limitations.

In the language of a PDG, the "prohibit" strategy is the dominant strategy for both of our imaginary players. Each player is better off choosing prohibit no matter what the other player does. Yet, as can be seen in figure 10-4, the tragedy is that the prohibit-prohibit outcome is worse off for each player than is the allow-allow strategy.

Before complicating the commons dilemma—making it more realistic—we will pause to show conditions under which the dilemma will not result in tragedy. We need several assumptions. They are: (1) choice of the allow or prohibit strategy can be postponed, (2) choice need not be simultaneous, (3) each community will know of the choice of the other community, and (4) the game begins with no restrictions on mobility between communities. The payoff matrix remains as shown in figure 10-4. With the assumptions just introduced, the game is no longer a PDG. The game still has the payoff matrix of a PDG. But PDGs, strictly speaking, are defined not only by a type of payoff matrix but also by certain rules such as, the game is played only once and simultaneous choices are forced. Thus, we subsequently use the phrase "game with the payoff matrix of a PDG" instead of the simpler but inaccurate phrase "a PDG." The four assumptions introduced do allow for a solution of the commons dilemma in mathematical and normative senses.

The communities have to choose not only between the prohibit and allow strategies but must also decide whether they wish to be the first to choose or the second to choose. Either community, considering whether to make the first or the second choice, must consider the payoff matrix as viewed by the other

		Petaluma	
		Allow Growth	Prohibit Growth
Palo Alto	Allow Growth	(0, 0)	(−2, 1)
	Prohibit Growth	(1, −2)	(−1, −1)

Figure 10-4. Examples of Payoffs in a Growth Limitation Game in a Society of Only Two Communities

community. That is the essence of strategy. Each community will realize that if it makes the first choice—whatever that choice is—the other community will immediately decide to prohibit growth. If the other community did not do so, it would receive what is usually referred to—with good reason—as "the sucker's payoff."[14] Since the payoffs associated with the status quo are preferred to payoffs resulting after the first (and certain second) choice, neither community has an incentive to make the first choice. Both communities prefer to be the second to choose even though they know that the second choice will always be prohibit. Since the "rules" permit stalling and since both communities decide to be the second to choose, the status quo is stable. Both communities allow mobility. (Were the game begun with both communities prohibiting mobility, that status quo would also be stable.)

In previous examples, we have used the recognition of two interdependent PDGs to resolve apparent commons problems. The example just given illustrates another way in which a game having the payoff matrix of a PDG can be solved. Note several implications of this "solution." Players must stress that they are not committed to any choice. If one player is perceived to be committed to the allow choice, then the other player will immediately choose the prohibit choice. This problem may be insurmountable among "real" players; a postponement of choice may be misperceived as a commitment to the allow choice. Another implication is that a rule-maker (say, state government) should increase the difficulty of making a commitment to the allow choice and foster the clarity and irrevocability with which a player could become committed to the prohibit choice in order to promote the stability of the allow-allow status quo. This implication is counterintuitive. Yet, the status quo is upset if one player's actions (or inactions) could be perceived as a commitment to the allow choice. Similarly, the status quo is less stable if both players must fear that there is a chance the other player has adopted an unrecognized prohibit strategy. Thus, clarity is important. Promoting irrevocable commitment to the prohibit strategy reduces unsettling incentives to test the will of the other player through temporary prohibit strategies.

Nothing about the simple game precludes government from using the more conventional solution of "mutual coercion mutually agreed upon." When the game is expanded to include numerous strategy alternatives (degrees of prohibit) and many players, the status quo solution is still stable under previous assumptions. But the decreased certainty of knowing whether all players have or have not made a choice may lead to a "mutual coercion" agreement. In fact, one can observe such an outcome in Oregon. Municipalities are required to develop plans containing both "urban growth boundaries" *and* provisions for future housing needs (including low-income housing) and to allow for "orderly transition" of rural to urban land uses.[15] Note that such possibly inconsistent emphases in a plan are compatible with a role for state government deduced earlier. The requirement of an urban growth boundary makes commitment to a pure allow strategy rather difficult. The same requirement makes a clear, irrevocable commitment to a prohibit strategy a possibility but—because of provisions for housing needs and orderly transition—not a necessity.

The dilemmas considered so far do not lead to tragedy. But what about Petaluma? If the dilemma problems considered so far are applicable, Petaluma should not be limiting growth. The case of Petaluma can be explained by examining either of two unrealistic aspects of the games previously developed. Both will be examined.

Although it may seem paradoxical, one reason for limiting community growth is to make the community more attractive to certain potential residents and less attractive to others. The social and psychological implications of limited growth are attractive to some people. Such people may value the symbolic importance of a policy they think is environmentally "responsible." Others may value the intimacy of small communities. They may also find reassurance in the stability and predictability of community social structure, city services, educational curriculum, and the distribution of political power. Not everyone, however, might find such a community attractive, but judge it to be dull, stagnant, clannish, and socially "irresponsible." Controls or lack of controls on community size can be thought of as part of the bundle of goods and services which communities offer to prospective consumers.[16] This competition for residents works in another way. Limitations on community growth may raise the costs of housing in the community. Such limitations are a strategy for protecting the tax base; that is, increasing the chance that the taxes payed by the next addition to the community will exceed the marginal costs to the community of providing services for that additional resident. Adoption of limits on community growth can be thought of as one way in which communities compete to win the game of a "solvent" tax base.

Communities are limiting growth (or not limiting growth) in competition with each other. They are competing for supports from certain of their current residents and possibly trying to attract certain types of residents of other communities. There is a commons dilemma. It is similar to the earlier example of two producers trapped in a PDG (see page 117); both desiring to achieve the cooperate solution (that is, price fixing) but destined to compete (defect). Here, the danger for society occurs if the players can get together and collude. A state law requiring that all municipalities establish boundaries to limit growth without taking into consideration future housing needs would be an example of such a collusion. Competitors—or at least some forms of competition—are eliminated (municipalities seeking to offer unlimited growth and lower cost housing).

We have argued that when many communities compete through policies on community growth, there is a commons dilemma for the communities involved, but the dilemma has positive spillovers for society as a whole. Some cities offer limited growth (Petaluma). Some do not. There is no tragedy unless competition is limited (as it often is).

We have built the above analysis with an example in mind, suburbs in the San Francisco area. Now, bring in the central city. San Francisco may have no realistic alternative to an allow strategy. Population is already declining. San Francisco must choose allow. Petaluma can take advantage of that knowledge when calculating its best strategy. But there is no commons dilemma in the sense of a PDG payoff matrix. In fact, one can argue that the game is entirely cooperative. Central cities may prefer that suburbs limit growth. The tighter the limitations by suburbs, the more people there are left in central cities and the higher their average income (assuming limits on suburban growth raise costs of suburban housing).

There is no commons dilemma, but there is tragedy. To say the game is cooperative—each player chooses that strategy the other player would like them to choose—does not mean that both players "win." San Francisco is forced to play a game it can only lose. Petaluma gets limited growth and the citizens that can afford to live in the community. Other suburbs attract middle-income citizens and "clean" industries. San Francisco gets the leftovers. San Francisco has little with which to bargain. (Policies to deny central city services to suburbanites, or charge them through income taxes likely would only further diminish the amount of industrial and retail activity in the central city.)

The competitive or bargaining position of the central city could be improved by redistribution if society sought a more "equitable" distribution of payoffs. Here, we note an example of what seems to us to be a general principle. Redistributive policy situations do not arise from commons dilemmas. One aspect of PDGs which make them attractive to scholars is the notion that they ought to be solvable with no need for redistributions; one ought to be able to make at least one, perhaps both players better off without making either player worse off. As the case of the central city illustrates, commons dilemmas provide no guidance on one of the more difficult types of public policy, redistributive policy. An incorrect conceptualization of the central city problem as a commons dilemma may make its solution appear too easy.

Problems with Cooperative Solutions

The population issues described above indicate that the explicit recognition of spillovers often can identify potential policy alternatives for the resolution of population related conflicts. The implicit criterion used when policy alternatives are identified in this manner is efficiency. The utilization of a game theoretic approach makes the process more explicit in that the identification of the payoff matrix forces us to make more clear whose benefits and costs are included and how the benefits and costs are calculated. Caution must be exercised, however, in choosing policies on the basis of efficiency criteria. Although the payoff matrix makes more explicit what values have been included in the calculation, those values that have been omitted may be more easily overlooked.

A second, more important, reason for caution is that efficiency is an inherently conservative criterion. The expected utility of various outcomes is calculated using the existing distribution of rights in society. This distribution partially reflects prevailing social norms concerning what is fair and just; and, as these norms change, legally protected rights will also change. For example, in past years many persons accepted that paying a woman less than a man for equal work and giving preferences to men in employment was fair. The presumed role of the man as primary provider for the family furnished one justification for this discrimination. Men had a right to employment preference and higher pay. Schools, the media, and other institutions that socialize individuals into various roles buttressed these norms and associated rights by stereotyping certain roles as male or female. The women's rights movement and associated ideas of justice such as equal pay for equal work challenged this notion of equity. Recent textbooks, television programs, and other media reflect this challenge. Only after norms and values began to change did public policy attempt to redistribute rights and change social institutions to encourage greater equality among men and women.[17]

If analyses of policy alternatives using a game theoretic approach had been done prior to the changes in norms a quite different set of policies concerning employment and affirmative action would have been chosen than if the analysis were done now. When society changed the value placed on women staying home and the separate roles of men and women, what were once considered benefits came to be seen as costs. As norms and conceptions of equity change, efficiency also changes. Rights, and therefore, efficiency are partially products of social norms which in turn reflect dominant concepts of distributive equity and justice. However, as sociologists are fond of telling us (and empirical research throughout the social sciences has supported their claims), social norms, values, and conceptions of justice and equity are themselves partially products of the existing distribution of rights, duties, and privileges. Individuals growing up in a capitalist economy tend to see capitalism as equitable and just, while individuals growing up in a socialistic economy are likely to see socialism as more just. Efficiency, equity, norms, rules, and the distribution of rights and resources interact in a dynamic system. The system rarely changes rapidly because most of its elements reinforce the others. Because rights cause and are caused by prevailing practices, and because practices influence and are influenced by norms, there is a strong tendency in all societies to see what is as what is right.

Once it is recognized that the payoff matrix will change as norms and rights change, much of the normative attractiveness of purely cooperative solutions is diminished. Although the polity will "solve" commons dilemmas previously seen as intractable, the question of whether the purely cooperative solution is the "best" solution emerges quite strongly. What are the distributional impacts of purely cooperative solutions?

To illustrate the distribution issue, we reexamine our analysis of policies designed to reduce fertility. As is indicated in figure 10-3, when society chooses a purely cooperative policy, this does not mean that the policy program will attempt to prevent all ineffective decisions and all unwanted births. Rather, society would spend resources only to the point where the marginal social benefits of prevention would equal marginal social costs. It can be reasonably hypothesized, however, that persons requiring the most expensive forms of prevention (education, counseling, and medical treatment) would be the persons who would experience the greatest *individual* benefits from the reduction of ineffective decisions and the prevention of an unintended or unwanted birth and would experience the greatest *individual* harm from such a birth. However, society through its governmental institutions can be expected to choose those prevention programs that are purely cooperative and have the highest net *social* benefit. This is likely to mean, therefore, that those persons with the greatest individual needs will have the lowest probability of being helped.

The regressive distributional impacts of purely cooperative policies are not limited simply to monetary considerations. The current conflict over the federal funding of abortions provides an excellent illustration of how nonmonetary considerations limit the set of purely cooperative solutions and may do so primarily at the expense of the less advantaged sectors of society. When the Supreme Court decided that state intervention to prevent abortions during the first trimester of pregnancy violated the right to privacy and due process, the rights of the pregnant women, the fetus, and the society (the State) were redefined.[18] As indicated, above, such a change in rights would change the efficiency calculations regarding abortion programs. Given this new definition of rights and changed efficiency calculations, if the policy decisions concerning the prevention of unwanted pregnancies were made on the basis of monetary cost-effectiveness, subsidizing abortions would almost certainly be more efficient than sex education, counseling, and similar programs. In addition, abortions allow for an effective backstop to contraceptive programs and do not require the same level of planning as most contraceptive programs. Despite these monetary advantages, a policy to subsidize abortions will not be a purely cooperative policy solution even when vote trading is allowed. The political decision-makers must also enter the psychic costs that such a subsidy imposes on those who believe abortion is equivalent to murder and that a state policy to subsidize abortions forces them to contribute to an immoral act. It is highly unlikely that a sufficiently large side payment can be made to the opponents of abortion so that the benefits of a policy to subsidize abortions outweigh the costs to them.

The distributional consequences of allowing but not subsidizing abortion have been made clear by the proponents of medicaid payments for abortion. The middle and upper income groups will have greater access to abortions. At the same time, the persons who are most likely to need abortions to prevent unwanted pregnancies are more highly concentrated in the lower income groups.[19]

The above example is, of course, only one of many that can be cited to illustrate that solutions that meet the criterion of "no one is made worse off and at least someone is made better off" can be expected to benefit the more advantaged more often and to a greater degree than the programs will benefit the less advantaged in society. The example of individual mobility and growth restrictions by local jurisdictions also demonstrated the bargaining superiority of the more advantaged sectors of society. The "best" that the center cities may be able to hope for is that the suburbs will become sufficiently exclusive to force many in the middle income groups to remain in the center city.

The conclusion that use of an efficiency criterion and the commons dilemma paradigm will tend to increase rather than decrease the distance between the more advantaged and less advantaged in society should not come as a surprise. Economists as disparate as Friedman and Sammuelson have recognized this.[20] Research from almost every field of political science has indicated that public policy, particularly nonconflict-oriented public policy, will reward the rich and the organized substantially more often than it will reward the poor and the unorganized.

Summary and Conclusions

Population issues provide opportunities to reexamine the widely held position that environmental situations are typically commons dilemmas. Our analysis of several population problems indicates that many of these dilemmas are, in fact, closer to purely cooperative situations and can be resolved by existing institutions. Other situations are competitive; but they do not meet the definition of a commons dilemma. The basic reason that many population issues are incorrectly perceived as commons problems derives from the failure to distinguish between those users of the common resource who are capable of increasing demand on this resource and those who are not. Once this distinction is made, we often find that the negative spillovers from one group to another provide the basis for a cooperative resolution of the issue. The role of government in these situations often becomes one of providing a mechanism for the collection and payment of sufficient incentives to change the payoff structure so that fewer additional demands on the resource will be made. In addition, we indicated how purely cooperative solutions can overcome the problem of unrevealed preferences, and increase the probability that the policy will be enacted.

The examination of population issues also found that important problems remain even when the situation is not a commons dilemma. These issues include the changing efficiency calculation when the norms, values, and rights in society change; a predicted distribution of benefits that can be expected to favor the more advantaged sectors of society over the less advantaged; the problems resulting from unequal bargaining power among individuals or sets of individuals; and the inability to realize future gains because of an inability to invest in the present.

In many respects the conclusions that can be derived from our analyses indicate that the politicians have often been more adept at achieving resolution of population problems than those who do research on population issues. Political decision makers have already found that many issues which ecologists identified as commons dilemmas could be resolved in a cooperative manner. Examples include current family planning programs, safety programs, and mobility policies. Although the public sector may not have moved as quickly or as decisively as many would wish, it remains undeniable that policies to resolve many difficult issues have been developed and enacted. At the same time one cannot fail to note that the pluralist political system in the United States has continued to ignore many of the distributional aspects of population issues and that the policies that have been implemented may exacerbate prevailing social inequities. Whether dealing with abortion and medicaid or mobility through land use control the interests of the less advantaged have been relegated to secondary considerations.

Notes

1. A Pareto-efficient situation is one in which some change in the conditions can be made such that at least one person's utility is increased without subtracting any utility from another person. A Pareto-optimal situation is one in which any further changes would reduce someone's utility.

2. Garrett Hardin, "The Tragedy of the Commons," *Science* 162 (1968):1243-1248.

3. By "rationality" we mean that an individual choosing among alternatives will choose an alternative that he prefers over one that he does not. The individual is not choosing in an abstract situation, but in a particular situation. When we use the word "utility" we mean, "the subjective value that the individual subscribes to the goods and services available." R. Duncan Luce and Howard Raiffa, *Games and Decisions* (New York: John Wiley and Sons, Inc., 1957).

4. R.M. Dawes, J. Delay, and W. Chaplin, "The Decision to Pollute," *Environment and Planning A.* 6 (1974):3-10.

5. John Baden, "A Primer for the Management of Common Pool Resources," in *Managing the Commons*, Garrett Hardin and John Baden, eds. (San Francisco: W.H. Freeman & Co., 1977), pp. 137-146; Vincent Ostrom and Elinor Ostrom, "A Theory for Institutional Analysis of Common Pool Problems," in *Managing the Commons*, Hardin and Baden, eds., pp. 157-172.

6. Hardin's original essay included several historical errors. The most important was attribution of the reduction in commons lands to overgrazing. The reduction was not caused by overgrazing, but by changes in agricultural techniques and the increased profitability of commercial wool. These changes

led the feudal lords to enclose the commons and take away the peasants' grazing rights. Even today, however, approximately 1.5 million acres of common lands in England and Wales continue to be grazed in much the same way that they have been for centuries. In almost every case overgrazing was, and is, prevented by quotas by which the users of the commons abide. For further discussion of errors in Hardin's original article see S.V. Ciriacy-Wantrup and Richard C. Bishop, "Common Property as a Concept in Natural Resource Policy," *Natural Resources Journal* 15 (October 1975):713-727.

7. James Buchanan and Gordon Tullock, *The Calculus of Consent* (Ann Arbor, Mich.: University of Michigan Press, 1962).

8. Mancur Olson, *The Logic of Collective Action* (Cambridge, Mass.: Harvard University Press, 1965).

9. Buchanan and Tullock, *The Calculus of Consent.*

10. Theodore Lowi, "American Business, Public Policy, Case Studies, and Political Science," *World Politics* 16 (July 1965):677-715; Robert Salisbury and John Heinz, "A Theory of Policy Analysis and Some Preliminary Applications," in *Policy Analysis in Political Science*, Ira Sharkansky, ed. (San Francisco: Markham, 1970).

11. Lowi, "American Business"; Salisbury and Heinz, "A Theory of Policy Analysis."

12. David Falk and Herbert Franklin, *In-Zoning* (Washington, D.C.: Potomac Institute, 1975), pp. 14-15.

13. We emphasize that this section focuses on policies designed to achieve a limit on growth. We are not analyzing policies which "guide" or "direct" growth. The distinction is important because the two policies are quite different when analyzed as commons dilemmas. Growth limitation is a policy which produces a commons dilemma (negative spillovers). Policies to direct growth are designed to reduce negative spillovers and other inefficiencies.

14. Steven Brams, *Paradoxes in Politics* (New York: The Free Press, 1976), p. 83.

15. Oregon Land Conservation and Development Commission, *Statewide Land Use Goals and Guidelines* (Salem, Ore.: Oregon Land Conservation and Development Commission, 1975).

16. C.M. Tiebout, "A Pure Theory of Local Expenditures," *Journal of Political Economy* 64 (October 1956):416-424.

17. R. Miller and K. Godwin, *Psyche and Demos: Individual Decision Making and Population Policy* (New York: Oxford University Press, 1977); David Ervin, James Fitch, Kenneth Godwin, Bruce Shepard, and Herbert Stoevener, *Land Use Control: Evaluating Economic and Political Effects* (Cambridge, Mass.: Ballinger, 1977), p. 32.

18. *Roe* v. *Wade* 410 U.S. 113, 93 S. Ct. 705 (1973).

19. The Alan Guttmacher Institute, *Abortion 1974-1975: Need and Services in the United States* (New York, 1976).

20. Gerald Dworkin, Gordon Vermont, and Peter Brown, eds., *Markets and Morals* (Franklinville, N.Y.: Hemisphere Publishers, 1977).

**Part III
Population Policy:
State and Local
Perspectives**

11 The Demographic Impact of School Desegregation Policy

Karl E. Taeuber and
Franklin D. Wilson

In a courtroom in Dallas in March 1976, a federal judge heard testimony from sociologists retained by each party in a remedy hearing on school desegregation.[1] The expert witness for the school district presented an analysis showing that full desegregation with extensive busing would spur rapid and sustained white flight, quickly turning the public schools into a system serving primarily black and Mexican American children. The school district proposed a limited desegregation plan that it claimed would avoid excessive white flight and thus permit the maximum feasible amount of desegregation. The plaintiffs opposed a plan that preserved a substantial amount of uniracial schooling. Their expert took issue with the unpublished and incomplete analysis of the other expert, and presented unpublished and incomplete evidence that showed no consistent relation between desegregation and white flight. The judge reached his decision only a few days after the conclusion of hearings.[2] He expressed dismay at his inability to resolve "the battle of the sociological experts." But he accepted a limited plan that had as one of its perceived virtues the avoidance of massive white flight.

Social science research on white flight is becoming a growth industry, but it has yet to return significant policy dividends. The judge was right to express bewilderment. Despite the recent flurry of studies, there is as yet little scholarly consensus.[3] The news media have publicized particular experts who are willing to express policy conclusions, and protagonists have seized upon those scholars willing to present evidence in judicial or legislative hearings. Presentation of evidence in scholarly publications is increasing, but cumulation of trustworthy evidence occurs at a glacial pace. Our purpose here is to indicate certain complexities in the study of white flight that make it extraordinarily difficult to analyze, and to suggest some data sources and modes of analysis that should prove helpful.

This paper is one in a series, "Studies in Racial Segregation," supported by funds granted to the Institute for Research on Poverty at the University of Wisconsin by the Department of Health, Education and Welfare pursuant to the provisions of the Economic Opportunity Act of 1964, by Contract No. HEW-100-76-0196 from the Assistant Secretary for Planning and Evaluation, DHEW, and by Grant No. 5 RO1 MH 27880-02 from the Center for Studies of Metropolitan Problems, NIMH. Data acquisition and processing were supported in part by Population Research Center Grant No. 5PO1-HD-0-5876 awarded to the Center for Demography and Ecology of the University of Wisconsin by the Center for Population Research of the National Institute of Child Health and Human Development. Conclusions and interpretations are the sole responsibility of the authors.

The redistribution of metropolitan population has long been affected by a variety of governmental actions, among which central city school desegregation actions are a recent addition. The call for a coherent national policy on population distribution is a recurring one in the United States (and many other nations), but the United States has been no more successful at developing a distribution policy than it has been at developing a comprehensive population growth policy or an integrated national urban policy.[a] Massive suburbanization of the white population is a fundamental feature of twentieth-century social change. It has been spurred by numerous governmental actions, often in ways not fully anticipated. At the federal level, public housing, slum clearance, highway construction, urban renewal, transformation of residential mortgage markets, public assistance regulations, facility location, and other programs, together with pervasive racial discrimination in the conduct of each, all contributed to shaping the current urban crisis and its racial dimensions. State and local governmental actions similarly contributed. Inactions at each level of government in the regulation of private racial discrimination (redlining, restrictive covenants, and so forth) may also be cited.

Interest in school desegregation as a possible contributing cause of the suburbanization of white families has not developed out of a broad concern for a coherent distribution policy, but springs rather from political maneuvering over school desegregation policy. The narrow policy framework within which questions about white flight have been posed is one explanation for the narrowness of the social science research on this topic. We believe a broader perspective is both feasible and more enlightening.

Varieties of White Flight

In its decision mandating implementation of school desegregation with "all deliberate speed," the Supreme Court ruled that "the vitality of these constitutional principles cannot be allowed to yield simply because of disagreement with them."[4] The Court did not then recognize the ingenuity that would be displayed in devising ways to inhibit application of these principles. In the 1960s and early 1970s the Court struck down one after another technique of delay and evasion. As public school systems increasingly desegregated their formal operations, avoidance of central city public schools became one of the most effective techniques by which individual white families could evade "unyielding" constitutional principles.

The immediate objective of most school desegregation programs is to effect a redistribution of pupils among schools. Although school districts have the authority to assign pupils to specific public schools, not all of the pupils need

[a]For a discussion of the institutional and political factors inhibiting policy development, see chapter 6 by James L. Sundquist.

attend as directed. In the early stages of desegregation in many districts, a simple boycott disrupted the intended attendance patterns. Usually organized for the purpose of keeping white children out of racially mixed schools or off the buses, boycotts and the agitation that often accompany them could induce such fear and concern among black parents that minority as well as white enrollments were diminished. Under local compulsory attendance laws and with the continued high valuation by the public of universal education, boycotts have invariably been temporary phenomena. Their effectiveness, however temporary, suffices to demonstrate that a carefully devised desegregation plan can, upon implementation, result in a greatly diminished and still totally segregated pupil enrollment.

The transfer of pupils from public to private schooling is another constitutionally permissible form of white evasion of public school desegregation. Many hastily organized and poorly financed "segregation academies" have proved to be only somewhat less temporary than school boycotts. In a few school districts, with Memphis a leading example, large-scale private educational systems have persisted for several years. Previously existing parochial schools, especially in cities with a large Catholic population, have also received recruits from public schools. In some districts, with Boston a prime example, religious authorities have sought to avoid use of parochial schools as a haven for white flight from desegregation. In other districts new pupils have been welcomed, if only covertly, as the basis for overcoming problems associated with a steadily declining enrollment.

The most permanent type of white flight is movement to another school district. If the district undergoing desegregation is the central city of a metropolitan area, there may be many suburban districts that offer schooling with few or no minority pupils. Nearly all northern suburban districts and many southern suburban districts have an overwhelmingly white enrollment. Their schools are nearly uniracial even if the suburban district has implemented its own desegregation plan.

Residential mobility to escape undesirable effects of a desegregation plan may be possible within a city. A change of residence may permit a family's children to attend a nearby school or a racially unbalanced school, depending on the details of the plan and its completeness. In other situations, moving may be of little effectiveness as flight from desegregation. In Florida, for example, school districts are county-wide, most counties contain a sizable proportion of black pupils, and all counties have desegregation plans in operation.

A Cohort Perspective on Enrollment Changes

Most studies of white flight from school desegregation have taken as their index a measure of change in the enrollment of white pupils in public school systems.[5]

The energy that has been put into assembling data and undertaking complex multivariate time-series analyses has not been matched by sufficient attention to the key variable. The change in white enrollment from one year to the next is a composite reflection of several types of change. In standard demographic parlance, it is a measure of "net" change rather than "gross" change. Use of net change glosses over the separate types of change and conceals information that would be revealed by appropriate specific measures.

To illustrate the limitation imposed by using net enrollment change as an index of white flight, consider any central city school district. Each year some families move to the city and some from the city, and some pupils transfer from public to private school or the reverse. Each year some pupils graduate from high school or drop out at an earlier stage, and others first enroll in kindergarten or first grade. Assume that this normal flow of pupils into and out of the public schools amounts to a 10 percent annual turnover in white pupils. Each year about 10 percent of the pupils from the previous year do not return and about 10 percent of the pupils are new to the system. Now assume that a desegregation program is begun, and that as a result of public controversy the supply of new white pupils dries up. No white parents moving to or within the metropolitan area locate so that they have to enroll their children in the desegregated system, and no five or six year olds enroll for the first time. Even if all of the pupils in the public school system comply fully with the desegregation action, there will be an annual percent decline in white enrollment. There is in this hypothetical situation a strong demographic response to school desegregation. To label that response white flight rather than white avoidance encourages a simplistic misidentification of the process.

Most studies of white flight have been sensitive to the problem of demonstrating that postdesegregation enrollment changes differ from predesegregation enrollment changes, but have overlooked the possibility of identifying separately any of the components of change. A diagram of the main linkages between desegregation actions and enrollment changes is given in figure 11-1. A desegregation action can affect aggregate enrollment by its influence on migration or private school enrollment. (The diagram simplifies by omitting the possibility of an effect on dropout rates, on annexation to or from the school district, on the pattern of interdistrict pupil changes, or on schools, grade spans, and special students included in the district enrollment court.) A change in pupil migration patterns may take several forms, as suggested in the hypothetical example of a district with a 10 percent turnover rate: (1) parents of currently enrolled pupils may move to another district; (2) parents of preschool children or potential parents may leave the district (note that parents may fit in categories (1) and (2) simultaneously); or (3) parents or potential parents who live in other districts and might have moved to the desegregated district may decide not to do so. An increase in enrollment in private schools may occur from: (1) an increased rate of transfer of pupils from public schools; (2) higher-

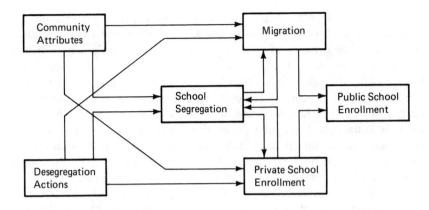

Figure 11-1. Model of School Enrollment Responses to Desegregation Actions

than-expected rates of enrollment of new pupils in private rather than public schools; or (3) lower-than-expected rates of transfer of pupils from private to public schools.

The second set of three modes of desegregation action affecting enrollment patterns was couched in terms of higher or lower enrollments than expected; the first set could have been phrased in similar conditional terms. Each of the distinct enrollment effects occurs in the "normal" course of events in the absence of desegregation actions. To identify the causal effects suggested by figure 11-1 requires a complex analysis of trends and the determinants of deviations from trends. Much enrollment change arises from causes other than desegregation actions. Unless these are well specified and well measured, there is a severe danger of overinterpretation of the impact of desegregation actions. The greater the reliance on aggregate measures of net change rather than on disaggregated or gross measures of specific components of change, the greater the interpretive difficulties.

Many of the analytic problems we have raised are not subject to resolution with the kinds of data generally available, nor are they all soluble within the techniques of contemporary social science. We shall return to these issues later, but first we wish to indicate that simple improvements in the measurement of enrollment change are feasible with data that often are available, and that these simple improvements may increase the interpretability of desegregation analyses.

The task of describing and assessing components of change in public school enrollment is formally similar to tasks routinely encountered in demographic studies of population change. Demographers have developed a variety of techniques for assessing components of change. One of the most powerful is cohort analysis. A cohort is a group of people defined on the basis of some common event during an initial period (for example, being born in year T). Cohort members are traced through succeeding years as they are exposed to the risk of sequential events (in the most elementary demographic example, the risk of death, which may be viewed as one form of departure from the initial population). The entrance of children into grade 1 of a public school district may be used as the defining event for a cohort. In a school population unaffected by migration, failure, mortality, and other changes, the number of pupils in grade 2 in year $T + 1$ should equal the number initially observed in grade 1 in year T. In fact, of course, there will be additions to and subtractions from the initial cohort that alter the numbers observed year by year. And if our data source is enrollment data rather than longitudinal information on the schooling and residential experience of each individual child, then we cannot identify all of the components of change nor exploit the full potential of cohort analysis. But administratively gathered data do permit a partial cohort analysis that improves upon analysis of aggregate net enrollment change. We shall illustrate the technique with published data from annual reports of the State Department of Education of Louisiana.

In Louisiana, public education is organized by parishes (counties). The East Baton Rouge Parish School District serves the population of the Baton Rouge metropolitan area (as defined at the time of the 1970 census). The Shreveport metropolitan area is served by the Bossier Parish and Caddo Parish School Districts, and we have combined data for these two parishes. Data for these school districts are displayed in tables 11-1 and 11-2. Each of these districts implemented a partial desegregation program in fall 1970.

In table 11-1, selected enrollment data for the years 1968 to 1975 in the East Baton Rouge Parish School District are organized to permit tracing the enrollment history of cohorts. The cohorts are identified by the year in which the pupils who progressed normally entered first grade. The first row of the table refers to the cohort of white pupils that entered first grade in fall 1961. We first observe them in this data set in fall 1968, when they are in eighth grade. They numbered 3,319 when the official enrollment count was made. In fall 1969, the official enrollment count of white ninth grades was 3.9 percent greater. The tenth grade count, in fall 1970 (upon implementation of the partial desegregation plan) was 5.5 percent lower than the year before. Between tenth and eleventh grades, this cohort experienced a net loss of 8.9 percent of its members. Throughout the table, the first entry for each row shows the size of the cohort of white pupils when it first appears in this data set, and subsequent entries in each row show the percentage change in enrollment from the previous year.

The principal question for which these data were assembled is whether grade by grade changes in white public school enrollment are associated with the implementation of a desegregation program. In table 11-1 and in table 11-2 the entries in the 1970 column are uniformly negative and are among the largest negative percentages in each row. Each cohort experienced a large loss in the year of desegregation.

Another question raised in the white flight literature is whether an apparent

Table 11-1

Initial Public School Enrollment and Annual Percent Change, for Selected Cohorts of White Pupils, East Baton Rouge Parish School District: Fall 1968 to Fall 1975

Cohort and Grade[a]		1968	1969	1970[b]	1971	1972	1973	1974	1975
1961	8th	3319	3.9	−5.5	−8.9	−2.5			
1962	7th	3678	−2.0	−4.3	−0.9	−11.8	−0.4		
1963	6th	3549	6.9	−9.2	4.9	2.8	−10.1	−18.6	
1964	5th	3362	1.6	−0.6	−1.6	−0.1	0.1	−16.1	3.3
1965	4th	3623	0.6	−6.3	3.9	−1.9	2.4	−5.7	−1.5
1966	3rd	3625	0.8	−7.7	3.3	−3.2	0.1	5.9	7.0
1967	2nd	3680	−0.9	−5.4	−0.3	0.2	7.6	7.9	7.2
1968	1st	3734	−1.7	−6.4	0.8	−2.3	1.6	−4.4	18.7
1969	1st		3650	−10.2	1.3	0.3	2.1	−4.5	9.5
1970	1st			3410	−1.3	−0.7	2.0	−7.2	6.4
1971	1st				2947	−0.2	1.9	−7.5	8.7
1972	1st					2931	1.9	−8.6	8.1
1973	1st						3111	−8.4	8.4
1974	1st							2988	9.5

Source: Annual Reports of the State Department of Education of Louisiana.

[a]Cohorts are identified by year (Fall) that most entered 1st grade. Grade identified is that at time of first observation in this data set (Fall 1968 or later).

[b]A large-scale pupil desegregation plan was implemented in Fall 1970.

first year white enrollment loss is matched by unusually high losses for several succeeding years, whether the pattern for subsequent years returns to "normal," or whether there is a drift back to public schools of some of those who left the first year. Examination of experience in the years after 1970 shows an erratic pattern of gains and losses for the East Baton Rouge cohorts, and an inconsistent pattern of small declines for the Bossier/Caddo cohorts.

The data in tables 11-1 and 11-2 provide other opportunities for browsing to discern patterns in enrollment trends. In both tables there are substantial enrollment declines associated with the transition from tenth to eleventh grades; perhaps this reflects dropouts of children exceeding compulsory attendance ages. The numbers at the bottom of each column show the size of the successive cohorts entering first grade. These numbers display a general downward trend. We cannot determine from these data how much of this downward trend is accounted for by previous fertility declines and the consequent annual declines in the number of children in each parish reaching age six, how much stems from increasing utilization of private schooling, and how much reflects migration patterns of families with young children.

Table 11-2

Initial Public School Enrollment and Annual Percentage Change for Selected Cohorts of White Pupils, Bossier and Caddo Parish School Districts (combined): Fall 1968 to Fall 1975

Cohort and Grade[a]		1968	1969	1970[b]	1971	1972	1973	1974	1975
1961	8th	3944	−1.6	−6.9	−9.8	−8.1			
1962	7th	4069	−3.3	−5.3	−4.2	−6.9	−9.5		
1963	6th	4127	−1.1	−9.9	2.7	−3.8	−7.4	−7.6	
1964	5th	4064	−2.7	−6.4	−3.3	7.1	−6.8	−7.2	−9.5
1965	4th	4232	−4.2	−6.6	−5.0	1.4	3.4	−3.2	−8.2
1966	3rd	4305	−4.9	−9.4	−3.3	0.4	−2.5	5.6	−3.0
1967	2nd	4207	−4.0	−10.1	−3.2	−0.4	−0.3	−1.2	7.8
1968	1st	4580	−9.1	−11.1	−2.9	−2.0	−2.0	−1.6	−0.7
1969	1st		4284	−12.6	−3.6	−1.4	−4.5	1.6	−1.7
1970	1st			3525	−4.8	−1.8	−4.0	0.2	−0.6
1971	1st				3026	−3.0	−3.6	0.7	−3.4
1972	1st					2725	2.0	1.7	−3.5
1973	1st						2590	0.4	0.0
1974	1st							2780	−2.8

Source: Annual Reports of the State Department of Education of Louisiana.

[a]Cohorts are identified by year (Fall) that most entered 1st grade. Grade identified is that at time of first observation in this data set (Fall 1968 or later).

[b]A large-scale pupil desegregation plan was implemented in Fall 1970.

Annual counts of enrollment by grade are often produced and used in educational administration. Standard computer programs have been prepared to permit use of such data in projecting future enrollments.[6] It is common experience that these numbers and the associated grade-to-grade transition rates fluctuate in erratic patterns. One expert recommends using a ten-year trend to establish a base from which to make a projection..[7] Clearly the task of establishing "normal" trends from which to identify deviations attributable to school desegregation actions is extraordinarily difficult. If it is assumed that parental flight responses may occur during the period that desegregation is a controversial issue before any action has been taken, at the time of actions, and for some years following, identification of effects would require extraordinarily rich data sources and ingenious and meticulous statistical methodology.[8]

Flight to Where

If pupils flee from public schools in a desegregating district, they must alight in some other school system. One way to work the puzzle of interpreting complex

enrollment trends in the desegregating district is to find evidence of complementary enrollment trends in private schools or adjoining districts. Of course, it
is not necessarily any easier to identify unusual enrollment increases in suburban
districts than it is to identify unusual enrollment declines in a central city
district. Indeed, for those central city districts in which the number of white
public school pupils declined greatly before desegregation, use of enrollment
data to identify destinations of fleers may be much harder. A 10 percent decline
in public school whites in the central district may represent only a 2 or 3 percent
rise in public school whites in suburban districts. If the suburban territory is
divided into many small school districts, the enrollment in each may be too
small and trends too erratic for reliable interpretation.

To illustrate the utility of pairing outflow with inflow data, we may use the
Louisiana districts. Because these are metropolitan districts, the principal
destination of white fleers from public schools must have been private schools.
(Unfortunately for our example, each of these metropolitan areas has been
expanding into adjoining parishes, and the formal definitions of the Standard
Metropolitan Statistical Areas have been altered since 1970 to include additional
parishes. To keep our example simple, we ignore this real-world complication.)

Annual data on private school enrollments, by race and grade, are provided
in the annual reports of the State Department of Education of Louisiana. To
permit a summary comparison of public and private enrollment trends, without
sacrificing all of the benefits of the cohort approach, we have summed together
data for five cohorts, those that were in first through fifth grade in fall 1968
(seventh through eleventh grades in fall 1975). Public and private school totals
are arrayed side by side in table 11-3. The first pair of data columns shows the
aggregate enrollment in the five-grade span for each year, 1968 to 1974. The
middle columns present the annual numerical changes in enrollment, and the
final columns present the change figures as percentages.

During the years 1968-1975 public school enrollments for these cohorts
were generally declining. Private school enrollments increased to a peak in 1970
and subsequently declined. We must examine the middle columns for evidence
of complementarity in public and private enrollment trends. The most striking
result is the change accompanying the partial desegregation in Bossier/Caddo
from 1969 to 1970. Public enrollment for our cohorts declined by 1,879 and
private enrollment increased by 1,822. The prima facie case for a significant
white flight to private schools could not be stronger. But there is more than just
this one piece of evidence, and the other pieces do not fit so easily into a white
flight interpretation. The year prior to desegregation in Bossier/Caddo also
reveals a matched transfer from public to private schooling, of a large magnitude.
The second year after desegregation there is an increase in public enrollment and
a somewhat greater decrease in private enrollment. Is this evidence of a return to
the public system once desegregation is implemented successfully? No other year
shows such a pattern, and the last two annual observations reveal declining
enrollments in both public and private schools.

The data in table 11-3 for East Baton Rouge contain evidence of a

Table 11-3

Annual Change in Enrollment of Selected Cohorts of White Pupils in Public and
Private Schools, East Baton Rouge Parish and Bossier and Caddo Parishes
(combined): Fall 1968 to Fall 1975

School Year (Fall)	Initial Enrollment		Changes in Enrollment			
			Number		Percent	
	Public	Private	Public	Private	Public	Private
East Baton Rouge Parish						
1968 to 1969	18,024	4,581	14	−135	0.1	−2.9
1969 to 1970	18,038	4,446	−969	459	−5.4	10.3
1970 to 1971	17,069	4,905	254	−378	1.5	−7.7
1971 to 1972	17,323	4,527	−14	−242	−0.1	−5.3
1972 to 1973	17,309	4,285	434	−379	2.5	−8.8
1973 to 1974	17,743	3,906	−1,382	−638	−7.8	−16.3
1974 to 1975	16,361	3,268	808	107	4.9	3.3
Bossier and Caddo Parishes						
1968 to 1969	21,388	1,205	−1,084	1,008	−5.1	83.7
1969 to 1970	20,304	2,213	−1,879	1,822	−9.3	82.3
1970 to 1971	18,425	4,035	−749	−71	−4.1	−1.8
1971 to 1972	17,676	3,964	251	−378	1.4	−9.5
1972 to 1973	17,927	3,586	−341	124	−1.9	3.5
1973 to 1974	17,586	3,710	−309	−411	−1.8	−11.1
1974 to 1975	17,277	3,299	−568	−427	−3.3	−12.9

Source: Annual Reports of the State Department of Education of Louisiana.
Note: Enrollment figures for all years are for those cohorts present in 1st through 5th grade
in Fall 1968 (identified in tables 1 and 2 as the 1964 through 1968 cohorts).

public-to-private transfer upon implementation of desegregation and a subsequent return movement, but again there is much other evidence not so readily interpreted. The public school loss with desegregation is twice the size of the private school gain. The subsequent pattern of return from private to public schooling shows up in the first and third years after desegregation, but not in the second year.

In East Baton Rouge Parish, 20 percent of white pupils in these cohorts attended private schools in fall 1968. This increased to 22 percent with desegregation, but had dropped back to 17 percent by 1974 (a drop that may reflect a general tendency to utilize private schooling more during the early grades when children are younger and costs are lower). In Bossier/Caddo Parishes, only 5 percent of white pupils in these cohorts attended private schools in fall 1968, and this increased in two years to 18 percent. By 1974 this had dropped only to 16 percent.

Enrollment data collected by governmental agencies cannot be expected to provide complete information on where parents flee to when desegregation occurs. Longitudinal data for individual pupils seem, in principle, to be needed. Such data are difficult and expensive to collect, and the only extant body of repeated interviews of parents in a district undergoing desegregation is the Boston study.[9] Alas, even this massive body of data has proven intractable to simple analysis of white flight, and no unambiguous findings have yet been reported.

Identifiability of Desegregation Effects

During the Dallas desegregation remedy hearings, a sociologist testified about the ambiguities in the evidence for desegregation-induced white flight. During the morning recess he was corralled by two persons who presented themselves as living proof that white flight exists. In a search for other living proof, we present in tables 11-4 and 11-5 sample survey data on the "main reason" given by white heads of households with school-age children for moving from the central city to elsewhere in the metropolitan area. These data are from the Annual Housing Survey, a recently inaugurated innovative program sponsored by the Department

Table 11-4
Percentage Giving Each Main Reason for Moving from the Central City to the Suburbs, White Households with School Age Children, Selected Metropolitan Areas: 1974 to 1975

Metropolitan Area	Employment	Family	Housing	Neighborhood	Schools	Other
Minneapolis-St. Paul	8.7	9.1	36.5	0.0	0.0	45.7
Newark	0.0	13.6	43.2	26.8	0.0	16.4
Phoenix	28.6	0.0	29.1	14.5	0.0	27.8
Pittsburgh	13.4	13.1	33.3	6.4	7.2	26.6
Boston	0.0	17.3	41.4	23.2	5.7	12.4
Detroit	22.7	8.7	36.4	23.3	4.3	4.6
Anaheim	8.2	8.1	39.9	15.9	7.8	20.1
Albany	0.0	4.9	50.0	24.4	4.9	15.8
Dallas	24.1	11.2	32.2	0.0	3.7	28.8
Fort Worth	14.9	6.5	32.3	18.8	15.3	12.2
Los Angeles	0.0	13.7	34.0	19.4	6.3	26.6
Washington	13.1	25.6	49.6	0.0	0.0	11.7

Source: U.S. Bureau of the Census, Annual Housing Survey for Metropolitan Areas, 1974/75.
Note: Each row sums to 100 percent.

Table 11-5
Percentage Giving Each Main Reason for Moving from the Central City to the Suburbs, White Households with School Age Children, Selected Metropolitan Areas: 1975 to 1976

Metropolitan Area	Employment	Family	Housing	Neighborhood	Neighborhood Racial Change	Schools	Other
Atlanta	11.5	4.5	56.8	6.8	2.2	0.0	18.2
Chicago	7.5	14.6	26.8	10.7	14.7	3.6	22.1
Philadelphia	0.0	36.9	36.9	8.9	0.0	8.6	8.7
San Francisco	0.0	10.8	22.5	45.1	0.0	10.6	11.0
Paterson	0.0	49.8	50.2	0.0	0.0	0.0	0.0
Rochester, NY	0.0	15.6	54.7	11.1	3.7	3.6	11.3
Miami	7.0	30.6	28.0	3.4	3.2	0.0	27.8
Cincinnati	9.1	36.3	32.3	4.6	4.7	0.0	13.0
Columbus, OH	22.5	30.1	34.7	4.3	0.0	4.1	4.3
Milwaukee	5.9	12.2	37.7	18.4	0.0	0.0	25.8
New Orleans	6.6	24.0	31.7	0.0	6.6	6.2	24.9
Kansas City	0.0	13.1	62.7	0.0	0.0	0.0	24.2
San Bernardino	14.5	4.5	47.7	9.0	0.0	0.0	24.3
San Diego	6.8	0.0	40.2	26.7	0.0	0.0	26.3
Portland, OR	5.3	7.3	43.7	10.1	0.0	4.9	28.7

Source: U.S. Bureau of the Census, Annual Housing Survey for Metropolitan Areas, 1975/76.
Note: Each row sums to 100 percent.

of Housing and Urban Development and conducted by the Bureau of the Census. Each year a subset of the nation's largest metropolitan areas is oversampled so that data for those individual areas can be reported in addition to national estimates.

Results for the metropolitan areas included in the 1975 and 1976 surveys are presented in tables 11-4 and 11-5. In each year, the interviewer was instructed to write all reasons mentioned and to mark the main reason. Reasons were subsequently coded into a specific set of about thirty categories, which we have collapsed into the groupings shown in the column headings. There was one change in coding of particular interest to us. In 1975, "neighborhood" was a single category, while in 1976 it was subdivided into "neighborhood overcrowded," "change in racial or ethnic composition of neighborhood," and "wanted better neighborhood." In both years, "schools" was a single coding category.

Housing considerations—needed larger house or apartment, wanted to own or rent, wanted better house, wanted residence with more conveniences, and so forth—dominate as the main reason for a suburban move. Family reasons—

change in marital status, change in size of family, wanted own household, moved to be closer to relatives—were cited frequently in many metropolitan areas. Employment reasons include job transfer or change and commuting reasons. The "other" category in the tables includes displacement by urban renewal, highway construction, fire, or disaster, along with a few miscellaneous categories.

The reasons of principal interest in the study of white flight from desegregation are "schools" and "neighborhood." The percentage of families indicating schools as the main reason for moving to the suburbs is small, ranging from zero for twelve of the twenty-seven places to above 10 percent for only two. Both Fort Worth and San Francisco have school desegregation programs, with a major implementation occurring one year and four years prior to the housing survey, respectively. Even in Boston with its history of bitter and sustained public controversy over desegregation, schools are cited as the main reason for moving by only 6 percent of white families who moved to the suburbs.

Perhaps white parents are reluctant to cite schools because that might tend to identify them as prejudiced. Judging from the public controversy in many cities, and from the national turmoil over busing, we would expect "schools" to be regarded by most whites as a legitimate and respectable answer. In the 1976 survey, neighborhood racial change was singled out as a separate category; it was cited by 15 percent of Chicago area movers (Chicago did not yet have a desegregation plan) and a much lower percentage of families in five other places. Wanting a "better neighborhood" may entail racial considerations, even if unspoken. Neighborhood reasons are relatively common for some metropolitan areas and infrequent for others. Unfortunately for simple interpretation, the search for better neighborhoods has been a motivating force for suburbanization for many decades, and hence cannot be regarded with any confidence as an indicator of racial concerns. To the extent that racial concerns are subsumed in broader reasons such as wanting a better neighborhood or better house, the racial considerations may reflect white flight from black neighbors—a process that has also been an active suburbanizing force for many decades—rather than a direct or immediate concern with school desegregation. Indeed, the opinion that suburban schools are better than city schools predates the controversy over desegregation.

Surveys designed more specifically to tap sentiments toward school desegregation could provide better information for our purposes than is available from the Annual Housing Survey. Even if such data were available, the analyst would be faced with a difficult task of inferring motivation. There are many reasons for moving to the suburbs and each family may have a mixture of motives. In this sense the behavior of most families is "overdetermined." If a concern with desegregation is identified as one reason among a larger set of reasons, how is it possible to specify whether it is one more straw on the pile or the straw that broke the back of residential inertia? Self-perceptions of motivation and public opinion polling on reactions to school desegregation are informative, but they do not provide a simple solution to the task of identifying desegregation effects.

Any specific effects of desegregation actions taken by a school district on migration patterns within, to, or from that district, occur in a context of many other political, social, economic, and psychological forces. National concern over white suburbanization and black ghettoization predates the recent decade of controversy over urban school desegregation, and the scholarly literature on the causes of these residential transformations is enormously rich and complex. Trends in public and private school enrollment have also been analyzed, incorporating such causes as trends in the birthrate, city-suburb and white-black differentials in fertility, the changing role of parochial education and of Catholicism in American life, the declining availability of nuns as teachers, educational finance, increasing educational attainment of parents, changing parental perspectives on the constituents of quality education, and many more.

To identify a specific impact of desegregation actions on public and private school enrollment and on the residential distribution of racial groups, we must be able to demonstrate either that the changes in these variables could not have occurred as they did in the absence of desegregation actions, or that some temporal or spatial variation in these processes can be attributed statistically to variations in desegregation actions. The first alternative can be dismissed, for racial enrollment and residential patterns clearly can and do change enormously in the absence of desegregation actions. Thus the task of identifying the impacts of desegregation actions requires sophisticated multivariate analysis.

If the effects of a desegregation action are direct and large, it should be feasible to disentangle their influence from the milieu of other forces. David Armor's recent work purports to demonstrate such a consistent pattern of massive white flight (when there is extensive mandatory busing in large districts with substantial minority populations and developed suburbs to accommodate residential flight) that no entanglement of other forces could possibly account for the results.[10] Gary Orfield's conclusion is similar to ours, that "to firmly establish any argument about white flight one would need some kind of general theory of urban racial change."[11]

Most studies of white flight, even when they have incorporated some kind of multivariate model, have been ineffective in controlling for the full range of known factors that should form part of a general theory of urban racial change.[12] Consider the two most noteworthy published studies. Coleman, Kelly, and Moore estimated equations in which changes in white public school enrollment were evaluated as a function of change in school segregation, number of pupils in the district, proportion black, segregation between districts in the metropolitan area, region, and certain interaction terms.[13] Farley added variables reflecting the metropolitan residential structure (city/suburb housing ratio, percentage of homes built before 1940, population density) and economic structure (white unemployment rate).[14] Neither study included measures of the administrative structure of school districts, the fiscal situation of municipalities and school districts, social and physical characteristics such as crime rates, fire and bond ratings, history of racial disturbances, and other such components of a general theory of urban racial change. In both studies the variable to be explained was aggregate net change in white public school enrollment, and desegregation action was characterized by a single measure (decline in the value of a segregation index). Orfield's mandate has not yet been fulfilled.

A Policy Research Agenda

Much social science research on contemporary society can be regarded to some degree as policy analysis. Narrowly focused evaluation research obviously seeks to influence policy choice, but even general social research is often carried out in the hope that better understanding of social change will enhance the design and implementation of social policy. In the case of school desegregation and white flight, neither is prime cause or consequence of the other. There are many reasons for undertaking school desegregation, and white flight is but one of many outcomes in need of assessment. There are many facets to white flight, and each has a number of causes. Many of these are the direct or indirect consequence of governmental policies of diverse sorts beyond the explicitly educational. As students of urban racial patterns in migration, housing consumption, residential location, and schooling, we can design an array of further studies of the demographic impacts of school desegregation. Some of these would be considered policy analysis only to the extent that they help set a realistic social context for the policy discussion, whereas others respond more directly to questions that legislators, judges, school board members, and citizens think need answering. We shall describe a few prospective studies to illustrate the range of types of policy relevance.

What is the response of white families to the presence of minority pupils in communities that have not implemented desegregation programs? The literature on residential succession abounds with instances of neighborhood racial turn-over.[15] How are residential change and school change linked in this process? Can annual racial enrollment data provide a richer data resource for neighborhood turnover studies than is available from decennial census data? Is there anything distinctive about the presumed white flight from desegregation that is not already embraced in the white avoidance of "changing" neighborhoods and schools? Why should a concern with white flight lead to a policy focus on school desegregation rather than on racial functioning of the metropolitan housing market, economic shifts between cities and suburbs, and the like?

Somewhat less far-reaching would be studies differentiating the private school and migration components of white flight. Moving one's children to private schools is much less permanent than moving one's family to the suburbs, and does not entail the same range of fiscal and residential impacts on the city. Further knowledge is needed of the circumstances under which existing or new private school systems serve as havens, and of the circumstances that are conducive to a return to public schooling.

The white population has been treated throughout our discussion as an undifferentiated aggregate. The socioeconomic differentiation within the white population is of great concern in the assessment of policy implications. Socioeconomic activity in private school enrollment and residential relocation is to be expected, yet has been ignored in most studies.[16] The socioeconomic selectivity of the response bears on the degree of conflict between seemingly independent federal policies. Urban development policy is concerned with attracting and retaining middle class persons as central city residents, with the avowed aim to alleviate the fiscal crisis of the cities and to reduce the city/suburb racial separation. To what extent is the federal effort to improve the education of city residents through desegregation working at cross-purposes with other urban policy goals? Within the domain of education, what are the potential conflicts in methods and aims between (1) desegregation actions that seek to disperse pupils according to race, (2) educational assistance programs aimed at schools with concentrations of disadvantaged children, and (3) programs designed to meet the special needs of non-English-speaking children and others of minority ethnic identification?

The attempt to use studies of white flight as a specific basis for changing public policy on school desegregation reached a peak in 1975 with extensive press coverage given to statements by James S. Coleman. There has been controversy over the methodology of the study conducted by Coleman and his colleagues, but let us ignore shortcomings of the research and consider two of his primary conclusions:

The effect of desegregation on white loss has been widely different among different cities where desegregation has taken place.

Because, insofar as we can estimate, the loss of whites upon desegregation is a one-time loss, the long-term impact of desegregation is considerably less than that of other continuing factors. The continuing white losses produce an extensive erosion of the interracial contact that desegregation of city schools brings about.[17]

The second of these conclusions might have been used as the rationale for undertaking broader-based research of the type we have presented and proposed. The import of this conclusion was largely overlooked in the effort to reach immediate specific policy conclusions regarding school desegregation.

The first of these conclusions is even more intriguing, for it has also been largely overlooked but pertains directly to the information needed for appropriate policy modification. The most immediately pertinent policy research on demographic impacts of school desegregation actions would be identification of the sources of differentials in the impacts. Of particular interest is whether the character of the desegregating agent (court, HEW, state, school district) or of the desegregation action affects the demographic impact. Katzman's review of a few case studies suggests that these policy choices do not affect the outcome,[18] but Armor's previously cited report suggests that the agent and the action are of fundamental import.[19] If it could be demonstrated that some controllable features of the desegregation process had a significant effect on the demographic impact—for example, the number of schools affected, the speed of implementation, the specific techniques used, the character of community education about the plan, reliance on court order or other federal pressure—then educational administrators could better plan to desegregate and avoid or minimize white flight.

Press coverage of Coleman's research and even subsequent scholarly research focused on the finding of an average effect of school desegregation on white enrollment. No judge, superintendent, or school board really cares much about average effects. They seek to discern what choices within their power can make the outcome of their actions more favorable. If social research is to aid in resolving America's continuing racial dilemma, its protagonists should seek to increase the stock of information about the effects of alternative policy choices. Otherwise the battles of the sociologists will continue to be dismissed in favor of personal intuition.

Notes

1. One of us (K.T.) testified as an expert witness for the plaintiffs.

2. *Tasby* v. *Estes*, 416 F. Supp. 644 (1976).

3. See, for example, Charles T. Clotfelter, "School Desegregation, 'Tipping,' and Private School Enrollment," *The Journal of Human Resources* 11 (December 1975):28-50; James S. Coleman, Sara D. Kelly, John A. Moore, *Trends in School Segregation*, 1968-73, (Washington, D.C.: Urban Institute Paper 722-03-01, 1975); Michael W. Giles, Everett F. Cataldo, Douglas S. Gatlin, "White Flight and Percent Black: The Tipping Point Re-examined," *Social Science Quarterly* 56 (June 1975):85-92; Reynolds Farley, "Can Governmental Policies Integrate Public Schools?" (Paper presented at the Annual Meeting of the American Sociological Association, New York City, September 1, 1976); Thomas F. Pettigrew and Robert L. Green, "School Desegregation in Large Cities: A Critique of the Coleman 'White Flight' Thesis," *Harvard Educational Review* 46 (February 1976):1-53; David J. Armor, "Declaration of David J. Armor," *Carlin et al.* vs. *San Diego Board of Education* (San Diego, 1977); Martin T. Katzman, *The Quality of Municipal Services, Central City Decline and Middle Class Flight* (Boston: Department of City and Regional Planning, Harvard University, 1977).

4. *Brown* v. *Board of Education*, 349 U.S. 294 (1954).

5. Coleman, Kelly, and Moore, *Trends in School Segregation*; Christine Rossell, "School Desegregation and White Flight," *Political Science Quarterly* 90 (Winter 1975/76):675-695; Armor, "Declaration of David J. Armor."

6. Donald N. McIsaac, Dennis W. Spuck, and Lyle Hunter, "Enrollment Projections: ENROLV2," Department of Educational Administration, University of Wisconsin, September 1972.

7. Ibid., p. 2.

8. Armor, "Declaration of David J. Armor."

9. J. Michael Ross, "Changes in Public Preference for Alternative School Desegregation Policies: Theoretical Formulations" (Paper presented at the Annual Meeting of the American Sociological Association, 1976). See also D. Garth Taylor and Arthur L. Stinchcombe, *The Boston School Desegregation Controversy*, Draft Report (Chicago: National Opinion Research Center, 1977).

10. Armor, "Declaration of David J. Armor."

11. Gary Orfield, "White Flight Research: Its Importance, Perplexities and Possible Policy Implementations." *Symposium on School Desegregation and White Flight* (Notre Dame, Ind.: Center for Civil Rights, 1975), pp. 48-49.

12. Katzman, *Quality of Municipal Services.*

13. Coleman, Kelly, and Moore, *Trends in School Segregation.*

14. Farley, "Can Government Policies Integrate Public Schools?"

15. Howard Aldrich, "Ecological Succession in Racially Changing Neighborhoods, A Review of the Literature," *Urban Affairs Quarterly* 19 (March 1975):327-348.

16. A study reported by Giles, Gatlin, and Cataldo does deal with the class issue as it relates to forms of protest against school desegregation. Michael W. Giles, Douglas S. Gatlin, and Everett F. Cataldo, "Racial and Class Prejudice: Their Relative Effects on Protest Against School Desegregation," *American Sociological Review* 41 (April 1976):280-288.

17. Coleman, Kelly, and Moore, *Trends in School Segregation*, p. 79.

18. Katzman, *Quality of Municipal Services*, chapter 3, p. 28.

19. Armor, "Declaration of David J. Armor."

12

The Political Economy of Growth Policies in Cities and Suburbs

Thomas R. Dye and
John A. Garcia

It is fashionable today to lament the correlates of urban population growth—congestion, pollution, noise, unsightly development, replacement of green spaces with cement slabs. There is no way to calculate accurately all of the dollar and nondollar costs of urban growth; in part these costs are closely intertwined with aesthetic preferences. Aesthetic preferences vary among social groupings and so do the benefits derived from urban development.

We do not propose to argue whose aesthetic preferences or whose economic benefits should take precedence. Rather, we propose to present some evidence of the dollar costs of urban growth to municipal governments and their populations. Specifically, we shall suggest that growth limitation policies do *not* necessarily produce economies in municipal taxing and spending. On the contrary, the evidence suggests that per capita costs of municipal government are only minimally related to size, and that growing cities have *lower* per capita costs than cities which are not growing or declining in population. In addition, effective growth limitation policies could be regressive in their impact, and would contribute to increased separation of needs from resources in metropolitan areas.[1]

To support these contentions about the political economy of growth rates, we have selected two separate samples of municipalities. The first "sample" is really the universe of 243 central cities of Standard Metropolitan Statistical Areas (SMSA) in 1970. The first part of this paper deals with these central cities. The second sample of 340 suburban municipalities was drawn at random from the universe of approximately 1200 municipalities of 10,000 or more population which are located within SMSAs but outside of the central city in 1970. Demographic data was derived from the *1970 Census of Population* and the *1970 Census of Housing*; data on municipal finances was derived from the *1972 Census of Government.*

Central Cities

Economies and Diseconomies of Size and Growth

For decades political and social scientists have been concerned with the impact of population growth on local government. Concern was generated for the

This research was supported by the National Institute of Child Health and Human Development, U.S. Public Health Service, Grant No. 1 RO1 HDO7629.

apparent diseconomies of large size and rapid growth, as well as the frustrations and maladjustments which frequently accompany rapid growth. But this analysis proposes that increasing size and rapid growth do *not* create insurmountable problems for local governments. On the contrary, the more serious problems appear to develop in cities which are stagnating or declining in size. It is not the highest growth rate cities—Las Vegas, Anaheim, Ventura, Santa Barbara, West Palm Beach, Fort Lauderdale, Colorado Springs, and Phoenix—which are "sick"; rather, it is the cities which are losing large numbers of people—Akron, Baltimore, Boston, Camden, Cleveland, Dayton, Detroit, Gary, Hammond, Johnstown, Jersey City, Newark, Philadelphia, Rochester, St. Louis, and Scranton.

It is true that larger cities spend more per capita than smaller cities, and that larger cities impose heavier tax burdens per capita than smaller cities (see table 12-1). In 1972, the six cities in the United States with a population of one million or more spent $636 per capita, and collected $292 per capita in taxes. In contrast, the 121 cities with populations of 50,000 to 100,000 spent only $212 per capita, and collected only $111 per capita in taxes. Moreover, larger cities are more dependent upon intergovernmental revenue than smaller cities. The contention that larger cities are uneconomic (and the implication that growth is expensive) rests primarily upon these contrasting averages for different size categories of cities.

But a different picture can emerge if we examine average per capita costs for categories of cities by *growth rate* (see table 12-2). The seven cities which lost over 15 percent of their population between 1960 and 1970 spent $308 per capita in 1972 and collected $175 per capita in taxes. In contrast, the forty-six cities which grew by more than 25 percent in the same period spent only $183 per capita and collected only $91 per capita in taxes. In short, the greatest diseconomies occur with population loss. Growth, even rapid growth, is associated with lower per capita taxing, spending, and intergovernmental aid.

If we plot the relationship between growth rate and per capita spending we obtain a shallow L-shape curve, as shown in figure 12-1. The highest per capita costs occur in cities losing more than 1 percent of their population per year. The

Table 12-1
Taxing and Spending of City Governments, Per Capita, by Size Categories, 1972

	1 Million and Over	500,000 to 1 Million	300,000 to 500,000	100,000 to 300,000	50,000 to 100,000
General revenues	$620	$387	$296	$262	$202
Intergovernmental revenues	257	142	92	81	50
Tax revenues	292	181	131	132	111
Total expenditures	636	398	296	271	212
	(N=6)	(N=20)	(N=27)	(N=69)	(N=121)

Table 12-2
Taxing and Spending of City Governments, Per Capita, by Growth Categories, 1972

	Loss		Growth		
	Over 15%	0 to 15%	0 to 10%	10 to 25%	Over 25%
General revenues	$280	$264	$222	$191	$183
Intergovernmental revenues	83	82	58	41	41
Tax revenues	175	136	116	103	91
Total expenditures	308	271	234	202	194
	(N=7)	(N=84)	(N=45)	(N=61)	(N=46)

"optimum" growth rate appears to be about 1 percent per year, if we define optimum as the growth rate which produces the lowest per capita costs. Surprisingly, there is no significant increase in cost associated with even rapid growth rates—5 or 10 percent per year. We expected to find a U-shaped curve with diseconomies occurring among cities with large losses and large gains in population. But cities appear to adjust very well to population increases; there were no significant diseconomies encountered in even the highest growth rate cities.

We can also observe the impact of growth rates on taxing and spending in table 12-3, which presents simple correlations coefficients between growth and per capita general revenues, intergovernmental revenues, tax revenues, and general expenditures. The coefficients are not high, but they are consistently negative: increases in growth rates have different impacts on different size cities. If we divide our central cities into small (50,000 to 100,000), medium (100,000 to 300,000), and large (over 300,000), we can observe the relationships between growth rates and taxing and spending in each size capacity of the city. The results were unchanged; growth rates have the same negative effect on per capita taxing and spending in small, medium, and large central cities. Population stagnation or decline is costly for small cities as well as large cities.

So far we have observed only relationships or associations between population decline and higher municipal costs and tax burdens. It is more difficult to sort out causal linkages. Population decline may "cause" increased taxing and spending directly because municipal services and costs remain at the same level despite population decline, and therefore smaller numbers of people must support the same municipal bureaucracy and physical plant. Or population decline may "cause" increased taxing and spending indirectly because the people left behind are poorer, unskilled, and in need of more costly social services than those who moved out. Thus, population decline may raise taxing and spending through its impact on the social and economic composition of the population. Or, the causal direction may be reversed; increased taxes and high costs for

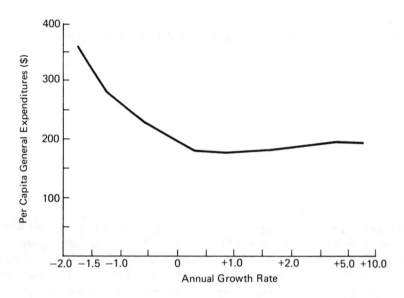

Figure 12-1. The Relationship between Growth and Municipal Expenditures

municipal services may drive some businesses out of the central city and their employees and supporting businesses follow them. Finally, all of these forces may be acting simultaneously.

Sorting Out the Independent Effects of Size and Growth

However, a closer examination of the determinants of taxing and spending levels in cities suggests that factors other than size and growth rate are responsible for most of the variations in per capita taxing and spending. For example, the relationship between size and per capita costs may be a product of the fact that larger cities are burdened with more functional responsibilities—notably schools, welfare, and hospitals. In most medium size and smaller cities these additional functional responsibilities are performed by separate school district, county, or state governmental agencies. Thus, a large proportion of the increased costs of big city government can be attributed to the fact that their budgets are enlarged by these additional responsibilities—responsibilities which are shifted to other governments in smaller cities.

We also know that size and density are related; the possibility exists that some of the increased costs of big city government might be attributed to density rather than size itself.[2] Moreover, big cities have larger nonwhite and ethnic population percentages; the possibility exists that these demographic characteristics, rather than size itself, produce the increased costs we observe in

Table 12-3

Relationships between Growth Rates and Taxing and Spending in Small, Medium, and Large Central Cities

	All Cities	Large Cities (over 300,000)	Medium Cities (100,000-300,000)	Small Cities (under 100,000)
General revenue	−.16	−.22	−.23	−.07
Intergovernmental revenues	−.20	−.19	−.28	−.15
Tax revenues	−.13	−.21	−.22	−.06
Total expenditures	−.15	−.20	−.20	−.07

Note: Figures indicate the simple correlation coefficient with growth rate.

large cities. We also know that big cities have larger populations of nonhomeowners than smaller cities. Perhaps it is nonhomeownership that contributes to the increased costs of city government; home ownership in medium and small cities creates resistance to increased taxing and spending. Large cities also tend to be older cities, and the age of development may contribute to increased costs, independently of size. Finally, we know that large cities house larger proportions of the poor, and carry heavier burdens in crime and social dependency, than smaller cities. Increased costs of big-city government may be attributable to these social problems rather than to size per se.

Let us try to sort out the independent effects of size and growth rate on municipal taxing and spending, from effects of functional responsibilities, density, homeownership, race, ethnicity, age, and social problems. Table 12-4 presents multiple regression problems on per capita taxing, and per capita spending, for 243 central cities of SMSAs. These cities range in size from 50,000 to 7,000,000. The simple correlation coefficients (r) are presented together with the standardized b values (Beta) for each variable which we believed might contribute to increased municipal costs. The total explained variances by all variables considered collectively are also presented at the bottom of table 12-4 as percentages. Note that we can explain 73 percent of the total variation among cities in tax levels, and 65 percent of the total variation among cities in spending levels, with reference to relatively small numbers of variables.

It is interesting to observe differential impact of size and growth rate on municipal taxing and spending. Size and growth rate are unrelated. (The simple correlation coefficient between population in 1970 and growth rate in 1960 to 1970 is −.04.) There are positive relationships between size and municipal taxing and spending. But the relationships between growth rate and municipal taxing and spending are negative. Even though size and growth rate both involve numbers of people, size measures a static condition, while growth rate measures change over time. It is possible to say that increasing size (cross-sectionally) contributes to increasing municipal costs. But one cannot say that increasing growth rates (changes over time) contribute to increasing municipal costs.

Table 12-4
Determinants of Taxing and Spending in American Cities

	Taxes Per Capita		Spending Per Capita	
	r	B	r	B
Population				
Size (no. of persons)	.28	.17	.36	.16
Growth rate (% increase '60-'70)	−.13	−.05	−.15	−.06
Density (pop./sq. mi.)	.47	.19	.49	.24
Life Style				
Youth (% under 18)	−.18	−.21	−.23	−.13
Aged (% over 65)	.24	.20	.21	.04
Homeownership (% owner-occupied)	−.55	−.37	−.55	−.32
Ethnicity				
Nonwhite (%)	.13	−.09	.18	−.10
Foreign born (%)	.58	.19	.46	.22
Resources				
Property value (avg. dwelling)	.48	.27	.39	.28
Income (median family)	.28	.38	.20	.18
Social conditions				
Age of city (years)	.41	.04	.45	.02
Poverty (% below)	−.18	.33	−.11	.20
Crime rate (U.C.R.)	.26	.14	.28	.03
Public assistance rate (%)	.29	.13	.29	.07
Functional responsibility (number of functions performed by city)	.63	.42	.65	.41
Total explained variance	73%		65%	

Note: The central cities in the analysis represent the universe of cities greater than 50,000 population in the 1970 census. Thus, tests of significance are not required.

Indeed, just the opposite is true with regard to growth rates; increasing growth rates contribute to decreasing municipal costs. Or, to put it another way, "non-growth" increases per capita taxing and spending.

Perhaps the more important point is that factors *other than* size and growth rate are more influential in determining municipal taxing and spending. Indeed, the most important determinant of municipal costs is the number of functional responsibilities assigned to municipal government—especially whether the city pays the costs of welfare, education, and hospitals, or whether these functions are shifted to county governments, school districts, or state agencies.[3] Other factors which turn out to be more important than size or growth rates are: density, homeownership, percent foreign born, and property value. Other factors which turn out to roughly equivalent in importance to size are: youth, age, income, poverty, crime rate, and public assistance rate.[4] (We might speculate that the most effective way to relieve financially hard-pressed cities, is to have the federal or state governments take over all of the costs of welfare and hospitals, and contribute a larger share of the costs of education.)

Local governments appear capable of accommodating various city sizes and growth rates.[5] There is little variation in per capita taxing and spending which can be attributed to size or growth rate. Increased per capita taxing and spending are closely associated with differences among cities in functional responsibilities and socioeconomic composition. Limiting population growth does not save money. On the contrary, low growth-rate cities have slightly higher taxes and expenditures than high-growth-rate cities.

Suburbs

Suburbs, Growth and Costs

The suburbs utilized in this study were drawn from the 1200 municipalities in all 243 SMSAs which exceeded ten thousand inhabitants. This random sample of suburbs includes 340 communities with a mean population of 32,017. These suburban cities had a mean annual growth rate of 4.8 percent for 1960-1970. Whereas larger central cities spend more per capita than smaller cities, size and spending does not follow as clear a linear pattern for suburbs. Generally larger suburbs spend more than smaller suburbs, yet mid-size suburbs (20,000-35,000) are the biggest per capita spenders. In 1972, suburbs in the 20,000-35,000 category spent $194 per capita while larger suburbs (over 75,000) spent $183 per capita. A somewhat similar pattern occurs with tax revenues as larger suburbs impose heavier tax burdens per capita than smaller ones. Nevertheless, the middle-size suburbs (15,000-20,000) imposed a heavier tax burden per capita, than larger suburbs, $322 per capita. Moreover, large suburbs, in addition to mid-size (20,000-35,000) are more dependent on intergovernmental revenues than smaller suburbs (see table 12-5). The contention that size affects spending and taxing patterns does not follow a completely linear direction as central cities. Middle-size suburban cities behave similarly to large suburban cities, and many of the differences between suburbs in general are not statistically significant.

Table 12-5
Taxing and Spending of Suburban Governments Per Capita, by Size Categories, 1972

	10,000 to 15,000	15,000 to 20,000	20,000 to 35,000	35,000 to 75,000	75,000 and Over	F Ratio
General revenues	$152	$421	$270	$173	$275	.75
Intergovernmental revenues	31	33	145	36	185	1.06
Tax revenues	87	342	260	106	322	.69
Total expenditures	155	156	194	178	183	1.02
	(N=98)	(N=67)	(N=91)	(N=51)	(N=27)	

If we examine the same per capita costs by categories of suburbs by growth rate, a mixed and overall weak pattern emerges. That is, suburbs experiencing higher growth rates spend less than slower growing communities. Yet, the exception was the suburbs in the 10-25 percent range which experienced the highest expenditures. Again, a neat linear pattern is altered by this growth category. On the other hand, tax revenues increase with increasing growth rates (see table 12-6). This pattern differs from that of central cities as their per capita tax burdens were shown to decrease with increasing growth rates. Those suburbs which are experiencing population loss, spend and tax less than growing suburban communities. Thus, growth has an uneven effect on spending and taxing for suburbs, and again many differences are statistically insignificant. As a result, the question of diseconomies for suburbs was not as clearly defined as for central cities.

As growth rate was plotted with per capita general expenditures for central cities, the same operation was applied for suburbs (see figure 12-2). The highest per capita costs occurred in suburbs losing more than 2 percent annually, and those suburbs in the 0.5-1.3 percent growth category. Given the oscillating pattern of the curve, expenditures did not decline steadily until one reached the 7.5 percent growth rate and higher. Such a pattern did not indicate any optimum growth rate. Whereas central cities displayed a shallow L-shape curve, suburban communities with high growth rates (over 6 percent annually) appear to adjust well to population increases.

Another manner of observing the impact of growth rates on taxing and spending was the presentation of simple correlation coefficients between growth and per capita general revenues, intergovernmental revenues, tax revenues, and general expenditures (see table 12-7). None of the coefficients are very high, most are statistically insignificant, and most are negative; increases in growth are associated with lower per capita spending and taxing. The relationship was tested

Table 12-6
Taxing and Spending of Suburban Governments Per Capita, by Growth Categories, 1972

	Loss		*Growth*			
	Over 15%	*0 to 15%*	*0 to 10%*	*10 to 25%*	*Over 25%*	*F Ratio*
General revenues	$161	$163	$190	$221	$316	.31
Intergovernmental revenues	46	35	88	39	99	.24
Tax revenues	89	97	183	151	277	.30
General expenditures	183	168	153	223	151	2.90[a]
	(*N*=7)	(*N*=40)	(*N*=75)	(*N*=69)	(*N*=149)	

[a]*F* ratio significant at .05 level

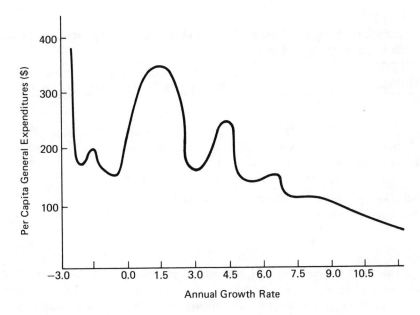

Figure 12-2. The Relationship between Growth and Suburban Expenditures

also with different size suburbs. The negative association was more common among large and small suburbs, but positive associations (although insignificant) were present in medium suburbs. The data again indicate a weak level of association between growth rate and financial aspects of suburban governments.

Suburbs: Sorting Out Key Factors

The preliminary examination of the effects of size and growth rate on taxing and spending levels in suburbs suggest that other factors are more responsible for variations in per capita taxing and spending. Just as functional responsibilities proved important for central cities' financial patterns, these responsibilities are an important factor for suburbs. Functional responsibility is the most crucial variable (R^2 = 31.4 percent and 33.6 percent respectively) in determining both taxing and spending in suburbs. The assumption of more functions, particularly schools and hospitals, enlarges the cost of suburban government.

Other factors that affect suburban per capita taxes are density, median property values, crime rate, and public assistance rate (see table 12-8). As median property values increase, so do per capita taxes. Density and crime rate have a negative impact on tax levels. Age, density, percent nonwhite, median property value, and income have a tendency to lower the expenditures of suburban cities. The total explained variance by all variables considered is 53.3

Table 12-7

Relationships between Growth Rates and Taxing and Spending in Small, Medium and Large Suburban Cities

	All Cities	Large Suburbs (over 65,000)	Medium Suburbs (35,000-65,000)	Small Suburbs (10,000-30,000)
General revenues	−.009	−.14	.06	−.02
Intergovernmental revenues	.03	−.06	.09	−.02
Tax revenues	.003	−.16	.07	−.02
Total expenditures	−.11[a]	−.13	−.16[a]	−.09
	(N=317)	(N=52)	(N=104)	(N=159)

Note: Figures indicate the simple correlation coefficient with growth rate
[a]Significant at .05 level

percent for tax levels, and 54 percent for spending levels. The amount of explained variance was noticeably smaller for suburbs than central cities. This indicates that other factors, such as aesthetic values and community norms, may play an important role in taxing and spending levels, in addition to demographic factors.

Finally, the relationship between growth rate and size in suburban communities produced similar impacts. Size and growth rate proved to be unrelated ($r = .03$). There is a positive relationship between size and suburban taxing, and a negative relationship between size and suburban spending. But the relationships between growth rate and taxing and spending are negative. In other words, increased growth rates do not necessarily increase taxing and spending and appear to decrease municipal costs. Thus, the impact of growth rate has a minimal impact on suburban taxing and spending, and other demographic and structural factors (most importantly, functional responsibility) affect suburban costs.

Discussion

The Regressivity of Growth Limitation Policies

What implications do these findings have for municipal population policy—direct efforts on the part of cities to limit size and growth rate? Generally, growth limitation policies have little economic justification. In most cities across the nation, limiting size or growth rate will *not* result in lower per capita tax levels of lower per capita expenditures. This does not mean, of course, that the aesthetic preferences of individuals or groups in the community might not be

Table 12-8
Determinants of Taxing and Spending in American Suburban Cities

	Taxes Per Capita		Spending Per Capita	
	r	B	r	B
Population				
Size (no. of persons)	.01	−.02	−.13	.01
Growth rate (% change '60-'70)	.00	.08	−.11	−.13
Density (pop./sq. mi)	−.06	−.13	−.01	−.14
Life style				
Youth (% under 18)	−.01	−.02	−.04	.65[a]
Aged (% over 65)	.02	−.12	.11	.12
Homeownership (% owner-occupied)	−.08	−.04	−.04	−.23
Ethnicity				
Nonwhite (%)	−.03	−.01	−.08	−.48[a]
Foreign born (%)	.12	−.01	.15	.16
Resources				
Property value (avg. dwelling	.27	.36[a]	.00	−.23[a]
Income (median family)	.04	−.11	−.13	−.36[a]
Social conditions				
Poverty (% below)	—	—	—	—
Crime rate (U.C.R.)	−.25	−.24[a]	.16	.42[a]
Public assistance rate (%)	.11	.21[a]	.01	.02
Functional responsibility (no. of functions performance by city)	.56	.63[a]	.58	.60[a]
Total explained variance	53.3%		54.0%	

[a]Significant *F* ratio at the .05 level

advanced by limiting size or growth rate. But from an economic standpoint, municipal governments would be better advised to act, insofar as possible, to maintain a modest growth rate, and certainly to avoid population loss.

Larger cities do not need to restrict growth. Indeed, cities in most of the larger, older metropolitan areas of the Northeast and Midwest are likely to face problems of population stagnation and decline in the 1980s, not problems of growth.

Nonetheless, there may be a few upper-middle-class suburban municipalities in metropolitan areas that will view growth restriction as in their own best interest.[6] They may employ zoning laws, subdivision control restrictions, environmental regulations, and even municipal land purchases to restrict growth. They may do so fearing that additional growth would: bring in poorer people and change the local social structure and life style; increase congestion and pollution; or alter the aesthetic quality of the community, including the trees, green areas, and open expanses. Today, the euphemisms of upper-class exclusion seek to obscure the social and economic bias of "growth" policy. The rhetoric of "environmental quality," "quality of life," and "preservation of scenic beauty," obscures the impact of growth limitation policies on the working classes and the poor who need jobs and places to live.

What happens when a suburban municipality restricts growth? There are no effective methods by which municipal governments in America can reduce local birthrates; all that municipalities can do is try to keep "outsiders" from moving in. Even an effective municipal "growth" policy is really a "distribution" policy, because it merely deflects population to other parts of a metropolitan area or region. The people kept out do not cease to exist, they merely find housing elsewhere in the metropolitan area or region. They probably end up imposing their costs on municipalities—central cities or larger, close-in, suburbs—which are less able to afford their burden than the wealthier, upper-class residents of the communities which succeeded in excluding them. What appears to be a local "growth" issue is really a metropolitan "distribution" issue.

A metropolitan area as a whole, or even a large city or suburb, probably cannot enforce a growth policy, even if it decides to try to do so. The consequences of deliberate restrictive policies are clearly regressive. Consider the traditional instruments available to a municipality to limit growth: zoning laws can keep out multi-family dwellings, small lots, and heavy or "dirty" industrial development; municipalities can refuse to participate in public, subsidized housing; high local taxes, especially for a high quality, college-oriented school program, can be imposed; public utilities needed for large-scale, high-density developments can be halted; restrictions on industrial development, including strong pollution control regulations, can inhibit the growth of jobs; and opposition to street widening and highway building can also be used to restrict development. Note that the burden of each of these policies is regressive. It is not the upper classes whose lives are adversely affected by the environmentalists, ecologists, and no-growth advocates, but rather the poor and the working class.[7]

Not only are these policies regressive, they are ineffective in the larger metropolitan area. People or industry excluded from one municipality will find another place within the metropolis. Overall levels of metropolitican growth or decline are determined by economic and demographic forces at work on the national level. A suburban municipality can only halt or restrict growth by directing it to other suburbs or keeping it isolated in the central city. The effect is likely to be inefficient and unjust. The metropolitan-wide impact is to contribute further to the separation of needs and resources within the metropolis.

Notes

1. The analysis to follow is based upon the universe of 243 central cities of Standard Metropolitan Statistical Areas in 1970. The figures on general revenues,

intergovernmental revenues, tax revenues, and total general expenditures, were obtained from the *1972 Census of Governments*.

2. There are several methods of measuring "density," the most common is population per square mile, but persons per household (household density) and persons per room (room crowding) can also be employed with effectiveness. See Thomas R. Dye, "Population Density and Social Pathology," *Urban Affairs Quarterly* 11 (December 1975):265-275; Robert E. Mitchell, "Some Social Implications of High Density Housing," *American Sociological Review* 36 (February 1971):18-29. One may also control for recent annexations by examining the number of persons in 1970 living in the 1960 area of the city. But central cities which are losing population are also declining in density over time. Northwestern and midwestern cities have largely ceased annexation; western and southern cities continue to annex.

3. The importance of functional responsibility in the determination of municipal taxing and spending is described in detail in Roland J. Liebert, "Municipal Functions, Structure, and Expenditures," *Social Science Quarterly* 54 (March 1974):765-783.

4. The literature on the general determinants of municipal taxing and spending is found largely in economics. For a summary and analysis of this research see John C. Weicher, "Determinants of Central City Expenditures," *National Tax Journal* 23 (December 1970):329-396.

5. While our research has focused on growth rates, research on city size is clearly summarized by Richard P. Appelbaum, "City Size and Urban Life," *Urban Affairs Quarterly* 12 (December 1976):139-170.

6. For an interesting essay on the use of population growth restrictions by upper-middle-class suburbs, see Michael N. Danielson, "Differentiation, Segregation, and Political Fragmentation in the American Metropolis" in Commission on Population Growth and the American Future, *Government and Population*, vol. 4 (Washington, D.C.: U.S. Government Printing Office, 1973).

7. The increasing separation of city and suburban municipalities by class and race is discussed at length by Richard Child Hill, "Separate and Unequal: Governmental Inequality in the Metropolis," *American Political Science Review* 68 (December 1974):1557-1568. See also Frederick M. Wirt, et al., *On the City's Rim: Politics and Policy in Suburbia* (Lexington, Mass.: Lexington Books, D.C. Heath and Co., 1972).

13 The Ecological and Political Determinants of Suburban Development

John Logan and
Mark Schneider

Research on the determinants of the growth patterns of suburban communities, with few exceptions, has been bifurcated into two major traditions, which closely parallel boundaries between academic disciplines. Following the ground-breaking work of Burgess and the Chicago School, sociologists have been primarily interested in the effects of such *ecological* factors as spatial location, economic function, and age of community. Political scientists and economists, on the other hand, have concentrated on a set of variables—primarily controls on land use and fiscal policy—which represent the *political* forces operating in the development process. Our purpose here is to juxtapose these alternative theoretical traditions within a single empirical investigation of change in two significant characteristics of suburban communities, economic function and population density, in the period 1960-1970.

Ecological Determinants of Growth

The principal statement of the ecological determinants of metropolitan development predicted through a model of concentric zones,[1] a monotonic decline of both employment activity and population density with distance from the central business district (CBD).[2] Further, by assuming a process of development through expansion from the metropolitan center into fringe areas, the Burgess model also suggested greater economic activity and population density in older parts of the metropolis. Subsequent research has shown the general validity of these predictions.[3] Thus both age and distance from the center are known to be important correlates of the pattern of development of various parts of the metropolis at any given time.

As a model of *change over time*, the concentric zone theory presumes a natural life-cycle of transition from low to high density and residential to employment land uses.[4] In addition, it predicts that the zone of transition will move progressively further from the city center as the metropolis continues to develop. Basil G. Zimmer has summarized evidence for such a development

The authors would like to thank Avery Guest of the University of Washington, Seattle, for making available the data upon which the research is based. Funds from the Graduate School of SUNY, Stony Brook, made this research possible.

167

pattern, which he characterizes as "centrifugal drift."[5] It has also been noted that this ecological model implies that the rate of increase in density or economic activity (as distinguished from the absolute level of either) is greatest in newer areas, relatively distant from the CBD.[6]

The continuing work of Leo Schnore on metropolitan differentiation suggests other ecological factors which impinge on the suburban development process. First, Schnore has shown that there was a general tendency for residential suburbs to grow faster and have higher rates of increase in density than employing suburbs during the period 1940-1960 and for a growing specialization in economic or residential development to occur between suburbs.[7] Second, Schnore suggests systematic variations in the emergence of the classical metropolitan pattern across regions, in accordance with the "maturity" (that is to say, age, size, and location) of the metropolis.[8] Newer central cities, located mostly in the South and West, partly because of their aggressive annexation policies, stronger fiscal base, and availability of undeveloped land within their boundaries, may continue to experience relatively high rates of development; growth rates in their suburban rings, therefore, may be correspondingly low.

Political Determinants of Development

In contrast to the body of literature based on ecological models, there does not exist a dominant model of the political factors affecting suburban growth. However, the most obvious characteristic of suburban political structure usually identified as affecting growth is its fragmentation into multiple governmental jurisdictions.[9] In general, these incorporated suburban communities (whether municipalities, villages, or towns) have a variety of formal powers with which they may attempt to influence the pace and pattern of their own development. Of these the most important seem to be their control over zoning, development timing ordinances, subdivision controls, and their discretion in budget and service allocation.[10]

Causes of Suburban Incorporation

It is reasonable to assume that suburbs frequently incorporate specifically to gain these powers over patterns of growth, although there may be no clear uniformity in the way in which they are used. Robert Warren has documented the range of purposes of incorporation among California suburbs in the 1950s: to avoid annexation by a central city or neighboring suburb, to slow the rate of population growth, to protect a wealthy residential or industrial tax base, and so forth.[11] In general most of these incorporations were designed to protect some value held by the community and to exclude possible land uses or development that would challenge this value.

The general use of "protective" incorporations may be inferred from the historical pattern of their timing. Of 2,356 incorporated suburbs appearing in the 1970 census, about 25 percent had incorporated during 1890-1910.[12] This spate of incorporations occurred as new transportation technologies, especially the increasing efficiency of electrified railroads, allowed central cities to extend their dominance into previously isolated fringe areas. Incorporation may have been a means for native upper-class fringe communities to protect themselves from absorption into an expanding, immigrant, working-class central city. State governments apparently cooperated in this "protective incorporation" movement by relaxing restrictions on incorporations while making annexation of incorporated areas by central cities more difficult.[13] The next peak in the number of incorporations, the decade of the 1920s, took place in a period of massive suburbanization stimulated by the diffusion of the automobile and truck. Coincidentally, it was in 1926 that the U.S. Supreme Court in *Euclid* v. *Ambler* upheld the constitutionality of zoning and, in fact, Seymour I. Toll argues that suburban communities were among the first to adopt zoning ordinances, specifically to control the suburban growth of the 1920s.[14]

The last major wave of incorporations occurred during 1950-1960, again in response to large-scale suburbanization, which in this period included significant proportions of working-class households.[15] Many of these incorporations were partly motivated by the need to provide basic public services to entire new communities, but again it can be argued that incorporations of previously settled suburban communities were largely protective, and a means of achieving maximum local benefit from the development process.

Suburban Growth Policies in the 1960s

The most widely held belief is that suburbs, in reaction to change and growth pressures, use their powers to exclude undesirable residents through large lot zoning and stringent building codes that restrict high density development and that force up the cost of housing. This strategy is in part fiscally motivated; the large lot zoning produces a high status community with a strong residential tax while the resulting low density limits the demands for municipal services. The use of this approach to community development and fiscal strength is well documented,[16] and has been subject to intense public debate, mostly through challenges generated in the courts (for example, Mt. Laurel (1972), Ramapo (1972), Petaluma (1974), Madison Township (1976), and Arlington Heights (1977)).

The visibility of these court actions reinforces the prevailing notion that suburbs seek to maintain their semirural, low-density settlement patterns and to exclude low-income residents, and shows that the outcome of this exclusion has severe implications for the financing of local services. However, by focusing almost exclusively on population density and housing exclusion, this line of argument neglects the considerable decentralization of business and industry (beginning in at least the 1920s) which has been perhaps the most distinctive characteristic of suburban growth since 1950.[17] In particular, the emphasis on the fiscal benefits of low-density zoning, benefits which may in fact be overvalued,[18] neglects the substantial fiscal rewards that can accrue to communities from attracting industrial-commercial development. The defining characteristic of fiscal zoning is the attempt to maximize the tax base in relation to service demands. In fact, industrial and commercial land uses represent a greater concentration of taxable resources than most residential development. To the extent that the service demands of new business development can be regulated and to the extent that employees tend to find housing in other communities, industrial-commercial development has been found to be fiscally attractive to local jurisdictions.[19]

We believe that, despite the emphasis on large lot zoning, an attractive alternative to community development and fiscal well-being now exists, that is, a strategy based on commercial development. But the way in which communities respond to these alternate growth strategies is variable. Most importantly, it is likely that exclusionary residential zoning involves both fiscal and social status motivations, while the industrial-commercial development strategy is more explicitly a fiscal policy. The higher status value of residential development is due partly to the persistent suburban life-style ideal of the semirural estate. This value is challenged by the pressures for multi-family, more socially heterogeneous development that often accompany industrial-commercial development. As a result, affluent low density communities frequently exclude otherwise fiscally attractive development.[20] We hypothesize that, in fact, the use of local government powers to affect growth patterns may be more variable than the unidimensional drive for low density development the existing literature implies. We suggest that there may have been a shift over time in growth policies as more communities have sought the tax advantages of industrial-commercial development. This shift in local government policy is due both to the pressures and opportunities caused by the decentralization of metropolitan employment since 1950 and to the need to finance the increasing costs of local government. We hypothesize that more recently incorporated suburbs are the most likely to follow policies which allow increases in both employment and population density: (1) because they are less attached to the values associated with exclusive residential growth; (2) because many suburbs may have incorporated after 1950 specifically to protect an existing employment-related tax base, the resulting low taxes and existing supporting services may make these suburbs particularly attractive to new industry; and (3) because recently incorporated suburbs may be less densely developed and have more open land available for new construction, or be located in parts of the metropolis which are newly accessible to development.

It should be clear that the first two of these reasons reflect the outcomes of local policy, while the third represents ecological variables with which the period of incorporation may be associated. Clearly, therefore, the policy differences among suburbs cannot be tested without controls for ecological factors.

In this paper we provide a test of the hypotheses from the ecological literature, demonstrating the impact of age of suburb, distance from central city, economic function, and metropolitan "maturity" on change in employment activity and population density during 1960-1970. In addition, we test the effect of period of incorporation on suburbs' growth experience during the 1960s, controlling for the ecological factors. We propose that both political and ecological processes affect suburbanization. In particular, we hypothesize that recent incorporation will be positively associated with increases in both employment activity and density, and that this effect of a political process will act independently of the ecological forces which structure suburban growth.

Research Design

This research involves a time-series analysis of both population density and employment activity during 1960-1970. The sample on which this research is based includes 643 incorporated suburbs of at least 2500 population within the 1970 boundaries of SMSAs for which complete data on 1967 employment are available. In practice, because of census reporting constraints, this sample is heavily weighted toward larger communities, and includes only those with at least 450 manufacturing employees. The theoretical implication of this sampling bias is that we are unable to study the causes of growth in the many smaller communities in the urban fringe, and that the possible use of local government to create strictly residential enclaves—by both newer and older communities—cannot be reflected in these data. The sample does, however, represent the experiences of those suburbs which participated in the decentralization of employment during the postwar period, and it does allow us to determine the causes of differential development of those communities which housed the majority of suburban residents in 1970.

The major explanatory variables introduced below are straightforward. Period of incorporation has been divided into five categories: pre-1880, 1881-1910, 1911-1940, post-1940, and New England towns. The New England towns are communities which were formed before 1890 and share the governmental powers and responsibilities of other incorporated suburbs; they are treated as a separate category because of their rural pattern of land development in comparison with other suburbs. Distance from the central city is divided into four distance zones (contiguous, less than 10 miles, 10-20 miles, and over 20 miles). Metropolitan maturity (or age of SMSA) is indicated by year at which the central city reached 50,000 population; this measure is highly correlated with other components of Schnore's concept of maturity. Initial economic function is measured by a variant of the 1958/60 Employment/Residents (E/R) ratio. Finally, age of suburb is measured by the proportion of existing housing units built before 1939 as reported in the 1960 Census of Housing.

This last indicator was chosen with difficulty. In the ecological literature, age of community is often meant to indicate the condition of the housing stock and propensity to enter into transition from residential to more commercial land uses or to more densely settled residential development. The age of housing is a plausible measure of this concept.[21]

The measure of population density is total population divided by total land area as reported by the census in 1960 and 1970. In the present sample, few suburbs annexed significant land areas during the 1960-1970 decade, so that most change in population density resulted from population increases within the original 1960 boundaries. The measure of employment activity is a slightly modified version of the E/R ratio, the total number of employees and proprietors in manufacturing, wholesaling, and retail trade as reported by the Census of Business and Manufacturing (1958 and 1967) divided by the size of the local population. This measure is conceptually identical to the traditional E/R ratio and is highly correlated with it. The version used here was necessitated by the absence of census data on the employment of residents for a significant number of suburbs, thereby making the computation of the denominator of the traditional E/R ratio impossible.

The measurement of the E/R ratio for 1960 deserves comment. While complete data for all cases is available for the 1970 E/R ratio from the 1967 Census of Business and Manufacturing, such data is incomplete in the 1958 census. This absence of data results from Census Bureau restrictions on release of data that may violate confidentiality. Since we are concerned with change, 1960-1970, this lack of data presented a considerable problem—no base line for about one-third of our sample existed. Rather than delete these cases, we have employed a technique for approximating the number of sales and manufacturing workers in suburbs lacking employment data in 1958. The size of both sales and manufacturing work force is highly correlated to the population size of a community ($r = .81$ for sales force 1958 and population 1960; $r = .52$ for manufacturing 1958 and population). By regressing separately the size of 1958 sales force and the size of the 1958 manufacturing work force in 1960 population for all communities with complete data, we arrive at estimating equations to predict the size of the work force in communities lacking employment data. Thus we estimate the size in 1960 of a community's sales force to be $41.617 + .075$ (population 1960) and that of its manufacturing work force to be $43.629 + .120$ (population 1960). In this last estimation the maximum figure is set at 450, the size above which the U.S. census routinely reports figures on manufacturing work force. These estimates take the place of missing data in constructing the numerator of the variant of the E/R ratio employed here.

Results

Tables 13-1 and 13-2 report the results of a multiple regression analysis of the effects of our several explanatory variables on suburban development. In this analysis, the 1970 value of the dependent variable (population density or E/R ratio) is predicted by the independent variables, controlling for the 1960 value of the dependent variable. Through this procedure, we are studying causes of change in the dependent variable, defined as 1970 deviations from the values which would be predicted from scores on that variable in 1960.[22] Estimates of the coefficients of this model are subject to error due to autocorrelation problems, but Hibbs suggests that in research designs of the present type the effects of the independent variables are likely to be underestimated, introducing a *conservative* bias to our parameters.[23] We will discuss first the causes of change in population density, and then turn to the determinants of change in economic function.

Table 13-1
1970 Density Predicted by Ecological and Political Variables

	Unstandardized Regression Coefficient (B)	Standardized Regression Coefficient (Beta)	Standard Error of B	F Ratio
Ecological Variables				
Density 1960	.9268	.9119	.0174	2841.143
Distance from central city	−157.9249	−.0339	75.6508	4.358
Age of housing stock	−360.3231	−.0223	337.6163	1.139
Age of SMSA	−5.9346	−.0520	1.7861	11.040
E/R ratio 1960	525.7760	.0220	365.0821	2.074
Date of Incorporation				
Pre-1880 (N=252)[a]	11585.4044			
1881-1910 (N=195)	458.0380	.0503	164.1921	7.182
1911-1940 (N=106)	520.3589	.0461	226.2227	5.291
1941-1970 (N=56)	158.5865	.0107	279.1483	.323
New England Towns (N=34)	96.8338	.0052	300.6968	.104

[a]Pre-1880 suburbs are the "reference category" to which the other categories are compared.

Table 13-2

1970 Employment/Residents Ratio Predicted by Ecological and Political Variables

	Unstandardized Regression Coefficient (B)	Standardized Regression Coefficient (Beta)	Standard Error of B	F Ratio
Ecological Variables				
E/R 1960	.5156	.3077	.0639	65.172
Distance from Central City	−.0105	−.0322	.0132	.626
Age of Housing Stock	.1693	.1500	.0591	8.218
Age of SMSA	.0001	.0132	.0003	.113
Density 1960	−.0000	−.1271	.0000	8.835
Date of Incorporation				
Pre-1880	−.0418			
1881-1910	.0249	.0391	.0287	.752
1911-1940	−.0069	−.0088	.0396	.031
1941-1970	.1167	.1123	.0488	5.706
New England Towns	−.1006	−.0769	.0526	3.659

Population Density 1960-1970

The effect of employment concentration on density increase is not significant. This contrasts with results from previous decades, which showed that employing suburbs, while having a higher absolute density than residential suburbs, experienced the least growth of population. More consistent with previous findings, the effect of age of SMSA is highly significant; suburbs in newer metropolitan regions grew much less rapidly than those in older regions. This outcome is likley the result of two factors. First in newer SMSAs vacant land within the central cities is both available and attractive for new development. Second, the newer central cities are in states which provide them with considerable powers of annexation. Rapidly growing suburbs bordering on the central cities are likely to be candidates for annexation, thus depressing the average rate of growth for all suburbs in that region.

Consistent with part of the reasoning behind theories of centrifugal drift, there is a slight (but not significant) tendency for greater rates of increase in population density in newer suburbs with comparatively little old housing stock. But more important, increasing distance from the central city is negatively associated with density increase. Thus it appears that rather than a continued outward drift of urbanization into the suburbs, the decade of the 1960s produced an *infilling* of suburbia.[24]

Controlling for the effects of these ecological factors, there are significant differences among suburbs according to their period of incorporation. Among communities incorporated before 1880, there was an actual decline in average density, from 5,555 to 5,259 persons per square mile. Suburbs incorporated during the years 1880-1910 and 1911-1940 had the most rapid gains in density ($p < .001$), while there were relatively low increases in the New England towns and post-1940 suburbs. It is plausible that the stagnation of pre-1880 suburbs is due to their initial high density, but New England towns and newly incorporated suburbs had the lowest density levels of any type of suburb in 1960 (less than 3,000 per square mile for New England towns and less than 4,000 for newly incorporated suburbs, compared to an average density of more than 5,000 for the entire sample). Thus, it may be argued that their highly controlled growth rate during the 1960s represents their use of municipal government powers at least partly to restrict new development, and thwart normal processes of growth.

Economic Function 1960-1970

The determinants of change in economic function appear to be quite different from the factors which explain change in population density. The two ecological variables with the strongest effect on population density have no significant effect on change in economic function. Thus suburbs in newer regions experienced increases in E/R ratio equal to those of suburbs in older regions—a result which is surprising, in view of the argument that annexation powers of central cities in the South and West, and the relatively strong fiscal base of these cities, limit the incentive for suburbanization of employment. Also, there is only a slight tendency for greater increases in employment in suburbs closer to the central city, where there was also greater population growth.

As predicted by the Burgess model of transition from residential to employment land uses in older communities, suburbs with higher proportions of old housing stock experienced significantly higher gains in E/R ratio. Yet controlling for age of housing, new employment did not locate predominantly in the most densely populated suburbs. Rather increasing E/R ratio was negatively associated with initial population density, suggesting a spread of employment out of the most "urbanized" suburbs. This pattern may reflect the cheaper land costs in less densely populated communities, or the lower taxes and superior service levels which likely could be provided by communities with less residential service demands. This last interpretation introduces policy concerns of local governments not found in the ecological model.

Looking further at political effects, we find two political categories of suburbs experienced changes in economic function which were significantly different from the others. New England towns had relatively low increases in E/R ratio (from an average .14 in 1960 to .19 in 1970). More important, newly incorporated suburbs had by far the greatest increases in employment concentration, moving from an average E/R ratio of .09 in 1960 to .31 in 1970, as predicted in our theoretical discussion above.

Discussion

Following 1950, the decentralization of people and jobs from cities to the suburbs has been one of the most substantial demographic changes occurring in the United States. This process has been described as an urbanization of the suburbs, implying a gradual imposition of the high densities and employment concentrations found in the cities onto the semirural ideal of suburbia. The most influential conceptual framework which has been applied to suburbanization is the ecological model developed by the Chicago School and its descendants over the last four decades, a model predicting metropolitan development based largely on market forces creating a gradient in land prices.

Our research reported here has demonstrated a continued importance of the variables which are central to the ecological model. Geographic centrality, and the accessibility to the central city that it implies, is significantly associated with population growth and even somewhat linked to increasing employment concentration, despite the process of centrifugal drift noted in studies of city-suburban differentials. There is evidence of residential to employment transition in older suburbs, but with no corresponding increase in population density (possibly because much population growth in the 1960s was through construction of new single-family housing rather than conversion from single-family to multi-family dwellings). However, increase in E/R ratio was negatively associated with initial population density, and the determinants of change in density and economic function are distinctly different.

We have noted that some of the effects of ecological factors—particularly the employment growth in low-density communities—can be interpreted in terms of government fiscal strength and the provision of local services, which is an economic factor quite distinct from the free-market basis of ecological theories, and one more related to the structure of local government financing and taxes. In addition, our data show the importance of political determinants of suburban development above and beyond ecological effects. In particular, New England towns and suburbs incorporated after 1940 have experienced a development pattern which is significantly different from that of other suburbs, independent of their differences in centrality, age of housing, age of region, and initial density and economic function.

New England towns had relatively low increases in population density and far below average gains in employment. One might interpret this growth pattern in terms of the general outmigration of people and jobs from New England during the 1960s. We suggest that another factor which may be operating is the effort by these communities to maintain their nearly rural environment through local government action.

Suburbs incorporated after 1940 began the last decade with low population density and a predominantly residential land use distribution. During the 1960s, they remained relatively low in population density while attracting considerable growth in local employment. This development pattern contradicts the normal market considerations which link employment with high-density residential development (resulting from the high land values associated with each). Our findings, while tentative, suggest a breaking of this traditional pattern. As noted by Toner, local government—through the use of its legal authority and land use controls—can operate as a monopoly force to contradict the free-market process.[25] We suggest that the newly incorporated suburbs operated in such a fashion during the 1960s, working to concentrate the fiscal resources based on employment land uses while limiting the in-migration of persons. This process was successful because of the convergence of the interests of these local governments in successful fiscal zoning with the desire of industry to locate in areas with a strong fiscal base.[26]

Thus, the study of suburbia, focused mainly on ecological processes, and concentrating on market forces determining land values, seems to be somewhat less than adequate. Political considerations can affect these "natural" growth processes. We know that at the current time, these political forces do operate to institutionalize differences in a pattern of "separate and unequal" development.[27] But if government power can be used to create fiscal advantages for successful suburbs and fiscal burdens for others, and can be used, in general, to create inequalities, it should also be possible to use those same government powers to violate market and ecological forces to further desirable social conditions, and to create greater equality in metropolitan development.

Notes

1. E.W. Burgess, "The Growth of the City," in R.E. Park, E.W. Burgess, and R.D. McKenzie, eds., *The City* (Chicago: University of Chicago Press, 1925).

2. Leslie Kish, "Differentiation in Metropolitan Areas," *American Sociological Review* 19 (1954):288-98; Edgar M. Hoover and Raymond Vernon, *Anatomy of a Metropolis* (Garden City, N.Y.: Doubleday, 1962).

3. Hal Winsborough, "City Growth and City Structure," *Journal of Regional Science* 4 (1962):32-49; Leo F. Schnore, "The Functions of Metropolitan Suburbs," *American Journal of Sociology* 61 (1956):453-58; Avery M. Guest, "Employment and Suburban Residential Character," unpublished paper (Seattle: University of Washington Center for Studies in Demography and Ecology, 1976).

4. Avery M. Guest, "Neighborhood Life Cycles and Social Studies," *Economic Geography* 50 (1974):228-243.

5. Basil G. Zimmer, "The Urban Centrifugal Drift," in Amos Hawley and Vincent Rock, eds., *Metropolitan America* (New York: John Wiley & Sons,

1975). For an earlier discussion of the phenomenon, see Amos Hawley, *Human Ecology: A Theory of Community Structure* (New York: The Ronald Press Co., 1950).

6. Brian Berry, James W. Simmons, and Robert Tennant, "Urban Population Densities: Structure and Change," *Geographical Review* 53 (1963):389-405; Bruce Newling, "Urban Growth and Spatial Structure: Mathematical Models and Empirical Evidence," *Geographical Review* 56 (1966):213-25.

7. Leo F. Schnore, "Satellites and Suburbs," *Social Forces* 36 (1957):121-27; "The Socio-Economic Status of Cities and Suburbs," *American Sociological Review* 28 (1963).

8. Leo F. Schnore, "The Timing of Metropolitan Decentralization: A Contribution to the Debate," *Journal of the American Institute of Planners* 25 (1959):200-06; *Class and Race in Cities and Suburbs* (Chicago: Markham, 1972).

9. Committee for Economic Development, *Reshaping Government in Metropolitan Areas* (New York: Committee for Economic Development, 1970).

10. Robert C. Wood, *1400 Governments* (Cambridge, Mass.: Harvard University Press, 1961).

11. Robert D. Warren, *Government in Metropolitan Regions: A Reappraisal of Fractionated Political Organization* (Davis, Calif.: Institute of Governmental Affairs, University of California, 1966).

12. Avery M. Guest, "American Suburban Development" (Seattle: University of Washington Center for Studies in Demography and Ecology, 1977).

13. Ira Kaufman and Leo F. Schnore, "Municipal Annexations and Suburbanization, 1969-1970," CED Working Paper 75-4 (Madison, Wisc.: Center for Demography and Ecology, 1975).

14. Seymour I. Toll, *Zoned America* (New York: Grossman Publishers, 1969), pp. 192-93.

15. Bennett Berger, *Working-Class Suburbs* (Berkeley, Calif.: University of California Press, 1969).

16. James G. Coke and John J. Gargan, *Fragmentation in Land Use Planning and Control* (Washington, D.C.: National Commission on Urban Problems, Research Report #18, 1969); Michael N. Danielson, "Differentiation, Segregation, and Political Fragmentation in the American Metropolis," in A.F. Keir Nash, ed., *Governance and Population*, vol. 4 of Research Reports of the Commission on Population Growth and the American Future (Washington, D.C.: Government Printing Office, 1972), pp. 143-76; Anthony Downs, *Opening Up the Suburbs* (New Haven, Conn.: Yale University Press, 1973); Michelle J. White, "Fiscal Zoning in Fragmented Metropolitan Areas," in Edwin S. Mills and Wallace E. Oates, eds., *Fiscal Zoning and Land Use Controls* (Lexington, Mass.: D.C. Heath, 1975).

17. Douglass Commission, *Building the American City* (Washington, D.C.: U.S. Government Printing Office, 1969); John D. Kasarda, "The Changing Occupational Structure of the American Metropolis," in Barry Schwartz, ed., *The Changing Face of the Suburbs* (Chicago: University of Chicago Press, 1976).

18. Marion Clawson and Peter Hall, *Planning and Urban Growth* (Baltimore: The Johns Hopkins Press, 1973).

19. Wood, *1400 Governments*; Dick Netzer, *Economics of the Property Tax* (Washington, D.C.: Brookings Institution, 1966); Richard C. Hill, "Separate and Unequal: Governmental Inequality in the Metropolis," *American Political Science Review* 68 (1974):157-68; James W. Hughes and Franklin James, "The Dispersion of Employment: Planning Implication," in James W. Hughes, ed., *New Dimensions in Urban Planning* (New Brunswick, N.J.: Center for Urban Policy Research, 1974).

20. John R. Logan, "Industrialization and the Stratification of Cities in Suburban Regions," *American Journal of Sociology* 82 (1976):333-48.

21. Winsborough, "City Growth."

22. George Bohrnstedt, "Observations on the Measurement of Change," in Edgar Borgatta, ed., *Sociological Methodology 1969* (San Francisco: Chandler Publishing Company, 1969).

23. Douglas A. Hibbs, Jr., "Problems of Statistical Estimation and Causal Inference in Time-Series Regression Models," in H. Costner, ed., *Sociological Methodology 1973-74* (San Francisco: Jossey-Bass, 1974).

24. Guest, "Employment and Suburban Residential Character."

25. William J. Toner, "Introduction to Nongrowth Economics," in Earl Finkler and David L. Peterson, eds., *Nongrowth Planning Strategies* (New York: Praeger Publishers, 1974).

26. John R. Logan, "Industrialization and the Stratification of Cities"; Lawrence Sagar, "Tight Little Islands: Exclusionary Zoning, Equal Protection and the Indigent," *Stanford Law Review* 4 (1970); Robert W. Burchell, David Listokin, and Franklin James, "Exclusionary Zoning: Pitfalls of the Regional Remedy," in James W. Hughes, ed., *New Dimensions in Urban Planning: Growth Controls* (New Brunswick, N.J.: Center for Urban Policy Research, 1974).

27. Hill, "Separate and Unequal."

14 Population Policy Implementation: Local Growth Management Strategies

Marilyn W. Whisler

Local government officials in rapidly growing sections of the United States are increasingly addressing the population policy issue by considering a variety of growth management strategies. This paper examines the context in which the policy formulation of alternatives has occurred and discusses difficulties and questions encountered in the implementation of these strategies. The factors contributing to the consideration of policy alternatives are explored.

In a recent survey on environmental management and local government, land use and growth were rated as the two most severe environmental problems facing communities.[1] The previous pattern has been that of the state government delegating this policy responsibility to local governments. The standard local mechanisms used for managing growth were zoning ordinances, subdivision regulations, and master plans. The last decade has been one of increased concern about environmental issues; interest groups have moved aggressively in this policy arena, and many political actors involved in environmental issues also have been involved in the formulation of growth management strategies.[2] The political climates at national, state, and local levels have been more receptive than ever to the definition of growth issues.

Federal Activity

Recently adopted and proposed federal legislation has increased policy activity and functioned as an inducement to local governments to consider growth management strategies. The Housing Act of 1954 provided for the first broadly based urban planning program. Under the Section 701 program, metropolitan planning commissions were eligible for grants, and in 1966 councils of governments (COGs) were encouraged to seek 701 planning assistance. OMB Circular A-95 gave to regional planning agencies and COGs the authority to "review and comment" on key proposed federal projects, including those assisted by federal grants.

A new source of federal aid for general planning assistance and coastal zone management programs is available to thirty-four states under the Coastal Zone Management Act of 1972. Under the Federal Water Pollution Control Act Amendments of 1972, grants are available for areawide waste treatment management plans. The Section 208 grants really involve general planning and land use controls since almost all uses of land cause some discharge.[3]

181

None of the bills considered by Congress in this decade with an explicit concern for national land-use policy has passed. Early in 1970 Senator Henry Jackson introduced a bill proposing the creation of a national planning council to establish national land use goals and priorities and to encourage coordination or federal activities having an impact on land development. State planning was to be encouraged through available grants with the provision for a reduction in federal grants for certain programs if a state failed to submit an acceptable plan by a specified date.

The Land Use Policy and Planning Assistance Act passed the Senate in 1973, after several amendments imposing sanctions on noncomplying states were defeated.[4] However, the act was not adopted by the House. The act would have required some type of direct state role in land use decisions that affect areas of critical environmental concern and large scale projects that affect more than a local area. In 1974 similar legislation was passed by the Senate but defeated on a procedural vote before it could be debated on the House floor.[5] The consideration of such legislation has had an impact on the quantity and quality of the land-use control activity at the state and local level.

The Housing and Community Development Act of 1974 provides for changes in federal planning assistance; a land-use element and a housing element are required in project applications. Planning organizations are to consider the intensity and timing of growth and are to "integrate all existing land-use policies . . . and planning activities impacting land use." Communities are expected to confront the question of balance between environmental concerns and social equity concerns as they try to meet simultaneously the objectives of satisfying urgent community development needs and giving "maximum feasible priority" to low- and moderate-income families.

Initial assessment of the program suggests that local community development programs are placing a limited emphasis on low- and moderate-income families. An interpretation of policy issues based on the first year findings of the National Association of Housing and Rehabilitation Office (NAHRO) Community Development Monitoring Project found "a notable shift in emphasis in the first year's experience from low- and moderate-income tracts to moderate- and middle-income tracts."[6] In addition to the continuation activities in the categorical programs, local community activity choices centered on rehabilitation loans and grants, public works, public facilities, and site improvements.

State Activity

In the last decade, there have been major changes in state-local relations in the area of land use and growth policy.[7] State proposals have involved new partnership roles for states and their local governments, with varying degrees of state versus local authority and responsibility in the partnership. The general thrust has been to place a greater responsibility on state governments to exert authority directly or indirectly over land use policy decisions having more than a local impact. Those states which have the most to lose ecologically and economically (namely, Florida, Colorado, Oregon, Hawaii, Vermont) through deterioration of their environments have been the most active in formulating controlling legislation.[8]

Since land-use planning and management reemerged as an issue requiring some form of state participation, a number of approaches have been proposed and adopted. A method gaining acceptance is that by which local governments are required to develop comprehensive plans based on guidelines which have been established by the state. By adopting this procedure, states give local governments the flexibility to plan for identified state concerns as well as unique local goals. If the local government fails to act, the state usually can develop the comprehensive plan for the locality. States which have adopted variations of this approach are: Colorado, Florida, Idaho, Maine, Maryland, Montana, Nebraska, Nevada, Oregon, Vermont, Virginia, and Wyoming.

The Florida Local Government Comprehensive Planning Act requires that all counties and municipalities adopt a comprehensive plan for future growth by 1 July 1979.[9] City and county governments were permitted considerable flexibility in deciding what group or person could be designated as the "local planning agency."[a] The required elements in the comprehensive plan are the following: land use, traffic circulation, conservation, recreation and open space, housing, intergovernmental relations, utilities, sewage, drainage, and water. There are other specified elements which may be included at the option of the local government, such as: mass transit, aviation facilities, off-street parking, bike paths, public services, public buildings, community design, area redevelopment, safety, and historical preservation. Although the legislation specifies certain required elements, it does not establish any firm guidelines for the content of those elements.

The plan is to be submitted to various government agencies for review, but each government clearly has the right to adopt whatever plan it deems best, regardless of the comments or objections of those agencies. The sanction for noncompliance is the possible withholding of state revenue or tax funds in the amount necessary to pay for formulating a plan.[10]

Regional mechanisms represent another approach. California created the Coastal Zone Conservation Commission and six regional commissions. In addition to permissions obtained from agencies of the state, local, and county governments, permits also are required from the commission for a zone which extends three miles out to sea and a thousand yards inland. Vermont has a state environmental board and seven district commissions which function under the board as a local hearing body for initial applications under the permit issuing procedure.

[a]The agency may be a local planning commission, the planning department, or some other instrumentality, such as a council of local governments.

The American Law Institute has prepared a Model Land Development Code which will likely increase the role of the state in local growth policy. The model code gives that state land planning agency the power to intervene in local land development regulation. In the code, state intervention is provided for when necessary or appropriate because of the potential impact of some development activity. The ALI code identifies three specific land uses that properly require state intervention: (a) land around major growth-inducing public investments, (b) developments with potential impact on critical environmental or natural resources, and (c) developments of regional or statewide importance.

Two complementary methods of state review of local land development control powers have been introduced—first, designation and control of areas of critical state concern, and second, state review of "developments of regional impact." Sections of the state may be designated as areas of critical state concern because of environmental or ecological significance. The state land development agency may define categories of development which, because of their size, nature, or effect on surrounding land, constitute "developments of regional impact." The Florida Environmental Land and Water Management Act of 1972 is based on the American Law Institute Model.

One of the most interesting innovations in control techniques is that found in the Colorado legislation, which contains substantive guidelines for the administration of controls in areas, and over activities, of state interest. The state land-use commission may adopt guidelines for the designation of areas and activities of state interest. However, local governments both designate these areas and activities and adopt guidelines for their administration. Although the state agency makes recommendations, the affected local government can reject the state's proposed designations.

The question of distribution of population within the state is being addressed by the state of California. On 23 May 1977, Governor Edmund Brown, Jr. released his urban growth plan which would tend to hold the state's future development close to the boundaries of existing cities. Proposed incentives include giving cities and their closest suburbs the priority when doling out allocations of state water and of state and federal funds for roads and sewers, and a streamlined building permit process for industries that would choose to build in areas designated by state and local governments as the most appropriate sites for new industries.

The more active role of the state raises questions for local officials about their own roles. Much of the state legislation represents an attempt by the state to force local governments to take action in areas in which they previously have been reluctant to act.

Dissatisfaction with Standard Mechanisms

Professionals involved with land regulation, cognizant of the need for providing means of control that permit more individualized treatment than past strategies, and dissatisfied with the standard regulatory mechanisms, have searched for new techniques. The traditional regulatory techniques are failing to inhibit undesirable development. Critics of the traditional mechanisms charge that they are based on unrealistic assumptions.[11]

The critics also charge that many land-use tools escalate housing costs. The most notable of these devices are: density controls which increase the cost of land per dwelling unit, minimum floor area requirements, requirements for accessories such as garages regardless of market requirements, architectural controls, and administrative delays that add time and increase the capital costs.[12]

The new strategies have as major objectives the inducement of particular types and mixes of development and the provision of public amenities in connection with construction activity. These approaches include: "(1) stimulating coordinated development of large areas in multiple ownership rather than lot-by-lot development; (2) providing for more flexible administrative reaction to development proposals rather than relying on detailed pre-stated regulation; and (3) requiring developers to contribute land or money, or to undertake particular development, as a condition for desired permits."[13]

The following evolutionary changes can be identified. Local governments are moving in the direction of the English system, one of individualized regulation of most proposed development. Various public costs created by development are being placed on developers who normally shift these costs to consumers. Public officials are "seeking to stimulate large-area development which can be more carefully designed to reflect higher levels of amenities and to provide more stimulating relationships between different uses."[14]

Growth Management Techniques

One of the specific techniques used is development district zoning.[15] The land is divided into development zones, based on readiness for development; the provision of capital and service improvements can be coordinated with defined developed zones.

A "development timing ordinance" is used in Ramapo, New York; it requires that anyone who wishes to use land for residential development must obtain a special use permit. The permit is granted only if standards are met for minimum facilities and services available for the new development, and the ordinance sets out standards in the form of a point system.[16]

Petaluma, California has adopted a widely publicized residential control system. The development policy of the city establishes a quota of new residential units per year, and the city's land use plan specifies the type, location, and density of all future development. Each year applications for development allotments are ranked by a Residential Development Evaluation Board; it makes recommendations to the city council which has the authority to award the allotments.

An approach to the problem of extensive costs arising from growth is the requirement that developers pay money or contribute land to compensate for extra public facilities resulting from new housing construction. It is becoming increasingly common to require land, or money in lieu of land, for parks and for schools. A slightly different method of obtaining developer contributions to the public costs of development is to levy some form of fee or charge for services provided. San Jose, California uses a two-part development tax, a construction tax on all new development and a real property conveyance tax on property transfers.

A common short-range approach is the imposition of a moratorium on building permits, water and sewer connections, or requests for rezoning. Moratoria can be used by local officials to analyze alternatives and to develop effective programs or to postpone the resolution of a problem. The strategy is frequently chosen as a result of a crisis; there is little evidence that moratoria work to discourage the interest of developers.[17]

The sewer moratorium has emerged as the favorite of the ad hoc legal mechanisms used by local and state governments to control complicated environmental, economic, and equity problems.[18] Local governments may choose to upgrade treatment systems and receive the promise of federal and state assistance; or they may refuse to cooperate. The no-action alternative has been chosen by some communities as a form of fiscal zoning and by others as a means of achieving no growth or severely controlled growth.

The legal basis for imposing a moratorium varies with the level of government. Local governments usually justify intervention through the police power; states use potential violations of state quality standards. The vast majority of moratoria since 1972 have been applied by local governments to suburban and suburban fringe areas. More than 60 percent of the moratoria have been applied in Florida, New Jersey, California, and Ohio.[19]

Water supply was a key factor in determining the limitations taken in Morro Bay, California, Westminster, Colorado, and Pinellas County, Florida. Morro Bay and Pinellas County limit access to water facilities. The growth ordinance in Westminster provides for water conservation incentives. The building permit formula provides that builders may have additional permits for water conservation devices and for water-conserving landscaping.

Some communities have investigated growth controls designed to produce an optimum population for their areas. The city government in Boca Raton, Florida decreed that no more than 100,000 people would be entitled to settle in that city and chose to achieve that goal through a limit on the number of dwelling units.

The official city policy of San Diego is not to limit growth but to determine which locations are developed and built up first, on the basis of a five-tier designation of city land. Incentives are offered to developers for the first two tiers; a developer building in the third tier will have to pay for development costs; the fourth tier is not considered necessary for development during the next eighteen years; the fifth tier is classified as land that should never be developed. The city is emphasizing growth where city services are already available, as well as redistribution of development for a better balance between old and new sections.

The development rights transfer technique is being used in St. George, Vermont. With this tool

zoning ordinances allocate to each parcel of land a certain potential for development. The development rights transfer process permits the transfer of unused development rights of one parcel to another within a defined district in exchange for the payment of a fee as determined by market value. Under the DRT process owners of land designated for open space or land on which older buildings are located can sell their development rights to other property owners.[20]

New Jersey is using the technique for a model farmland preservation project. The state may buy development rights from farmers in four townships. Farmers who participate will still own their land and pay property taxes on it after they sell their development rights. Once the state buys the rights, it will retire them and permanently hold the land for farm use. Money for the project comes from the state's Green Acres Fund, aimed at keeping open space in the state.[21]

Interest in growth management has coincided with interest in environmental protection. Environmental impact assessments are now required by many local governments.[22] Criteria used to determine whether a statement must be prepared include: public or private origin, dollar value, number of dwelling units, and type of action required by the local government. The California Environmental Quality Act requires an impact statement for projects within a city or county which could have a significant effect on the environment.

Among the most popular recent innovations are planned unit developments (PUD). The PUD alternative is a means of providing a mixture of residential, commercial, and industrial land uses; unified development control on a greater than single lot basis; and consolidated administrative review of specific development proposals.

It involves specific plans that require administrative discretion and does away with the lot-by-lot approach found in standard zoning and subdivision regulations. The technique can be used as an incentive for better development by enabling complete schemes to be worked out and approved ... Developers typically are permitted to develop under PUD provisions when the proposed development exceeds a minimum number of acres, five for example, or a minimum number of housing units—perhaps 20. Further, PUDs are included within a zoning ordinance but usually are not mapped districts.[23]

Babcock and Bosselman argue that an ordinance that permits Planned Unit Development is the most convenient means of ensuring that high-quality housing can be made available at lowest cost to the residents and with maximum fiscal benefits to the local government.[24]

Problem Perception and Adoption

The adoption of growth management strategies can be viewed as a response to problems perceived by decision makers. The types of strategies chosen can be expected to vary with the nature of the perceived problem. Environmental variables are critical in shaping the problems encountered by policy makers.

Residents often view differing housing types and higher densities as threats to the structure of the community, as disruptive of the status quo, and as a disturbance to existing life styles. In the public's mind, there is a seeming connection between growth and higher costs, inconvenience, environmental damage, and lower quality public service.[25]

The PUD alternative is particularly attractive to legislative bodies politically concerned with tax rates and balanced development. It is viewed as an excellent merchandising vehicle for townhouses, a vehicle which provides the fiscal packaging of a variety of housing forms which otherwise are anathema to suburbs with rising tax rates. It permits a local government to control the staging and timing of local development while maintaining an essentially stable tax base. PUDs have served a dichotomous market, providing primary housing within commuting range of existing employment concentrations and housing for the recreation/retirement market. The high urban growth states and the states with warm or specialized climatic features have been the most receptive to the Planned Unit Development alternative.[26]

Growth management strategies have been a significant issue of local politics, occupying part of the campaign platforms of candidates for local office in recent years. The 1975 San Diego mayoral election was a classic confrontation between two articulate candidates with growth as the issue. The winner linked his controlled growth philosophy to a "hold the line" position on taxes.

An issue often raised in such campaigns is whether or not the community can afford a no-growth future. However, it is recognized increasingly that population growth does not automatically bring with it desirable economic growth for most residents. Furthermore, studies indicate that whether or not economic growth at the local level leads to increased economic welfare for all citizens of the community depends upon the specific economic and demographic characteristics of that growth.[27]

Other research suggests that it is useful to make a distinction between economic problem perception and population problem perception in seeking to understand the attitudes of officials toward the adoption of growth management strategies. In a study of attitudes toward the Florida Local Government Comprehensive Planning Act of 1975, a state policy to be implemented by local officials, this writer found that perception of population growth as a problem at the local level was related to support for the planning legislation, while perception of economic growth as a problem was not.[28] An assessment of attitudes toward an increased role for the state in population distribution policy found those concerned about population growth supportive of an increased state role while those concerned about economic growth at the state and local levels tended to oppose an increased state role. They may fear that state action would discourage economic growth.

Local officials who are the most dissatisfied with present local strategies seem to be the most supportive of increasing the responsibility and leadership of state and regional actors in this policy domain. They appear to lack confidence in the capability of local government to respond appropriately to the needs they perceive.[29]

Problem perception of local officials can be influenced greatly by planning consultants. For example, the utilization of professional expertise in an advisory and evaluative fashion either prior to or subsequent to a developer's inquiry appears to be an important factor in local acceptance of planned unit development legislation.[30] Local governments usually adopt this alternative after a developer has assembled land with an option to purchase and has questioned a government about possible approval of this innovative development idea.

There is a need to investigate further how and why certain policy options are chosen as a government's response to specific problems. Research in Florida indicates that local officials who perceive population growth as a problem and those who want to attract more industry favorably assess the land dedication strategy as an effective mechanism.[31] Local economic problem perception and interest in industry are related to a favorable assessment of PUDs.

Implementation Difficulties

Local governments are at present the key implementors of population distribution policies, whether those policies are formulated at the federal, state, regional, or local level. The experience of governments in implementing growth management strategies suggests important obstacles to be considered by those making policy choices.

Challenges in the judicial system constitute an important obstacle. The grounds used for these challenges depend on the nature of the strategy in question as well as the specific circumstances. Major issues raised include the exclusionary effects of some strategies, appropriate compensation for the "taking" of land, and the right to travel from one community to another.

The impact of the judiciary on growth management strategies is unclear. Consistent patterns are difficult to discern. There appears to be a growing split between federal and state courts in the treatment of land use cases. Federal courts have relied heavily on the presumption of legislative validity afforded governmental actions and have placed a heavy burden on challenges to overcome that presumption. It is the state courts which are increasingly examining the intent and effect of local government actions, reviewing in detail the land use decision-making process. In New Jersey and Pennsylvania, state courts have handed down decisions directing local governments to issue permits to plaintiff-developers. In Pennsylvania a municipality with a zoning ordinance excluding apartment buildings found its ordinance overturned in the courts. When the municipality then created an apartment district without including the plaintiff's land, and the plaintiff sought to compel issuance of a permit, the government announced that it would condemn the property for a park. The issuance of a permit was eventually ordered by the state supreme court. In New Jersey a municipality was ordered by the state's supreme court to approve a planned unit development proposal which includes moderate-income housing units.[32]

Although the above examples are ones in which the courts dealt with housing allocation questions, efforts to show injury appear to be far more successful in environmental cases than in housing equity cases.[33] "Whether courts can find analytically satisfactory ways of dealing with the new problems thrust upon them by challenges to local growth management is, at best, an open question. Thus far, the judicial responses have been inconsistent and uneven."[34]

Another obstacle faced in implementation is that growth management strategies often work to deter or discourage undesirable development but often do not provide sufficient inducement to attract the type of development a government wants. There is a strong possibility that the trend toward individualized treatment of development applications will reduce further the chances that specific strategies will acquire a reputation for attracting certain kinds of development.

The pattern of intergovernmental relations existing in a given area provides the environment for the implementation of growth strategies. The cooperation of adjacent governments may be essential for an effective policy. However, if the pattern has been one of intense conflict, experience suggests that the adoption of new growth policies is unlikely to increase cooperation unless there is a strong incentive involved.[35] Economies of scale in planning for a very large development may provide such an incentive. There is a need for more extensive study of what happens when governments in the same metropolitan market adopt different growth management strategies. Likewise, the consequences of a city and a county utilizing significantly different planning methodologies need to be explored.

If there has not been sufficient mobilization of support for a newly adopted strategy, the implementation process is particularly susceptible to organized opposition designed to alter the policy's effects. The plan to protect a portion of Brandywine Creek's watershed in the Philadelphia area failed because of a lack of local support. Local property owners and officials were upset by the proposal and responded by creating a new regional planning commission whose primary goal was the defeat of the plan.[36]

The long-range effects of these new growth management strategies are also unknown. The costs imposed by growth management apply to some individuals and business firms and not others. Some of those costs can be shifted to other individuals and business firms. It is important to discover how the imposition of those costs produces changes in the consumption of goods and services.

Planned unit developments appear to provide for the rapid infusion of middle class housing into the outer extremities of the metropolitan housing supply. Time-series research is needed to address the question of whether such PUDs will serve as catalysts for the drain of economic activities from the older urban centers similar to the drain of the white middle class populace. Similarly, development timing ordinances have been criticized as being exclusionary in class and race terms. Many of the solutions posed to the exclusionary problem take the recognition of the needs of the region as a minimum base from which to proceed. Those leading court decisions striking down local exclusionary zoning policies have generally adopted the perspective of regionalism. There is disagreement about the impact of the regional approach to considering land use decisions. Burchell, Listokin, and James argue that the regional approach may support rather than attack existing restrictive practices.[37] How do the actual consequences of a strategy coincide with the claimed effects?

Summary

The formulation of population distribution alternatives has occurred in a context of increasing federal and state activity in this policy arena and increasing dissatisfaction with traditional regulatory techniques. Local governments are adopting a more individualized regulation of development and are encouraging the provision of public amenities in connection with construction activity. The types of growth management strategies chosen vary with the nature of growth problems perceived by decision makers. Implementation difficulties and selected research needs have been identified.

Notes

1. International City Management Association, *Environmental Management and Local Government*, sponsored by the Washington Environmental Research Center, U.S. Environmental Protection Agency, 1973.

2. R. Robert Linowes and Don T. Allensworth, *The States and Land-Use Control* (New York: Praeger Publishers, 1975).

3. Donald G. Hagman, *1976 Supplement to Public Planning and Control*

of Urban and Land Development (St. Paul, Minn.: West Publishing Company, 1976).

4. Eric C. Freund, "Land Development Management: Revolution and Evolution," *The Municipal Yearbook*, 1974 (Washington, D.C.: International City Management Association, 1974), pp. 277-87.

5. Norman Beckman, "National Urban Growth Policy: 1974 Congressional and Executive Action," *Journal of the American Institute of Planners* 41 (July 1975):234-49.

6. Mary K. Nenno, "First Year Community Development Grant Experience: What Does It Mean?" *Journal of Housing* 33 (April 1976), 172. This interpretation of policy issues is based upon the report entitled, "A Summary of Major Findings of NAHRO's Community Development Monitoring Project," prepared by Robert L. Ginsburg, Deena R. Sosson, and Mary K. Nenno.

7. Fred Bosselman and David Callies, *The Quiet Revolution in Land Use Control* (Washington, D.C.: U.S. Government Printing Office, 1971).

8. Elizabeth Haskell and Victoria Price, *State Environmental Management: Case Studies of Nine States* (New York: Praeger Publishers, 1973).

9. *Florida Local Government Comprehensive Planning Act Statutes* (1975), chapters 75-257.

10. For a study of the first year implementation effort, see M.W. Whisler, "Implementation of the Florida Local Government Comprehensive Planning Act of 1975," (Paper prepared for delivery at the 1976 Annual Meeting of the Florida Political Science Association, May 7-8, Sarasota, Florida).

11. Dukeminier and Stapleton, "The Zoning Board of Adjustments: A Case Study in Misrule," *Kentucky Law Journal* 50 (1962):218ff.

12. Richard F. Babcock and Fred P. Bosselman, *Exclusionary Zoning: Land Use Regulation and Housing in the 1970s* (New York: Praeger Publishers, 1973), p. 17.

13. I. Michael Heyman, "Innovative Land Regulation and Comprehensive Planning," in Norman Marcus and Marilyn W. Groves (eds.), *The New Zoning: Legal, Administrative, and Economic Concepts and Techniques* (New York: Praeger Publishers, 1970), p. 23.

14. Ibid., p. 25.

15. Steve Carter, Kendall Bert, and Peter Nobert, "Controlling Growth: A Challenge for Local Government," *The Municipal Yearbook*, 1974 (Washington, D.C.: International City Management Association, 1974), pp. 265-76.

16. For a discussion of Ramapo's approach, see Randall W. Scott, ed., *Management and Control of Growth* (Washington, D.C.: Urban Land Institute, 1975), vol. 2, pp. 1-119.

17. ICMA, *Environmental Management and Local Government.*

18. Michael R. Greenberg, "A Commentary on the Sewer Moratorium as a Piecemeal Remedy for Controlling Development," in James W. Hughes, ed., *New Dimensions of Urban Planning: Growth Controls* (New Brunswick, N.J.: Center for Urban Policy Research, 1974), p. 189.

19. Ibid., p. 193.

20. Michael E. Gleeson, Ian T. Ball, Stephen P. Chinn, Robert C. Einsweiler, Robert H. Freilich, and Patrick Meagher, *Urban Growth Management Systems: An Evaluation of Policy-Related Research* (Chicago: American Society of Planning Officials, 1975), p. 38.

21. For a discussion of transfer of development rights, see Steven R. Woodbury, "Transfer of Development Rights: A New Tool for Planners," *Journal of the American Institute of Planners* 41 (January 1975):3-14.

22. Kenneth Pearlman, "State Environmental Policy Acts: Local Decision Making and Land Use Planning," *Journal of the American Institute of Planners*, 43 (January 1977):42-53.

23. Gleeson, et al., *Urban Growth*, p. 39.

24. Babcock and Bosselman, *Exclusionary Zoning*, p. 90.

25. Scott, *Management*, vol. 1, pp. 6-7.

26. Robert W. Burchell, *Planned Unit Development: New Communities American Style* (New Brunswick, N.J.: Rutgers University Press, 1972).

27. Earl Finkler, William Toner, and Frank Popper, *Urban Nongrowth: City Planning for People* (New York: Praeger Publishers, 1976).

28. M.W. Whisler, "Growth Management Strategies: Attitudes of Local Officials," (Paper prepared for delivery at the 1976 Annual Meeting of the Southwestern Political Science Association, April 7-10, Dallas, Texas).

29. Ibid.

30. Burchell, *Planned Unit.*

31. Whisler, "Growth Management."

32. Frank Schnidman, "Legal Notes," *Urban Land*, 36 (June 1977):26.

33. Mary E. Brooks, "Commentary—The Equity Concept in Land Use Decisions," in Robert W. Burchell and David Listokin, eds., *Future Land Use: Energy, Environmental, and Legal Constraints* (New Brunswick, N.J.: Center for Urban Policy Research, 1975), p. 109.

34. David L. Kirp, "Growth Management, Zoning, Public Policy, and the Courts," *Policy Analysis*, 2 (Summer 1976):434.

35. Whisler, "Implementation."

36. Ann L. Strong, *Private Property and the Public Interest: The Brandywine Experience* (Baltimore: Johns Hopkins University Press, 1975).

37. Robert W. Burchell, David Listokin, and Franklin J. James, "Exclusionary Zoning: Pitfalls of the Regional Remedy," in Hughes, *New Dimensions*, pp. 31-61.

Index

Index

About the Editors and Contributors

Neal E. Cutler is associate professor of political science, and laboratory chief of the Social Policy Laboratory, at the University of Southern California. His research interests focus upon age and generational patterns of social and political behavior, demographic parameters of political change, and political gerontology. He is co-author of *Aging, Social Policy, and Politics* (Brooks/Cole, 1978), and his articles have appeared in the *American Political Science Review, the Gerontologist, Youth and Society, Public Opinion Quarterly*, the *Urban and Social Change Review*, the *Annals*, the *Journal of Peace Research*, and the *Handbook of Aging and the Social Sciences*.

Thomas R. Dye (Ph.D., University of Pennsylvania) is professor of government at Florida State University. He has served as president of the Policy Studies Organization and president of the Southern Political Science Association. He is the author of *Understanding Public Policy, Who's Running America?, Politics in States and Communities, The Irony of Democracy, Politics, Economics and the Public, Policy Analysis*, and other books and articles on American government and public policy.

Jason L. Finkle, a political scientist, is professor of population planning at the University of Michigan. His research and writings have been mainly concerned with the politics and administration of developing nations and with comparative population policy.

John A. Garcia (Ph.D., Florida State University) is assistant professor of political science at the University of Arizona. He is serving as editorial member of *American Politics Quarterly* and vice chairman of the Committee for the Status of Chicanos in the Western Political Science Association. He is author of articles in *Atisbos, Journal of Health and Social Behavior*, and other chapters and articles on urban policy and minority politics.

R. Kenneth Godwin is associate professor and chairman of political science at Oregon State University. His research interests are political behavior, political economy, and public policy. He is coauthor, editor or coeditor of *Psyche and Demos* (1977); *Land Use Control* (1977); *Comparative Policy Analysis* (1975); *Research in the Politics of Population* (1972); and *Political Science in Population Studies*, (1972). His articles have appeared in the *American Political Science Review, Journal of Politics, Comparative International Development, Journal of Developing Areas*, and *Environmental Law Review*.

Michael E. Kraft (Ph.D., Yale University) is assistant professor of political science and environmental administration at the University of Wisconsin, Green Bay. His research interests include American population politics, the political consequences of population stabilization, and environmental policy analysis. His articles have appeared in *Polity*, the *Policy Studies Journal, Alternatives, Population and Politics* (Richard L. Clinton, ed.), *Environmental Politics* (Stuart S. Nagel, ed.), and *The Sustainable Society* (Dennis C. Pirages, ed.).

John Logan is assistant professor of sociology, SUNY, Stony Brook. He has published in the area of suburban growth and is working, with Mark Schneider, on a large scale study of suburban development between 1950 and the present in a sample of more than 50 large SMSAs.

Alison McIntosh is a research associate in the Center for Population Planning at the University of Michigan. Previously she worked with the World Health Organization, serving in the Eastern Mediterranean and African regions.

A.E. Keir Nash is associate professor of political science at the University of California, Santa Barbara. He served as Director of Political Research for the National Commission on Population Growth and the American Future, in which capacity he edited the Commission research volume, *Governance and Population* (1972). He is the senior author of *Oil Pollution and the Public Interest* (1972), and his writings have appeared in numerous journals, including the *American Political Science Review*, the *Journal of American History*, the *Virginia Law Review, Demography*, and the *Journal of Comparative Administration.*

David S. North is director of the Center for Labor and Migration Studies, New TransCentury Foundation, Washington, D.C. He is author of *Manpower Policy and Immigration Policy in the U.S.* (1977) and *The Characteristics and Role of Illegal Aliens in the U.S. Labor Market* (1976).

John M. Ostheimer is associate professor of political science at Northern Arizona State University. He edited *Politics of the Western Indian Ocean Islands* (1975) and wrote *Nigerian Politics* (1973) and several shorter works in the African and Comparative fields. In American politics, he coedited *Life or Death—Who Controls?* (1976) and has written shorter works on environmental affairs and land use planning.

William Petersen is Robert Lazarus Professor of Social Demography at Ohio State University. Among his works, the ones closest to the topic of this book are *The Politics of Population* (1964); *Population*, 3rd ed. (1975); "Some Postulates of Population Policy," *Population Review* (1971); "On the Relation between Family Policy and Population Policy," *International Journal of Comparative Sociology* (1975).

Mark Schneider (Ph.D., University of North Carolina, Chapel Hill) is assistant professor of political science at SUNY, Stony Brook. His current research focuses on the demographic and economic development of suburbia and governmental response to such growth. His work has appeared in the *Public Administrative Review*, the *Journal of Politics, Polity,* and *Social Indicators Research.*

W. Bruce Shepard is associate professor of political science at Oregon State University. His current research interests range from natural resource policy to urban politics and policy. He is a coauthor of *Land Use Control: Evaluating Economic and Political Effects*; has contributed to *Comparative Policy Analysis*; and has published articles in *American Political Science Review, Journal of Politics, Environmental Law Review, Urban Affairs Quarterly,* and *Social Science Quarterly.*

Dorothy M. Stetson is assistant professor of political science at Florida Atlantic University. Her research interests include comparative policy process and family policy. Her articles have appeared in *Journal of Comparative Family Studies, Journal of Marriage and the Family, Journal of Politics,* and *Population and Politics* (Richard L. Clinton, ed.). She has recently completed a major study of English family law reform.

James L. Sundquist is director of the Governmental Studies Program at The Brookings Institution. He is the author of *Dynamics of the Party System* (1973), *Making Federalism Work* (1969), and *Politics and Policy: The Eisenhower, Kennedy, and Johnson Years* (1968). The research for his latest book, *Dispersing Population: What America Can Learn from Europe* (1975), took him into five European countries and led to the comparative analysis presented in his chapter.

Karl E. Taeuber is professor of sociology and assistant director of the Institute for Research on Poverty at the University of Wisconsin. He is coauthor of *Negroes in Cities* and *Migration in the United States*, and has written articles on black population trends and residential segregation. He has testified as an expert witness in many school segregation trials.

Marilyn Whisler is an assistant professor of political science at Florida Technological University. She has written several papers on policy implementation and on growth management. Her current interests include state and local politics, comprehensive planning, program evaluation, and higher education policy.

Franklin D. Wilson is assistant professor of sociology and a member of the research staff of the Institute for Research on Poverty at the University of Wisconsin. He is the author of *Residential Consumption, Economic Opportuni-*

ties and Race, and has written articles on metropolitan structure and change. He is coprincipal investigator on a contract with the Department of Health, Education and Welfare to study the demographic impacts of school desegregation policy.